Practicing Empathy

Also available from Bloomsbury

A History and Philosophy of Expertise, Jamie Carlin Watson
A Philosophy for Future Generations, Tiziana Andina
A Philosophy of Comparisons, Hartmut von Sass
Comparative Approaches to Compassion, Ramin Jahanbegloo
Ethics and Insurrection, Lee A. McBride III

Practicing Empathy

Pragmatism and The Value of Relations

Mark Fagiano

BLOOMSBURY ACADEMIC
LONDON • NEW YORK • OXFORD • NEW DELHI • SYDNEY

BLOOMSBURY ACADEMIC
Bloomsbury Publishing Plc
50 Bedford Square, London, WC1B 3DP, UK
1385 Broadway, New York, NY 10018, USA
29 Earlsfort Terrace, Dublin 2, Ireland

BLOOMSBURY, BLOOMSBURY ACADEMIC and the Diana logo are trademarks of Bloomsbury Publishing Plc

First published in Great Britain 2022
This paperback edition published 2024

Copyright © Mark Fagiano, 2022

Mark Fagiano has asserted his right under the Copyright, Designs and Patents Act, 1988, to be identified as Author of this work.

For legal purposes the Acknowledgments on p. ix constitute an extension of this copyright page.

Cover image: francescoch / iStock

All rights reserved. No part of this publication may be reproduced or transmitted in any form or by any means, electronic or mechanical, including photocopying, recording, or any information storage or retrieval system, without prior permission in writing from the publishers.

Bloomsbury Publishing Plc does not have any control over, or responsibility for, any third-party websites referred to or in this book. All internet addresses given in this book were correct at the time of going to press. The author and publisher regret any inconvenience caused if addresses have changed or sites have ceased to exist, but can accept no responsibility for any such changes.

A catalogue record for this book is available from the British Library.

A catalog record for this book is available from the Library of Congress.

Library of Congress Control Number: 2022942519

ISBN:	HB:	978-1-3502-8166-0
	PB:	978-1-3502-8170-7
	ePDF:	978-1-3502-8167-7
	eBook:	978-1-3502-8168-4

Typeset by RefineCatch Limited, Bungay, Suffolk

To find out more about our authors and books visit www.bloomsbury.com and sign up for our newsletters.

To James Christiana

The perfect Form of a friend

Contents

List of Illustrations		viii
Acknowledgments		ix
Preface		xi
1	Empathy and Pluralism	1
2	*Pathos* and the Death of Dualisms	21
3	Empathic Projection	45
4	Empathic Connection	67
5	Empathic Care	89
6	Is Empathy Moral?	111
7	Can Empathy Be Developed?	133
8	Empathic Democracy as a Way of Life	157
Notes		179
Bibliography		215
Index		229

Illustrations

1	Oracle of Delphi, Greece	2
2	Thick Clouds over Emory University, Atlanta, Georgia	22
3	Near Agora, Athens, Greece	46
4	Tyson Coble, Gainesville, Florida	68
5	Hiking the Blue Ridge Mountains with C. D. Batson	90
6	Clouds of Northern Georgia, with Praphat Xavier Fernandes	112
7	Springtime in Knoxville, Tennessee	134
8	The Guiding Light Appears, walking with John Stuhr	158

Acknowledgments

Whenever I teach introductory or upper division ethics courses, I assign Marcus Aurelius's *Meditations*, which is a collection of aphorisms of the famous Roman emperor. Until recently, I have always told my students to skip over Book One of this collection of existentially relevant and insightful sayings. But after writing this book, I have come to realize the profundity of that first book of the *Meditations*, for it is there where Aurelius honors the people in his life that made him the type of person he was.

All of the people that follow have been instrumental in supporting my life as an academic and/or the development of my thinking as a scholar, and I am extremely grateful for their appearance in my life: Vasiliki Chatzipli, Robert Innis, Melvin Rogers, Vinny Colapietro, Praphat Xavier Fernandes, Edna Katunarich, Tyson Coble and the Coble family, Darrin and Shari Griffith, Sarah and Judy Bergeleen, Kristin and Billy Calderwood, Fran Swick, Ivan Arnold, John Muckelbauer, Brendan Hogan, Tony Misch, Otis Clay, Suleika Jaouad, Samantha Noll, Michael Goldsby, Travis Ridout, Tim Parker, Jim Dunson, Bret Bastain, Kelly Bulkeley, Hilary Martin, Alan Dundes, Noelle McAfee, Shawn McFarland, Chase and Oana Reynolds, Tyler Diaferio, Lidewij Niezink, Cyrus Zargar, Paul C. Taylor, Aaron Simmons, Santosh Kumar, Denis Grosz, Russ Kendzoir, Tricia Glazebrook, Jared Rothstein, Robert Campbell, Dom Barnard, Sophie Thompson, Eduardo Mendieta, and Steve and Jan Fagiano.

Many thanks also to Colleen Coalter, Suzie Nash, Goretti Cowley and their team at Bloomsbury Press for their unyielding assistance and patience with the formation of this manuscript. A sincere thanks to my friend and lifetime editor Victoria Scott, whose early edits of this manuscript—and overall patience with me—helped me hone my writing skills over the years.

While I was at Emory University and the University of Tennessee, four scholars greatly influenced the direction of this book, whether this was their intent or not: Cynthia Willett, Frans de Waal, C. D. Batson, and John Stuhr. A heartfelt thanks to Cynthia Willett, who not only helped me find my own writing style and voice but has been exceedingly helpful as I have waded through the waters of professional philosophy. Many thanks also to Frans de Waal for the encouragement and kindness he extended to me while I was at Emory University.

At the University of Tennessee, I was fortunate to enter into dialogue and become friends with C. D. Batson; the conversations I had with Dan while we hiked in Blue Ridge Mountains were very formative to many of the ideas I express here. Finally, I truly do not know where I would be today without the presence, support, and guidance of John Stuhr over the years. John is one of the greatest living American philosophers and without question the best interpreter of William James for the twenty-first century and beyond it; I am fortunate to have him as a very close friend.

Preface

Every person who is interested in the subject of empathy is confronted with a problem. Conflicting definitions of "empathy" abound, and this causes confusion whenever we turn to our own experiences to discover what empathy is. A practical approach to banish this problem is simply to stipulate precisely what one means by empathy, and, hopefully, by doing so the problem itself is dissolved. Many scholars find this to be satisfactory, for it assists them in making a specific argument about experience, but it doesn't help us in our attempts to know exactly which experiences qualify for being "empathic" and which do not. For throughout its history as an idea, "empathy" has been assigned different meanings, though most commonly, empathy has been and still is often thought to be primarily either a thing or an activity.

As a thing, empathy has been defined as a condition of possible knowledge of the outside world;[1] a natural capacity to share, an act of understanding and responding with care;[2] an inner perceptual mechanism that produces an involuntary co-feeling with others; an ability to identify and to respond;[3] a shared affective state;[4] or a complex form of psychological inference.[5] As an activity, empathy has been defined as feeling into—or feeling one's way into—an object;[6] perceiving the internal frame of reference within another person;[7] recognizing what another may be feeling or thinking;[8] imagining the narrative of another;[9] or responding to another with affect or emotion.[10] Given this tangle of dissenting voices, which is only a small sample of the disagreements, might it be possible to weave together these and other conflicting perspectives about empathy into a pluralistic, inclusive, and pragmatic theory? This is the question that prompted me to write this book.

In this work I put forth a new and unified theory of empathy as an answer to the above question. I call this theory relational empathy. I define *relational empathy* as the convergence of three relations between things and/or activities, rather than as a given activity or thing, though certain experiences of each of these relations has referred to different empathic habits. Specifically, I refer to three distinct though experientially overlapping relations of experience as the relations of (a) *feeling into*, (b) *feeling with*, and (c) *feeling for*. By "feeling," I signify the general and broad meaning of the Greek understanding of *pathos* as anything experienced,[11] and by "relation," I mean the mode or manner by which two or more things are interrelated or interact within experience. The term "relation" is nothing new in the language games of philosophy, but the philosopher William James's articulation and use of it was revolutionary. Relations, for James, are not simply the modes or manners by which things are connected. They are these, but they are also the fundamentum of experience itself, what James called "pure experience."[12] Noticing the myriad relations that connect our thoughts, words, and experiences, as James suggests we do, draws out the multiplicity and complexity of experience itself and directs our attention toward the functionality of our descriptions. James's turn to relations was pragmatic because it helped him dissolve several unnecessary philosophical debates. In the same spirit, turning to relations for the purpose of reconstructing empathy has provided me with an opportunity to include conflicting definitions rather than to exclude them. It also allows us to reject a few unhelpful, yet historically prominent, dualisms that have influenced contemporary empathy research.

Each of these three general relations are recognized in experience as different types of actions. For instance, the relation of *feeling into* is recognized in the act of projecting one's thoughts and feelings into an object for the purpose of becoming aware of it. Or, in a different context, the relation of feeling into is noticed in moments of trying to observe or perceive someone or something acutely and accurately. This notion of feeling into as an act of projection ought not be equated with the notion of projection as it is commonly described in psychology, as something pejorative. (Where would we be without our projections? We are always projecting; whether the projection is problematic depends upon whether we are distorting the reality of the thing perceived by means of our projections.) The second relation is recognized in experience in those actions by which we feel with other persons or things by experiencing a sense of connection, unity, or concord with them. This does not necessarily mean, as it is assumed with many understandings of empathy, that one's understanding is exact—or is the same—but rather simply that there is a feeling of being connected or united with someone or something. The third relation, as a general relation of relational empathy, is manifested in acts of feeling for others or something by means of extending care and concern, e.g., by showing compassion toward another or by demonstrating concern for some cause.

In chapter 1, I begin with a story that puts the reader in a hypothetical situation in which she/he experiences, what have been recognized in the literature as, nine different types of empathy. I then explain each of these types of empathy as they have been described within different academic disciplines and provide examples of our experiences of each. I then introduce a contested debate about the subject of empathy, concerning whether it is better to conceive and define empathy narrowly or broadly. How one answers question matters pragmatically, for if one decides to adopt a narrow conceptualization and definition of empathy, then one risks leaving out something about empathy that, perhaps, should not be excluded. However, if one is inclined to conceive and define empathy pluralistically and broadly, it is possible that this choice might create more rather than less ambiguity. Ultimately, I claim, the significance of this debate lies in the consequences produced by conceiving and defining empathy either narrowly or broadly. And upon this truth, I then introduce the pragmatic and pluralistic account of empathy I am adopting to interpret the meaning and value of our empathic experiences, i.e., *relational empathy*. Again, a relation denotes a mode or manner by which two or more things are connected in experience, and relational empathy signifies the unification of three conceptually distinct, though experientially overlapping, empathic relations in our experiences with persons or things. Each of these three relations, the relations of *feeling into*, *feeling with*, and *feeling for*, has been described historically as a type of empathy, and all definitions of empathy incorporate at least one of these relations. I conclude chapter 1 with the claim that relational empathy, as a broad, pluralistic, and historically rich understanding of empathy, represents the most accurate portrayal of empathy as an experience and ought to be adopted for practical purposes, a claim that I defend throughout this work.

In chapter 2, I turn to a historical-genealogical analysis of the Greek word *pathos*, the root word of empathy, examine the different significations of this word among the ancients, and trace the transformations of its meaning after it was adopted by theorists within different intellectual traditions. Despite the multiple meanings and usages of *pathos* among the ancients, the consensus among scholars today is that *pathos* most generally signified in the ancient world *anything experienced*. However, this general and neutral understanding of *pathos* gave way to more negative interpretations of it. Beginning with Aristotle and Epicurus, I note how their neutral conceptualizations of *pathos* have been ignored in favor of more negative portrayals of *pathos* engendered by the philosophy of Stoicism and the medical practices of the school of Hippocrates. I then trace the various meanings of *pathos* and its cognate/surrogate terms in different languages (e.g., *passio*, "passion," *affectus*, "sentiment," and *perturbio*, "emotion") and how these were employed to construct and support different philosophical theories, paying close attention to the different ways *pathos* was often set in opposition to reason, and how this habit throughout the history of philosophy led to the construction of numerous artificial dualisms that have distorted the nature of experience. The main goals of this chapter are to show how these dualisms have distorted experience, to explain why they must be rejected, and to describe how a relational understanding of empathy avoids falling prey to impractical dualisms, i.e., by conceiving the root word "*pathos*" in the word "empathy" to signify *anything experienced* rather than, for instance, simply an emotional or cognitive experience.

In chapter 3, I provide philosophical and historical interpretations of the German verb *sich einfühlen* and the German noun *Einfühlung*, noting how these terms were used to describe the relation of feeling into, which I define as the *mode or manner in which we feel into any object of our perception or reflection*. Beginning with Herder and Novalis in the late eighteenth century, I explore how these thinkers argued that certain experiences of this relation could help one overcome historical prejudices, the folly of unilinerar theories of human development, as well as one's feelings of separateness from nature. I then examine why these pragmatic aims of Herder, Novalis, and other Counter-Enlightenment thinkers were abandoned by aestheticians in the nineteenth century and investigate how these theorists began to use *sich einfühlen/Einfühlung* to describe how one comes to understand and appreciate the form, structure, and beauty of artworks. This aesthetic understanding and usage of "empathy" was eventually discarded by psychologists in the twentieth century, who instead contended that one's ability to feel into the experiences of others is useful for imagining and understanding their perspectives or psychological states. The aim of chapter 3 is to explicate and offer justification for the relation of feeling into as both a type of empathy and as one of the three relations of relational empathy. I accomplish this by providing historical evidence of its usage, describing this relation broadly via a historical reconstruction of it, and considering how the experience of feeling into things and people functioned in different ways, both as a skill of perception and as a means to solve something problematic.

During the rise of psychology in late nineteenth and early twentieth centuries, this tradition of *Einfühlung* as a relation of *feeling into* began to be described as a relation of *feeling with* others, most notably by psychologists who were interested in learning how they could more accurately understand and feel with the perspectives of their patients. It is within this moment of history that the English word "empathy" was coined as a surrogate term for *Einfühlung*. This development gave rise to a debate concerning whether "empathy" or "sympathy" was the appropriate term to denote the second relation of relational empathy, i.e., the relation of feeling with, which I define as a *mode or manner in which we feel with other persons or things by experiencing a sense of connection, unity, or concord with them.* After making my argument about the pragmatic importance of using empathy rather than sympathy to describe the relation of feeling with, I then explore in detail, and provide critical analyses of, different arguments about the value of this relation within the academic traditions of phenomenology, psychology, and sociology in the early twentieth century. As a consequence of these intellectual contributions, we find that empathy as *Einfühlung*, as the act of feeling into objects, is largely abandoned, and that empathy described generally as feeling with the experiences of others (e.g., empathic perspective-taking, empathic mimicry, empathic connection) became the dominant approach for understanding empathic experience. In chapter 4, I describe the interplay of the relations of *feeling into* and *feeling with* and provide an analysis of the practical benefits of empathy as an act of feeling with others, exploring a few ways in which this relation of empathy might be thought of as a skill.

Reflection upon our lives informs us that in certain contexts we can experience these first two relations, *feeling into* and *feeling with*, without experiencing the third relation, what I am calling *feeling for*, which I define as a *mode or manner in which we feel for other persons/things by displaying concern for them and acting primarily for their benefit and general well-being*. In chapter 5, I explore this last relation, differentiate it from the first two relations, and explain how it functions in our experiences of relational empathy. Acts of feeling for others are sometimes referred to as instances of sympathy or compassion. But from the middle of the twentieth century to the present day, we find that empathy has been increasingly used to signify this relation of feeling for others and to describe helping behavior, e.g., acts of showing concern and caring for the well-being of others. With these developments, we find yet another transformation in the meaning of empathy, and I provide evidence for this semantic shift by examining the contributions of psychologists, biologists, and social psychologists who conceptualized and defined empathy primarily *as the relation of feeling for*. I locate the beginning of this expansion of the meaning of empathy in the works and insights of Carl Rogers, and then show the continuance and predominance of this approach to thinking about empathy in the works of Martin Hoffman, C. D. Batson, Frans de Waal and, more generally, within the disciplines of evolutionary biology, social psychology, neuroscience, and primatology. At the end of chapter 5, I draw on these contributions and consider the pragmatic value of thinking that the act of feeling for other persons and things is a skill and explain how the experience of all three relations of empathy I have described constitute relational empathy.

In the chapter 6, chapter 7, and chapter 8, I put my theory of relational empathy to work by using it to address three contemporary questions about empathy concerning the morality, development, and political import of empathy. I begin chapter 6 with Williams James's famous story about a squirrel and a man encircling a tree for the purposes of introducing the main question of this chapter and to remind the reader of the pragmatic method and philosophy of language I have adopted to analyze empathic experiences. I then note that many unresolved questions about empathy today are questions concerning the morality of empathy and argue why the pluralistic approach I have adopted can help us to think about these questions pragmatically. Questions about morality are notoriously difficult to answer; for not only do people mean different things by the word "empathy," but they also disagree about what constitutes and/or justifies good or bad, and right or wrong actions and behavior. In light of this, I conduct a short critique of a philosophical tradition I am calling "principlism" and offer a different account of morality, i.e., a relational and pragmatic moral theory, that emphasizes the importance of both the context and the consequences of our actions. I then explore current theories about the morality value of empathy, noting that answers to questions about the morality of empathy are wholly contingent upon how one defines empathy, and how writings on the morality of empathy share a pluralistic and pragmatic account that explains empathy's morality or immorality. I then turn to the pragmatic benefits of relational empathy, providing everyday examples to elucidate how the contexts and consequences of our experiences shape the moral realities of our empathic experiences.

In addition to questions about the morality of empathy, questions concerning whether empathy can be developed have also been prominent among contemporary discourses. Since these questions are quite often parasitic upon the nature/nurture dualism, I begin chapter 7 by rejecting this dualism's role in discussions about the development of empathy, offering instead a few pragmatic reasons why the adoption of relational empathy—as a radical contextualist approach to thinking about and practicing empathy—provides a functionalist method for our considerations of the roles that both nature and nurture play in our empathic experiences. I then turn to the importance of habit formation for developing different habits of empathic action and describe how each of the three relations of relational empathy functions as a habit within a variety of contextualized experiences. These habits, I claim, are developed by means of learning several interpersonal and social skills (e.g., the skill of mindfulness, self-empathy, and the skill of empathic listening), and by practicing them daily.

After an exploration of how each of the three parts of relational empathy functions as a habit—and how each may be developed as a skill—I end chapter 7 by analyzing recent discourses concerning the rise of technology and its effects upon our experiences of empathy. Turning to some examples, I explain how virtual reality has been and can be used for simulating experiences of relational empathy and how these simulated experiences might function to help one develop empathy.

After providing pragmatic answers to the most popular questions today about the morality and development of empathy, I explore the numerous ways the habits and skills of relational empathy can be used instrumentally to live democratically. In chapter 8, I begin this task by introducing the idea that moral luck can serve as a foundation for practicing relational empathy; I also discuss how empathic democracy can serve as a way of life, as well as a foundational truth of social existence that legitimizes the democratic spirit. There have been many criticisms of democracy throughout its history, and I address a few of these noting how the most common criticisms focus on certain consequences and ignore the more social beneficial consequences engendered by the democratic process. I then turn to explicate the pragmatic notion of democracy as a way of life, noting how it helps us to both take seriously and overcome criticisms about democracy. I then explore pragmatism's philosophy of social hope as a source of inspiration and necessary starting point for practicing democracy as a way of life. The pragmatic notion of social hope is often referred to as meliorism, the idea that the world can be made better with human effort. I reconstruct this ideal of social hope by making a distinction between expectant hope and social hope in action for the purpose of explaining how the practice of relational empathy can be used instrumently and serve as a vehicle for social hope in action. Relational empathy, when combined with a pragmatically informed notion of social hope, provides us with the opportunity to widen the windows of our perception, challenge our biases, and practice democracy as a way of life. I conclude this book by considering how relational empathy, social hope in action, and the practice of democracy as a way of life can help overcome the consequences of moral luck.

Relational empathy and all other conceptualizations of empathy are identical to one another in one important way: they are all social constructs that aim not only to describe experience but to change the quality of our lived experiences. The value of any given notion of empathy, then, lies not in its "being right" in some abstract silo of truth apart from and unrelated to our lived experiences, but rather in what the notion does—the way, for example, it shapes habits, decreases the suffering of sentient beings, establishes a foundation for scientific inquiry, or contributes to the flourishing of our lives. Specifically, this book and the theory of relational empathy does a few important things. First, this work about relational empathy provides, in my estimation, the most exhaustive historical account of what people have meant by empathy/*Einfühlung* within different academic disciplines from the Age of Enlightenment to present-day neuroscience, and argues for a pluralistic account of empathy for the purposes of including rival, often conflicting, definitions of empathy, as well as for establishing a historically rich conceptual framework that is useful for addressing a number of conceptual problems that distort our understanding of empathic experiences, creating mere verbal disputes about what empathy is. It also directs recurring questions about empathy (e.g., Can empathy be developed? Is empathy moral?) away from abstract speculations about the "nature" of empathy and toward the contexts and consequences of different experiences. For more than simply a theory about empathy, I put this account of relational empathy to work by explaining how it, as a pluralistic and broad account, provides pragmatic answers to three outstanding questions: Is empathy moral? Can empathy be developed? And how, if at all, might relational empathy function as a skill for practicing democracy as a way of life? In addition to my own philosophical reasons for choosing these questions, I have selected these because, according to the data on internet searches, they are the most asked questions about empathy today.

It is my hope that what follows provides each reader with a greater understanding of the experience of empathy as well as a refined sense of what is at stake regarding philosophical disagreements about empathy. The pluralistic theory I introduce in this book, which is drawn from thoughts and theories on the subject over the last few centuries, provides, I believe, the most pragmatic approach for both understanding and practicing empathy. I also hope that by taking seriously the approach laid out in this work, readers will be able to nurture empathy for the purpose of flourishing in life and helping others to do the same.

1

Empathy and Pluralism

Imagine you are driving up a long and winding road in the mountains. It is daytime; the sun casts its rays of golden light down through a few gray clouds, illuminating both the hills as well as the path ahead of you. The quiet, serene scene of this sunlit, warm day, coupled with the scent of pine, reminds you of the wonders and beauty of nature.

As you begin to steer around a sharp turn, you notice that a large section of the guardrail is missing. Filled with curiosity and the uncomfortable feeling that something is amiss, you pull your car over to the side of the road and begin walking toward the cliff to investigate the situation. There are long skid marks on the street leading up to a damaged guardrail, and small parts of a car's front bumper are strewn all along the road's shoulder. From these signs, you begin to believe that someone must have recently driven through the guardrail and into the ravine below. As you arrive at the cliff's edge, you look down into the ravine and see a blue car stuck between two big boulders halfway down the mountainside.

You don't see anyone in the car, but then unexpectedly, you hear a few faint cries that sound like people moaning in pain. This is followed by someone whispering faintly, "Help us . . . please!" As you scan the slope of the mountainside, you see a man and a young girl attempting to crawl up to safety from their mangled vehicle. You notice that with one arm the man is holding onto the girl (whom you assume to be his daughter) and with the other he is trying, in vain, to grab ahold of something sturdy to prevent himself and the girl from sliding down the mountainside. To make matters worse, you see that they are slowly sliding toward another cliff edge and if you don't do something fast, they will both fall hundreds of feet to their deaths.

Then, in an instant, your body becomes tense, your heart rate increases, and you unconsciously mimic the expression of anguish on the man's face. You imagine, for a second, what you would do if you were in his shoes, then suddenly, you shift your thoughts and begin to imagine for a moment what it might be like to be him in this harrowing event. Then, as you are considering your best course

Figure 1 Oracle of Delphi, Greece.

of action to save these victims, the man almost loses his grip on his daughter's hand; you become fearful, and it seems to you as if you "caught" his fear automatically. Feeling one with each of them in their struggle, you and the man finally make meaningful eye contact. Without any words exchanged, you read his body language and believe that you know his thoughts: he is thinking that he can't do this alone. Without any hope that the emergency services will arrive anytime soon, you have a stark realization: You are the only one who can save them.

Seizing your chance, you descend the steep slope of the mountainside, but you keep losing your footing. Taking this into consideration, and to avoid becoming a third victim, you begin to slide down the slope on your backside. As you draw near to the victims, you position yourself upon a stable rock protruding from the mountainside. You reach for the man's outstretched hand, but he is finding it difficult to hold the child and reach for your hand at the same time. But then, after the girl screams in terror, her father intensifies his effort, manages to secure his footing, and grabs ahold of your hand. As you slowly begin to pull him and the little girl up to safety, you continually reassure them with comforting words. When you all finally reach the top, the man thanks you over and over, and the little girl, tears running down her face, leaps into her father's arms.

What Is Empathy?

Now, in which part of this story did you experience empathy? According to a very common way of thinking about it today, you experienced empathy *only* when you took the perspectives of the victims.[1] People often think of empathy in this way, as "walking in another's shoes," which signifies a type of empathy that is sometimes called *empathic perspective-taking*. Empathic perspective-taking denotes an act in which you obtain an understanding of another person's perspective and this is sometimes gained by means of an imaginative simulation of that person's experience(s). But there are two types of perspective-taking, and these are sometimes conflated. For example, you can imagine how you (as you) would think and feel if you were the other person *or* you can perspective take by imagining how that person thinks and feels about his/her situation. C. D. Batson refers to this first option as an imagine-self perspective and the second as an imagine-other perspective.[2]

In the story above, when you imagined what *you* would do if you were in the shoes of the victims, you experienced the imagine-self type of perspective-taking; then, when you shifted your thinking and imagined what it would be like to be the victims, you experienced imagine-other perspective-taking. The differences between these two types of perspective-taking might seem slight, but they are not. In the first case, one projects his/her thoughts, feelings, and senses into the other's perspectives, and this, occasionally but not always, leads to a distortion (or even an ignorance) of the real felt experience of the other. In the second case, one is trying to understand the perspectives of another by projecting his/her thoughts, feelings, and senses into the experience of the other person and imagines what the other person might be thinking, feeling, and sensing.

Here is an example of the difference between these two types of empathic perspective-taking. You and one of your friends attend a social gathering at the end of the work week. As you arrive at the function together, it becomes immediately clear to each of you that everyone at the event is wearing formal attire, and though you are dressed in this way, your friend isn't. As you watch your friend explain his misunderstanding to others at the party, you begin to imagine how you would feel in his position and you begin to feel pity for him, believing that he must be embarrassed, as you would be if you were him (imagine-self perspective). But as you continue to watch your friend converse with others, you notice that he seems to be quite at ease with the situation. As you notice this, you begin to simulate his perspective differently by imagining how he feels (imagine-other perspective) instead of how you would feel if you were him.

Returning to the story in which you saved the man and his daughter, some would say that you experienced empathy when you guessed what the man was thinking rather than when you took their perspectives. People often refer to this experience of empathy as *empathic inference*, namely, an act of reading or inferring the contents of another person's mind (sometimes called "mindreading"). This type of experience involves a process of inference in which one observes and *feels into* another person's experience to guess the contents of that person's mind. Often, the final goal of this act of feeling into is to *feel with* and accurately grasp the other person's thoughts, intentions, emotions, etc. Correctly inferring and understanding the thoughts of another is often called *empathic accuracy*.[3] Empathic perspective-taking, empathic inference, and empathic accuracy have all been called "empathy," but each one differs from the other two. Empathic perspective-taking involves the imaginative simulation of what it might be like to have another's experience; empathic inference is a process of inferring and guessing what others may be thinking or sensing, and empathic accuracy signifies those moments when our inferences and guesses match (or are at least extremely similar to) what the person is actually experiencing, thinking, and sensing.

In addition to these approaches to defining empathy as an experience, some might claim that you also empathized with the victims in other parts of the story and experienced three other modes of empathy—namely, *empathic contagion*, *empathic connection*, and *empathic mimicry*. Empathic contagion arises whenever we unconsciously catch and co-experience the emotions, feelings, ideas, or perspectives of others.[4] By "unconscious" here I mean that our catching of the experiences of others does not arise from our conscious awareness and judgment, so it is not a consequence of our choice; it is neither an act of inference nor an imaginative simulation of the experiences of another. Like the way we catch a virus, we sometimes "catch" and feel with the experiences of others, and it seems as if those experiences themselves are contagious. Empathic contagion has often referred only to emotional contagion, for instance, when we unintentionally catch another's sadness, elation, or anger. But a great deal of evidence also shows that beliefs, worldviews, values, principles, behaviors, and opinions are also sometimes contagious in this way.

To say that our emotions alone are contagious, then, seems to fall short of portraying the full breadth of this type of plural experience. In the story, you experienced empathic contagion when you caught the victim's experience of fear, an emotional state that was absent within you before that moment.

Empathic connection involves a sense of identifying with, feeling unified or being in sync with another person or thing. Historically this type of empathy has also been recognized as a sense of the connection we feel with objects as well as persons, and sometimes with objects and persons at the same time, for example, when two people simultaneously experience the disappearance of the sun as it slips gracefully under the distant horizon. When you rescued the victims from certain death, you experienced empathic connection both as a sense of "oneness" with the victims in their struggle as well as a feeling of being united with their goal to survive. Our feelings of empathic connection with other people and/or things occur daily, for example, when we smile, laugh, or cry with others, when we feel with and rejoice in the happiness of others, and when we are in sync with the bodily movements of another. Synchronic physical movements with other persons seem to strengthen our capacity for this type of empathy; as Frans de Waal points out, these types of experiences build "upon the ability to map one's own body onto that of another, and make the other's movements one's own," thus facilitating one's ability to coordinate and connect with others.[5] This physical act of being unified, in sync, and connected with others can, as a further consequence, build feelings of trust and create strong bonds between persons, especially when the experience of empathic connection with another person is mutual and/or reciprocated.

In addition to your feelings of empathic connection and contagion, many would say that you experienced another type of empathy called *empathic mimicry* when you imitated the man's facial expression of his anxiety.[6] Comics and impressionists have mastered this mode of empathy, recognized in their uncanny abilities to copy the personalities, body language, and vocal modulations of others. Likewise, great actresses and actors mimic—and imagine creatively—the personalities, temperaments, and overall psychological dispositions of the roles they adopt for a given performance. Depending upon the context of an experience, empathic mimicry may arise within us by either a conscious or unconscious mimicking or emulation of a person's behavior, perspective, or body language. By "body language" I mean any nonverbal form of communication in which one's thoughts, feelings, or intentions are expressed by physical behaviors and/or signs, including but not limited to gestures, facial expressions, bodily postures, and touch.

These six types of experiences that people call "empathy," have at least one thing in common: within certain contexts, we experience these without feeling concern or demonstrating care for others. Take, for example, certain experiences of empathic perspective-taking and empathic inference/accuracy. Imagine you are a member of a jury during the trail of man who, based on the overwhelming evidence against him, has clearly murdered at least twenty innocent victims. You could simulate imaginatively the experience of what it might be like to be the defendant (perspective-taking), and you might also be able to infer correctly her/his thoughts or senses when a guilty verdict is declared at the trial's end (empathic inference/empathic accuracy). But exercising these modes of empathy does not necessarily require that you care about this person's well-being. Neither would it be likely that any experiences of empathic connection, empathic contagion, or empathic mimicry would lead you to care about, feel for, or show concern for the killer's welfare. Thinking back to our story, however, it is clear that your helpful and heroic act was motivated by the concern and care you had for the victims. If you didn't feel for them—as helpless strangers in need of your assistance—you wouldn't have acted as you did. You could have, however cruel it may sound, simply driven away.

If you had done this, would it not be strange if later in the day you described your experience with the victims as empathic? Many people wish to say that only sympathy means feeling or caring for others, but if one examines contemporary academic discourses about empathy as well as common parlance, it appears as though empathy means more than simply perceiving, imagining, and understanding the experiences of others. It involves what people call *empathic concern* and *empathic care*. Different from other understandings of it, I define empathic concern as a feeling of being interested in or concerned about the importance of something or someone. This is exemplified, for instance, when we recognize the importance of a social cause, or show interest in the work of an artist, but it is more commonly recognized whenever we feel concern about the well-being of another. These and other feelings of concern sometimes provoke motivation within us to act for the benefit of others. In our story, you demonstrated such concern when you showed interest in the safety of the victims, assigned importance to their situation, and were motivated to help them. Your feelings of concern for the well-being of people in serious danger were distinctly different from feelings of personal distress, in that they were directed toward the victims and not yourself; they were primarily other-oriented rather than simply self-oriented, self-regarding, and instinctual.[7]

Different from empathic concern, empathic care is demonstrated by *acts* of caring for persons or things.[8] Though one may gain a sense of satisfaction from such acts, or in some other way benefit from these acts, empathic care denotes those actions that are intended primarily for the benefit of other persons or things rather than for oneself, even sometimes at great risk to one's own well-being (e.g., acts of altruism). Though experience shows us that empathic care is often recognized in solitary and short-lived acts of helping behavior (e.g., returning a lost item to someone), it also denotes a devoted and processional commitment to another over a long period of time. A person's devotion to the happiness, security, and flourishing of another's life involves these long-term acts of care, love, and compassion for the benefit and well-being of another. This second manifestation of empathic care is often selective and exclusive because it is only possible to provide such steadfast care and benevolence to a few individuals without access to significant resources.

These eight different, though sometimes overlapping, dimensions of empathy all seem to rely upon a ninth type of empathic experience: *empathic projection*, a mode of empathy commonly associated with the meaning of the German word *Einfühlung*. *Einfühlung* signifies the process of projecting one's senses into an object of perception or reflection and "feeling one's way into" it. The object can be anything, another's person's experiences, thoughts, emotions, such as the experience of a beautiful sunset, a Van Gogh painting, a situation at work, a state of bliss; you can even "feel yourself into" a combination of related objects, such as a person's thoughts and an important historical event. To be clear, this type of empathic experience *ought not* be confused with another understanding of empathy as "the projection of *one's own personality* onto the personality of another ... in order to understand them better."[9] Nor should it be confused with the way psychologists speak of projection as a defense mechanism, in which the human ego defends itself against unconscious impulses or qualities.

Even though recent scholarship has explored this type of empathy as an act of projecting one's consciousness into both animate and inanimate objects of one's perception or reflection,[10] I suspect that many people have never heard of this, and some might think this idea to be quite odd. After all, isn't empathy simply an interpersonal phenomenon? How can one possibly have empathy for an object? Though it may sound strange to our contemporary ears, the idea of *feeling into* both animate and inanimate objects was very common before the twentieth century. During the late eighteenth century, a number of philosophers, poets, and Counter-Enlightenment thinkers believed that empathic projection could help to combat the misgivings and assumptions of overly systematic, scientific, and rationalistic interpretations of nature.[11] For example, the poet Novalis (1772–1801) recognized that excessively rational and rigid scientific interpretations of nature (common during the Age of Enlightenment) have deadened our poetic and spiritual sense of the natural world. Empathic projection, he thought, helps to counter this trend of disenchantment, for by feeling our way into the beauty and magnificence of the natural world, we can overcome our feelings of separateness from nature by becoming "one" with it.

For Johann Gottfried Herder (1744–1803), empathic projection was also defined as one's ability "to feel into everything" in order to "feel with" things outside of oneself, including but not limited to feeling with and understanding others.[12] Empathy for certain objects of our reflection, such as the different ideals, goals, and ways of life expressed within cultures other than our own, is necessary for one to feel one's way into both similar and radically different experiences of others. For Herder, then, to feel oneself into the time, place, cultural conditions, and history of a people—all of which are objects not people—helps us feel with both the similar and different lived experiences of persons.[13] Herder's larger aim for thinking this way was to convince the historians of his time that feeling into these objects ought to be central in their attempts to understand the histories of people in different cultures and times. Herder contended that such acts could lead these historians to recognize the limitations of overly rational and scientific historical methods and could also expose the folly of constructing unilinear theories of historical development that guided such Western methods.

The Narrow versus the Broad: Contemporary Conceptions of Empathy

If you are inclined to be a bit philosophical, at this point you might be asking yourself whether these nine experiences are distinct types of empathy. After all, a process such as imaginatively simulating what it might be like to have another's experience is quite different from unconsciously "catching" another's perspective, emotional state, or belief. And these two experiences are not the same as empathic care, e.g., acts of helping behavior. Maybe we should simply select one of these common ways of thinking about empathy or even make the argument that many of these modes of experience are falsely called empathic. The philosopher Amy Coplan adopts this approach and makes the argument that a number of the empathic modes I have mentioned are falsely referred to as empathy. In her article "Will the Real Empathy Please Stand Up?" (2011), she suggests that we would be better served by narrowing our conceptualization of empathy rather than conceiving it more broadly.[14] According to Coplan, general accounts of empathy, which advance broad and all-encompassing views that apply to myriad processes, take "us in the wrong direction," and only a narrow conceptualization of empathy will help us to understand it better. For Coplan, empathy, or what she calls "real empathy," is "a complex imaginative process in which an observer simulates another person's situated psychological states while maintaining clear self-other differentiation."[15] Under her conceptualization, empathy has three key features: affective matching, other-oriented perspective-taking, and clear self-other differentiation.

Coplan deftly draws distinctions between what she calls "real empathy," and two other processes she believes are falsely referred to as empathy, namely pseudo-empathy and emotional contagion. Pseudo-empathy is a self-oriented mode of perspective-taking in which you imagine how you might feel if you were in another's person situation. This needs to be clearly distinguished from what I have called other-oriented perspective-taking in which you imagine how you would feel if *you were* the other person. Emotional contagion, as the tendency to feel and express emotions similar to and influenced by the emotions of others, involves what Coplan refers to as a "low-level" psychological and bodily process, which is an automatic, involuntary "bottom-up" process, occurring subcortically whenever we sense the emotions of others. According to Coplan, this low-level process is both conceptually and empirically distinct from the high-level processes of other-oriented perspective-taking, namely, the internal process of real and genuine empathy. These two processes—low-level, bottom-up processes and high-level, top-down processes—are often referred to as "emotional empathy" ("affective empathy") and "cognitive empathy," respectively, though as Coplan astutely notes, these distinctions are often conflated.[16]

Several theorists, however, contend that emotional contagion is either empathy or, at the very least, a fundamental part of it.[17] In addition, a number of neuroscientists think our emotions are a by-product of "top-down" cognitive processes as well as low-level, bottom-up processes.[18] Perhaps for these and other reasons, some have argued that empathy is something quite different from Coplan's understanding of it. For example, the philosopher Michael Slote describes empathy as being similar to what Coplan calls "false empathy" or emotional contagion, which "involves having the feelings of another (involuntarily) aroused in ourselves, as when we see another person in pain."[19]

Attempting to bring greater clarity to this definition, Slote contrasts empathy with sympathy, which he defines as the feeling for (or showing concern for) someone, such as when we feel for someone who is experiencing pain. In accordance with this understanding, empathy involves an instantaneous feeling with another's experiences, whereas sympathy arises when one cares about another's well-being. Based on this distinction, it follows that we can experience empathy without sympathy and vice versa. For example, if you were to see a stranger accidentally ride his bicycle into a brick wall, you would likely both immediately feel with (empathy) and feel for (sympathy) the stranger. Empathy, says Slote, is the "cement of the moral universe" because it helps create something like moral approval and disapproval, which he contends is crucial for understanding what moral claims, utterances, and judgments mean. Following Hume's account of sympathy but moving beyond it, Slote sees empathy as a mechanism that allows our moral approval and disapproval "to focus on moral agents rather than on the consequences of their actions."[20] But is empathy itself moral? Is it fundamentally moral? Is it ever necessary for morality?

The philosopher Jesse Prinz, although inspired by the same tradition of philosophy Slote adopts (i.e., Humean moral sentimentalism), defines empathy a bit differently. For Prinz, empathy is primarily "a kind of vicarious emotion: it's feeling what one takes another person to be feeling. And the 'taking' here can be a matter of automatic contagion or the result of a complicated exercise of the imagination."[21] By defining empathy in this way—which seems to be almost a synthesis of Coplan and Slote's definitions—Prinz shows his skepticism about Slote's and others' claims that empathy serves as the cement of the moral universe. A few studies, Prinz notes, have shown that, as a vicarious emotion, empathy does not substantially motivate us to act on the behalf of those in need. It is also highly selective, prone to in-group biases, and in some cases results in preferential treatment for those who are spatially close to us. Even when empathy serves as a moral guide, our acts of empathizing are often biased and partial, and we often have more empathy for the suffering and pain of those who seem to be similar to us.[22] Furthermore, within certain contexts, empathy-induced acts of altruism are unfair, immoral, and unjust.[23] Conclusively for Prinz, empathy is not necessary for the capacities that make up basic moral competence, and one can acquire moral values, make moral judgments, and act morally without empathy.[24] Prinz's arguments are convincing; however, any coherent answer to questions about the supposed morality of empathy is, of course, contingent upon how one defines the term "empathy" itself.

The psychologist C. D. Batson defines empathy somewhat differently from Coplan, Slote, and Prinz. For Batson, empathy is intimately linked with *empathic concern*, which he has consistently defined as an "other-oriented emotion elicited by and congruent with the perceived welfare of someone in need."[25] This mode of empathic sensing requires not only that you perceive or recognize the needs of another person but also that you intrinsically value that person's welfare. Empathic concern often produces the motivation to act for the benefit of others. However, Batson notes, helping others sometimes produces consequences that benefit us. For instance, when responding to others out of concern, we sometimes do so in order to relieve ourselves of our feelings of distress. Other times, we avoid feelings of guilt and shame by helping others; and on still other occasions, we receive praise from others and gain a sense of pride from acting on another's behalf. Batson's empirical investigations have demonstrated that experiences of empathic concern produce altruistic *motivation*, and these other-oriented emotional responses are undertaken neither for the purpose of relieving us of feelings of distress, guilt, or shame nor to feel a sense of pride from the praise of others.

Batson's reasoning for linking empathy to empathic concern, then, is to demonstrate empirically how feeling for another—perceiving, responding, and showing concern for the welfare of another—produces altruistic motivation. He calls this premise—namely, the idea that feeling for others produces the motivation to help them—the *empathy-altruism hypothesis*. The empathy-altruism hypothesis does not suggest that our feelings for others *causes* acts of altruism (although this is how many falsely interpret Batson's hypothesis); rather, it claims that feeling for another produces nonegoistic motivation to help that person in situations where the ultimate end is the benefit or increased welfare of her/him. Batson is aware of the multiple and conflicting definitions of empathy, or what he has called the many different "things called empathy."[26] And in accord with Prinz's sentiments, he has also noted that empathy, conceived solely as an imaginative simulation of another's experience, can be used to bring about malevolent ends, rather than to assist the well-being of others.[27]

With Coplan, Slote, Prinz, and Batson, then, we have four different understandings of empathy—namely, empathy as an imaginative process of simulating another's perspective (Coplan); an inner perceptual mechanism that produces an involuntary co-feeling with others (Slote); a kind of vicarious emotion, i.e., feeling what one takes another person to be feeling (Prinz); and a caring emotional response for a person in need (Batson). Each of these insightful scholars, stipulate her/his particular meanings of empathy for the practical purpose of gaining insight into or arriving at a particular end. If I am interpreting the intentions of these thinkers correctly, Coplan's definition of empathy aims to clear up the confusion surrounding the concept of empathy, to advance the process of scientific inquiry, and to understand how we gain experiential understanding of others. Slote's purpose is to show how empathy operates as a type of moral cement and plays an important justificatory role within ethics, which in turn helps us to make sense of moral distinctions, utterances, and judgments. One of the goals of Prinz's definition of empathy is to challenge the assumed moral superiority of empathic experiences and to call into question passive and unreflective beliefs about the benefits of empathy. Finally, Batson's objective is to test his empathy-altruism hypothesis by demonstrating that empathic concern produces a nonegoistic, altruistic motivation to increase the welfare of another person rather than one's own welfare.

Though clearly different from one another, each of these four scholars adopts a narrow conceptualization and definition of empathy that selects and names only a few processes and experiences as empathic. The word "narrow" here is not pejorative but descriptive of a pragmatic move in which one's stipulation of the meaning of "empathy" aims to delineate the parameters of an experience, to bring to light particular truths of experience, and to ground inquiry toward some end. Narrowing the meaning of empathy is clearly worthwhile when it produces insight; nevertheless, narrow approaches necessarily exclude what people have meant or could mean by empathy.

In contrast, broad conceptualizations and definitions of empathy are more inclusive, using very general terms with which one can label a variety of relevant processes and experiences as empathic. For example, in Stephanie Preston and Frans de Waal's work "Empathy: It's Proximate and Ultimate Bases," we find a broad conceptualization and definition of empathy, which they define as "any *process* where the attended perception of the *object* generates a *state* in the *subject* that is more applicable to the object's state or *situation* than to the subject's own prior state or situation."[28] For those who argue for narrow conceptualizations and definitions of empathy, the general terms used here are believed to be too vague to be helpful. Coplan suggests as much by claiming that "we need more specificity, not more generality" to grasp what empathy really is.[29]

Preston and De Waal's definition of empathy and the abstract terms they use, such as "process," "object," "state," subject," and "situation," I contend, should be interpreted as broad but not ambiguous. These nonspecific terms can refer to a wide variety of contextualized experiences. Rather than bringing added confusion and ambiguity to the meaning of empathy, these abstract terms and broad definition function as a pluralistic conceptualization of empathy that invites creative and useful understandings of the complexity and multidimensionality of empathy as a phenomenon. The abstract terms Preston and De Waal use serve as useful abstractions, each of which can refer to several nuanced and contextualized empathic experiences. For example, the term "subject" could refer not only to humans but also to other animals, who experience a number of modes of empathic sensing, commonly ascribed only to humans. This definition also invites one to consider the importance of the historically common meaning of empathy, in which the object of empathizing has referred to inanimate objects, e.g., works of art, nature, and the cultural dynamics that inform us of the experiences of others, rather than simply the experiences of and interactions between living beings. Likewise, a variety of contextualized activities within experience can be subsumed under the general terms "process," "state," and "situation" without limiting the meaning of empathy to only a few, select experiences. For instance, the term "process" can refer to any of the nine modes of empathic sensing I have noted, as well as to the combination of these modes within specific experiences. As a consequence of narrow definitions of empathy, the states of the perceiving subject and the observed object have been described most commonly as either emotional states and/or states of weakness or passivity. But by following Preston and De Waal's broad conceptualization, other commonly experienced states such as exhibiting a strong will, feeling bored, inducing perplexity—or even experiencing the sentiments of rational thought—can be subsumed under this general term, "state." Finally, the useful and general term "situation" can signify a number of unique circumstances in which empathic experiences occur. With these general terms, then, we are able to locate and evaluate a variety of interpersonal, interspecies, and social phenomena that are often ignored when we narrow our conceptualizations and definitions of empathy.

Appropriately broad definitions of empathy, then, offer a great deal of conceptual and semantic flexibility in relation to historical differences and the plurality or variety of experiences. Narrow approaches have other benefits, such as delineating the parameters of inquiry as well as bringing clarity and precision to a given stipulation of empathy as it relates to a given experience or the outcomes of a scientific study. Each approach has its weaknesses too. For if one decides to adopt a narrow conceptualization and definition of empathy, then one risks leaving out something about empathy that shouldn't be excluded. Yet, if one if inclined to conceive of and define empathy pluralistically and broadly, it is possible that this choice might lead to more rather than less ambiguity.

Since both narrow and broad approaches have pros and cons, which should one choose? Ultimately, the significance of this debate lies in the consequences produced by conceiving and defining empathy either narrowly or broadly. What conceivable consequences might arise or how might one's habits of action be transformed if one thinks of empathy narrowly or broadly, according to one definition rather than another? Which dimensions of experience will be excluded if one defines empathy from either a narrow or broad perspective, and what might be the consequences of such exclusion(s)?

Empathy through the Lens of Pluralistic Pragmatism

These types of questions are drawn from the philosophical bloodstream of pluralistic pragmatism—a American tradition of philosophy I favor, and from which I will draw throughout this work.[30] One who embraces this tradition, interprets thoughts, words, and theories to be instruments useful for enlarging our perspectives of experience and for provoking melioristic social change. It is pragmatic, therefore, to judge conflicting definitions of empathy in terms of what they do or might do rather than to declare one of them to be "real" outside of their contextualized meanings and the effects they produce. Pragmatism's focus on instrumentality and the actual or conceivable consequences of our actions relies upon both a conceptual pluralism as well as a linguistic relativity, each of which encourages us to consider, and then reconsider, the instrumental nature of our thoughts and speech and their usefulness for producing satisfactory actions and outcomes.

Pragmatists hold to the belief that the whole of life is fundamentally plural, superabundant, and in transition; life is always emerging, giving birth to new and different permutations of experience as time unfolds. Life has, as William James once described it, an "ever not quite" quality to it, and as new sensations, sentiments, perspectives, experiences, thoughts, feelings, actions, and events arise, life is transformed. Among this flux, the things of experience and the relations between them are likewise irrevocably plural and perpetually changing. This fact of experience requires us to reconfigure and reconstruct our thoughts, words, and theories when, as instruments, they do not serve the needs and problems of people. From a pluralistic pragmatic perspective, it follows from this that both searching for a singular and unchanging "phenomenon" called empathy and claiming that one has given the final word about the "essence" or "nature" of empathy, are wrongheaded from the start.

Pluralistic pragmatism's focus on the instrumentality of our theories, the consequences of our actions, and the plural, processional, and transformative nature of experience is a call to reorient our perception and understanding of life in light of different and emerging experiences within it. One way we can do this, James suggested, is by perpetually returning to the changing dynamics of experience in order to assess, reconsider, and even change the way we formulate our abstractions. James once lamented the fact that philosophers often cling to their abstractions (the names, definitions, and "essences" of things) even when they become unintelligible. This clinging to words and their meanings arises when we carry on in higher realms of abstraction, without seeing the need to redescend into the changing relations within life. Holding on to the abstractions of our thought that bear no intelligible relationship to experience, James believed, fails to finish the function of thought itself, which is to reinsert the conclusions of thought "into some particular point of the immediate stream of life."[31]

Grounded in this tradition of pluralistic pragmatism, my argument will invite consideration of a novel, perhaps provocative idea, namely, that empathy—in its most pragmatic form—is an experience of three general relations between activities and things, rather than simply a particular activity or thing in the world. I will use the term *relational empathy* to signify the merging of these three relations in one's experience toward an object or objects. The usefulness of this notion of relational empathy requires that we reject the false dilemma between narrow and broad approaches; that we think of empathy as a number of different, though interrelated, experiences rather than competing definitions; and perhaps even more radically, that we scrap the very common idea that empathy is a singular thing or activity in the world.

Empathy is generally believed to be either a *thing* or an *activity*. For instance, as a thing empathy has been described as a natural capacity,[32] an ability to identify and to respond,[33] a shared affective state,[34] and a complex form of psychological inference,[35] to name just a few examples. As an activity, empathy has been defined as recognizing what another may be feeling or thinking,[36] imagining the narrative of another,[37] using our imaginations to adopt a different perspective,[38] and responding to another with affect or emotion.[39] There is nothing wrong with describing empathy as a thing or as an activity. Many who have done so have produced amazing insights. However, since my concern is to bring clarity to the notion of empathy when so many people have defined it differently, I sense that this notion of relational empathy is not only novel and useful, but it also represents the most inclusive representation of what people have called "empathy" throughout history, within different academic disciplines, and among different societies. But what is a "relation" and why it is pragmatic to think of empathy relationally?

A relation is a particular mode or manner by which two or more things are connected in experience. By "things," here, I mean any broadly conceived thing, such as activities, objects, people, situations, ideas, concepts (and even relations themselves). Williams James's articulation and use of the notion of a relation was philosophically novel, and it helped him to dissolve a number of unnecessary philosophical debates.[40] For James, relations aren't simply the modes or manners that connect things; they are also the fundamentum (or the ground) of experience itself, what he called "pure experience"—a term that refers to the original, undifferentiated, and multivalent states of relations within experience.[41] Noticing the myriad relations that connect our experiences informs us of the multiplicity and complexity of experience itself. This in turn, awakens us to the fact that, depending on the contexts and circumstances of our experiences, we do not have access to certain relational experiences and we experience and interpret the relations between things in some ways but not others.

Nevertheless, when we consciously perceive, abstract, and represent certain relations between things out of a given context of an experience, we actively select these relations for particular purposes, aims, and interests, and out of necessity, ignore others. And since different people with different intentions and purposes select and represent relations in quite different ways, the self-same thing stands to be interpreted, perceived, and known from a variety of different perspectives. The selection of the relations of a given thing are formed by our conceptual distinctions and are made known by the distinctions we draw both from experience and between different words. And since distinctions have a functional rather than an ontological status, every particular form of knowing as an activity, as James elucidated, can be explained as a particular sort of relation toward one another. Conceptualizing and defining the social construction of empathy is no different. There is an inexhaustible flood of experiential relations from which different theorists have drawn and will continue to draw for the purpose of describing and redescribing empathy. My theory of empathy aims to embrace all of these descriptions for pragmatic purposes, and the success or failure of my goal is wholly contingent upon the actual consequences of accepting it as a theory and employing it as a practice. What a theory does is the whole of what it is.

Relational Empathy

Based on my exploration of the various historical meanings and usages of empathy, I find it to be pragmatic to think of empathy as *relational empathy*, which names an experience wherein there is a unification of three conceptually distinct, though experientially overlapping relations: the relations of feeling into, feeling with, and feeling for. Thus, relational empathy arises when all three of these general relations converge in one's relationship with an object. Each of these represents a general mode or manner in which we relate to persons or things, and each has been conceived historically and independently as a general mode of empathy, and as such may be conceived as different types of empathic experience and modes of feeling. By "feeling" here, I mean the general and broad meaning of the Greek word *pathos* (the root word of "empathy")—signifying, broadly, anything experienced.[42] My employment of the word "feeling" is also very similar to the plural and multiple meanings of the Latin term *sensus*. *Sensus* is very similar to the Greek word *pathos*, for each of these words has been understood according to a variety of different meanings and used for a variety of purposes to describe our bodily experiences and capacities. If the reader feels uncomfortable with the way in which I am employing the word "feeling," she/he may substitute the word "experience" here for the word "feeling."

The first general relation of empathy is a mode or manner in which we feel into an object of perception, observation, or sensation through acts of empathic projection, such as "feeling one's way" or feeling oneself into the experiences of others as well as into the dynamism of inanimate things. This relation is sometimes noted in experience as intentional and willful acts accompanied by, or often intended to produce, a feeling or sense of the object. But this is not always the case in view of the fact that this relation is experienced in disparate ways, as different modes of this general relation—for example, experiences of immediate perception, vigilant observation, intuitive sensation, as well as mindfulness (the sensation of lucid awareness of one's surroundings). Sometimes these experiences provoke an instantaneous feeling of the object, while other times they involve a process of feeling or sensing the object over an indefinite period of time. Here is an example of the former: imagine you are walking through a forest and, gazing upward, you feel yourself into the golden and dancing lights adorning the very tops of the trees and experience an immediate perception of nature's ephemeral beauty. As an example of the latter, think of the relationship between close friends, during the course of which the relation of feeling into is experienced over a period of time. Many friendships begin, in part, with mutual acts of feeling into the personality and character of the other. Then, as long as the friendship lasts, these acts of empathic projection are processional and recurring acts of feeling into the friend's experiences as well as the friendship relation itself.

The second general relation of empathy is a mode or manner in which we feel with other persons or things by experiencing a sense of connection, unity, or concord with them. Depending upon the context, this might involve a feeling of understanding or grasping the thoughts of another, a sense of being united with another's aims, a feeling of agreement with another's sentiments, copying another's bodily expressions, or a deeply felt emotional connection with some person or thing (e.g., a friend or spouse; a political movement; a painting). For pragmatic purposes, a number of different ways empathy is conceptualized in scholarship today, I contend, should be conceived as modes of this general relation, rather than as competing definitions vying for the final word on the nature of empathy (e.g., empathic connection, empathic perspective-taking, empathic accuracy, empathic contagion, and empathic mimicry). As it is with our experiences of the relation of *feeling into*, this second relation is actualized as either an instantaneous feeling or processional feeling. Moreover, experiences of one of these two relations often engender experiences of the other, while in other contexts, these two relations arise in experience simultaneously. However, and unlike the first relation, *feeling with* is experienced as either conscious or unconscious feelings of the body. For example, I can be aware of the fact that I grasp and feel with the actions of another (empathic perspective-taking), yet be unaware that I have adopted the body language of a close friend (empathic mimicry). In the first case, the act of feeling with is confirmed by my cognitive awareness of it, whereas in the second case I unknowingly copy my friend's body language and adopt it as my own.

The third general relation of empathy is a mode or manner in which we feel for other persons/things by displaying concern for them and acting primarily for their benefit and general well-being. By "concern," here, I mean something different from how others have employed this word in relation to empathy. For example, C. D. Batson operationalizes empathy primarily as empathic concern. I deviate from his understanding of this type of empathy by adopting a more general and pluralistic definition of empathic concern as a socially recognizable act of displaying interest in the experiences, circumstances, and general well-being of another person or thing. This broad understanding of concern includes Batson's conceptualization of it as well as our positive experiences with others (e.g., showing interest in the triumphs of others, not just people's pain), and even incorporates our experiences of displaying concern for things such as a political movement or social cause. When our social acts of empathic concern as well as our internalized feelings of concern are sufficiently strong within us, they sometimes motivate us to feel for persons and things through acts of empathic care. These socially recognizable acts of care, as another mode of the relation of *feeling for*, move beyond social displays of interest in that they are acts aimed primarily at benefiting someone or something other than oneself. We exercise empathic care in a variety of disparate contexts of experience, such as through acts of helping someone in need, celebrating someone's good fortune, or promoting a cause, etc.

These three relations of experience as relations of feeling are distinct in thought but not in experience. They are general abstractions of reflection that help us to make sense of the plurality and messiness of experience. In experience, however, each of these relations is recognized as a concrete experience that often overlaps, mingles, and blends together within the different contexts of our experiences; *each is only perceived as distinct through reflection*. Although sometimes all three of these relations come together in an experience, there are times when only one or two of these relations function during our interactions with other persons or things. Here are two concrete examples to clarify what I mean by this.

Imagine that you and a friend are walking on the boardwalk of a California beach, when suddenly, a man blindsides you and steals one of your belongings; and as a consequence, you and your friend are knocked down. Each of you are in a state of shock lying on the wooden pathway, but you manage to watch the person run away. He is running quite quickly, and as you consider whether or not it is a good idea to chase after him, you notice that the man steps on a nail protruding from the boardwalk and, as a consequence, is screaming in agony. At this moment, you would probably experience the first and second relations of empathy but not the third. That is, you observed the man stepping on the nail and "felt your way into" his experience as he was expressing his pain. With this conscious act you experienced a contextualized version of the relation of feeling into. By "feeling your way into" the man's agony, you then experienced the second relation as you immediately grasped that he was in pain and were able to imaginatively simulate what it might be like to feel his pain. But you probably didn't experience the third relation of *feeling for*. Now consider another version of the story. You and your friend are walking on the same boardwalk, but in this case, your friend steps on a nail. In this circumstance, you would most likely experience all three relations of empathy. You would have felt your way into the experience of your friend, grasped and imagined her/his experience, and acted to help your friend. In the first story, you likely didn't experience relational empathy, but in second, chances are you did. A second much shorter example that illustrates how these three relations are recognized in experience.

By calling experiences in which we find a convergence of all three relations of experience *relational empathy*, I do not mean to state that experiences of these relations within a given experience are morally superior to or even more practical than those experiences in which one only experiences one, two, or none of these relations. Rather, I mean to state that the notion of relational empathy reflects the plurality of meanings given to the word "empathy" throughout the history of it as an idea. It does appear, however, that our most intimate relationships often benefit from the coexistence and application of all three of these relations. The generality of the relations I have outlined may seem for some to be too abstract to accentuate the contexts and situatedness of unique, specific experiences, but just the opposite is true. Depending upon the context and circumstance of a given experience, these three general relations can be representative of a variety of contextualized experiences. For example, in one context, relational empathy might include an observation of nature, a feeling of being united with it, and the social act of displaying interest and caring for the natural environment. While in another context, it could function as a perception of one's pain, an imagined simulation of her/his pain, and a demonstration of concern for such a person through a social act of helping behavior aimed to alleviate the other person's pain.

The three relations I have described are recognized clearly within a variety of historical and cultural traditions dating from the late eighteenth century to the present day. Even though over this span of time people have given different names to signify each of these relations, they have also been labeled as types of empathy. To demonstrate this fact, it is necessary to conduct a thoroughly historical—and philosophically genealogical—investigation into the origin and varied meanings of *pathos* (the root word of empathy), the important historical-semantic differences between sympathy and empathy, the multiple meanings and functions of these three relations, and how all these historical edifices of meaning have influenced the idea of empathy in modern times.[43] Only then can we begin to provide satisfactory answers to a number of outstanding questions about empathy, such as: Is empathy moral? Can empathy be developed? Or, how might relational empathy be used as an instrument to help us to live more democratically?

2

Pathos and the Death of Dualisms

It has been over seven hours now, and although you arrived well before your scheduled departure. your plane has been delayed for five hours. Your plan was to arrive early to your destination, go for a walk in the afternoon, embrace the chill of the autumn air, and enjoy the charming colors adorning the tops of trees.

But your current situation is neither embracing nor charming; the atmosphere at this airport is thick with frustration, as frazzled customers can't stop expressing their disappointment. You start to "catch" the anxiety and distress of those surrounding you, but then you shift your attention to a nearby couple in an attempt to avoid absorbing the moods of disappointed—merely potential—passengers. The couple is having difficulty controlling their five kids, each of whom is mimicking the parents' facial expressions by feeling into and feeling with their undesired experiences. You begin to feel yourself into the parents' hopelessness and feel connected to them as you project your thoughts into their experience and imagine what it might be like to experience their current, seemingly hopeless, situation. You infer that they might need help, as one of their churlish, yet creative, children begins to write his name on the terminal window by squirting the milk out of his younger baby brother's bottle. Feeling waves of concern for the now cranky and cantankerous couple, you feel impelled to help them. You leap from your seat and gracefully grab the bottle out of the child's hands and return it to his parents. The father of the child thanks you for your assistance, though his mind is clearly elsewhere.

Despite your efforts, the couple, Nia and Cole, begin to fight over which one of them is to be blamed for their current unmanageable circumstance:

Nia "See, I told you last night that keeping the kids up late before a day of long travel would lead to this."

Cole "Listen, calm down, there is no reason to cause a stir."

Nia "Didn't I tell you to stop playing with the children at 9 p.m.?"

Figure 2 Thick Clouds over Emory University, Atlanta, Georgia.

Cole "Oh, so it's my fault!"

Nia "I didn't say that."

Cole "Maybe if your mothering skills were better, our kids would be more civil!"

Nia "Really? Can you be any more insulting?"

Cole "Also, whenever there is a problem, you become irrational."

Nia "What do you mean?"

Cole "Just please ... don't be so emotional! Be calm and use your reason!"

Nia "Wait a second, when you ask me not to be emotional, is that an emotional or rational request?"

Cole "Huh?"

In this scenario, you might have recognized a few experiences that we established in chapter 1 to be exemplary of different understandings of "empathy." You might have also noticed that Cole's depiction of Nia's perspective as irrational and emotional *seems to be rooted in his own emotional states of frustration, anger, and anxiety.*

Not entirely unlike Cole's specific understanding of the differences between rational and emotional experiences, we often tend to think that our experiences of reason and emotion are distinct, that is, we act either rationally or emotionally. Such a claim seems to be justified in certain circumstances. If one person is forming judgments about her business strategy by a process of logical thinking and another is crying hysterically because one of his family members has just passed away, clearly the former is for the most part *acting rationally*, while the latter is *reacting emotionally*. But the first person could also be joyous at the same time that she is utilizing her rational capacities; and the person who is crying profusely could also be thinking rationally about the possible ways he could honor the dead. It is often believed that reason is superior to and should be in control of our emotional experiences—at least, this has been the common trend, a recurring narrative, throughout the history of philosophy. But this idea seems to be untenable in consideration of the fact that although reason and emotion are distinct as thoughts, they are not wholly distinct in our experiences.

Long before the distinction between the words "reason" and "emotion" began to guide our judgments about the character and value of our thoughts and action, reason (*logos*) was sometimes opposed to *pathos*, which is the root word of empathy. *Pathos* didn't mean "emotion" (a word that was not yet invented); but rather, as contemporary scholarship has demonstrated, it meant something very broad, signifying *anything experienced*, any feeling of experience.[1]

By examining the original meaning(s) of the word *pathos* as well as the plurality of meanings *pathos* adopted when it was translated into other languages, we discover that *pathos* and its cognate terms (e.g., *passio, affectus,* and *perturbio*) signified a variety of different experiences depending upon the worldview of the person that employed them. These multiple meanings of *pathos* as an experience were often coupled with terms that were believed to signify opposing meanings. This led to the construction of ontological dualisms, such as the dualisms of *pathos/logos*, "passion/reason" and *passio/affectus*, "pathological/healthy," etc. These distinctions *as dualisms*, and others like them, are problematic, for they distort experience by making our conceptual distinctions rigid and leave our understandings of the complexity of experience wanting.

In order for what I am calling relational empathy to be able to evade the distorting effects of dualistic thinking, we must first conceive the root word *pathos* in the word "empathy" to signify *anything experienced*, rather than conceive it in terms of any existing dualism. And to accomplish this, it is necessary to provide a bit of historical and philosophical genealogy, which will allow us to become familiar with how different understandings of *pathos* were used to serve different purposes, and why these understandings and usages are relevant to our contemporary discussions about "empathy."

Pathos: Neutral Conceptualizations in Antiquity

Aristotle described *pathos* (pl. *pathé*) as a state and feeling accompanied by pain or pleasure. *Pathé*, as it is defined in *Rhetoric*, are "all those feelings that so change men as to affect their judgments, and that are also attended by pain or pleasure. Such are anger, pity, fear and the like, with their opposites."[2] Moderate and appropriate experiences of *pathé* were valuable for Aristotle, not as an end goal in life, but rather, for how they contribute to the ultimate end goal of life, namely human happiness (*eudaimonia*). The highest form of happiness is a flourishing life, a life of virtue or excellence (*arete*). *Pathé* are instrumental and beneficial when—cultivated and controlled by reason—they contribute toward this ultimate end goal of life. *Pathé* are disruptive, however, when they distort our ability to reason and/or when they contribute to irrational actions. Elsewhere in *Rhetoric*, Aristotle provides an example of how *pathé* are instrumentally beneficial by exploring three modes of persuasion: *pathos, ethos*, and *logos*. He notes that a speaker's ability to evoke the right *pathos/pathé* within an audience is a skill for arousing feelings that change people's judgments.[3] Evoking the right responses (*pathé*) in an audience, establishing the integrity or character (*ethos*) of the speaker, and the "proof, or apparent proof, provided by the words of the speech [*logos*] itself" are three modes of persuasion that contribute to the realization of virtuous ends.[4]

Pathé, conceived also as internal changes that affect our judgments, are morally neutral for Aristotle, but they become good or bad by how they hinder or help the actualization of virtuous ends and the way these ends contribute to a life of happiness.[5] When *pathé* are felt appropriately, i.e., they are neither excessive nor deficient, they are a mark of moral virtue. On the contrary, inappropriate feelings of *pathé*, i.e., having too much or too little *pathé* are marks of vice. This is what Aristotle refers to in the *Nicomachean Ethics* as the doctrine of the mean:

Moral virtue ... is concerned with *pathé* and actions, and in these there is excess, defect, and the intermediate. For instance, both fear and confidence and appetite and anger and pity and in general pleasure and pain may be felt both too much and too little, and in both cases not well; but to feel them at the right times, with reference to the right objects, toward the right people, with the right motive, and in the right way, is what is both intermediate and best, and this is characteristic of virtue.[6]

A life of virtue and particular virtuous acts are consequences of experiencing *pathé* moderately (i.e., by *metriopatheia*). *Pathé* are fleeting experiences, and we are sometimes unable to control their power over us. Other dimensions of experience are much less ephemeral, for example, *hexis* (our general disposition), or *ethos* (the consistent habits that form our character), each signifies something much more permeant and stable than *pathos*. *Ethos* cultivates our ability to moderate our *pathé* when it is informed by *logos*/reason or fixed logical truths. *Pathos* is fleeting and impermanent. Both one's general disposition (*hexis*) and character (*ethos*) are relatively stable and consistent, but *logos* (reason) is unchanging.

In the philosophy of Epicurus, *pathos* is defined a bit different than this. For Epicurus, *pathos* is a feeling or experience that is either pleasurable or painful.[7] Similar to Aristotle's account, *pathé* are neutral; they are intrinsically neither good nor bad. Rather, as senses or feelings within us, they aid our ability to discern between good (pleasurable) and bad (painful) experiences and help us to live a life of pleasure. "Pleasure is our first and congenital good, it is the starting point of every choice and avoidance, and we return to it since we make *pathos* the standard by which to judge every good."[8] For Epicurus, *eudaimonia* was also conceived as the highest good; but the ultimate goal of life is to live a life of pleasure.[9] Also quite different from Aristotle, *pathé* do not rely upon our rational capacities. They are themselves instinctive modes of awareness or sensations; they are senses or feelings within us. They are nonrational dynamics of the psyche or soul by which we recognize and grasp the quality of our experiences.

Pleasure and pain are two general *pathé*, in which "pleasure" is understood simply as the absence of pain, and "pain" includes all forms of pain, e.g., physical, psychological, and emotional pain. A life of pleasure for Epicurus, which is equal to both a life of happiness (*eudaimonia*) and the ultimate end goal of life itself, is easy to achieve if we are inclined to seek out and fulfill the desires that are easiest to satisfy. Pain often arises from our inability to fulfill desires, but certain desires, what Epicurus referred to as natural and necessary desires, such as the physical desire for water and food or the psychological need for friendship, are necessary to fulfill in order to achieve happiness. Natural but unnecessary desires (e.g., eating exotic foods) need not be fulfilled for happiness although they are natural, while vain desires (e.g., the desires for immortality, fortune, or fame) are neither natural nor necessary; they are very difficult to fulfill, and our failure to fulfill them culminates in the *pathos* of pain.

Pathos, Pathology, and *Eupathy*

Within two other traditions in antiquity, *pathos* was defined in pejorative rather than neutral terms. The first was the Hippocratic tradition of medicine, and the second was the philosophical school of Stoicism. Within the former, *pathos* is defined, in the same manner in which Epicurus defined it, as a feeling within our bodies; however, for Hippocrates, it is a both a feeling of physical suffering and a sign that the natural order and health of the body has gone awry. It should be no surprise, then, that words such as "pathological," "pathogen," and "psychopathy," are derived from this original, pejorative usage of the word *pathos* in the Hippocratic school. Within the latter tradition of Stoicism, *pathos* also referred to something that has gone awry, but for the Stoics it referred to the disorder, irrationality, and general ill-health of soul (psyche) rather than of the body. This pejorative understanding of *pathos* is the other source of negative terms today, such as "passivity," and "pathetic."

Common to each of these traditions of inquiry, *pathé* was contrasted with and set in direct opposition to health, reason, and order. And as it was believed, experiences of ill-health and irrationality, whether of the body or the soul, come and go, but reason stands unmoved, and the logical truths derived from it do not change. On a more cosmic scale, a number of ancient philosophers contended that our experiences of *pathos* resembled in form the material cosmos (*hyle*) in that, while the former was controlled by reason, the latter originated and is directed by the eternal, unchanging Reason (*Logos* or God) as well as the providential order of all things. On a more concrete level, *pathos* was also conceived as a deviation from the natural and proper functioning of the body and as a forerunner to sickness and disease.

Just as the aim of physicians was to use logical and rational thinking to cure the body of diseases and sickness, the goal of Stoic philosophers was to use logical and rational thinking to "cure" and eliminate the diseases (i.e., *pathé*) of the soul, which were likewise conceived to be contrary to nature.[10]

These two aims overlapped; and consequently, each of these narratives of *pathos* influenced one another. For example, the Hippocratic connection between *pathé* and the unnatural symptoms/affects (*pathéma*) of the body led the Stoics to draw analogies between the diseases of the body and those of the soul.[11] Chrysippus compared the weakness, sickness, and irrationality of the soul with the weakness of a body that "falls easily into sickness"; and he suggested that the souls of inferior men are "comparable to bodies which are liable to contract fevers."[12] Posidonius rejected this comparison claiming that "the soul's sickness ... is like either bodily health with proneness to sickness *or sickness itself*. For bodily sickness is a *tenor* already sick, but the sickness Chrysippus speaks of is more like proneness to fevers."[13] The word "tenor," which means a "prevailing character," suggests that the sickness of the body or of the soul is a *chronic condition* or *disposition*, namely that a person's soul is diseased when *pathé*, as false judgments, weak opinions, and/or excessive impulses, are sufficiently habitual as to constitute one's character (*ethos*). Despite the apparent difference between Chrysippus and Posidonius, Galen reports that Chrysippus held *pathé* to be both a disease/*noséma* and a sickness/*arróstmata*.[14] Both claims, namely that *pathos* is either proneness to sickness or that it is sickness itself, are recognized in Diogenes Laertius's account of Zeno, the founder of the Stoic school of philosophy, who seems to have held both positions.[15]

Stoics believed that the ultimate goal in life was happiness, which is the result of a virtuous life.[16] Though both Aristotelian and Stoic philosophies linked happiness with virtue, moral virtue for the Stoics is not achieved by experiencing the mean between excess and deficiency as Aristotle portrayed it to be; rather, it was described in general as a well-reasoned *harmonious disposition in life*.[17] Despite different interpretations of this phrase,[18] it means the alignment of one's reason and judgments with what is good in life, to live a life in accord with the eternal, unchanging *Logos*, which is synonymous with Reason, Nature, or Fate.[19] As the *Logos* or active rationality commands and directs all things, so too our reason/*logos* must be in command of our reaction to what befalls us.[20] *Pathé* thwart our ability to be in harmony with the rational structure of the eternal *Logos*. They are *passive* experiences in which reason lacks command over our souls/psyches; they arise whenever we are moved by an experience that would not move or affect us if we were acting rationally.[21] For most Stoics, *pathé* meant one of two things: (a) false judgments or weak opinions and (b) excessive impulses.

Pathé as false judgments or weak opinions are states of perverted reason with which we make incorrect judgments concerning the value of a present or future experience. *Pathé* are also irrational impulses, *excessive impulses*.[22] Impulses, as proper functions of the body controlled by reason, are healthy and normal when they contribute to a life of virtue, but they are unhealthy and abnormal when they are excessive, i.e., contrary to reason itself and the habits of reasoning during one's daily live.[23]

Pathé were categorized and subsumed under four main types: *appetite, fear, pleasure,* and *distress*. Appetite and fear are *future-oriented* irrational judgments; appetite is an excessive impulse, a movement of the soul/psyche toward something that appears to be good; fear is a movement toward something that appears bad. Pleasure and distress are similar types of judgments, impulses, and movements, but these are directed toward some experience in the present conceived as either good (pleasure) or bad (distress).

The goal of life for the Stoic was to live a life without these and similar *pathé*—and to do this, one must be apathetic. This might sound odd, but this simply means that you must control your responses and reactions to whatever happens, especially when you do not have the power to change the circumstances of experience in which you find yourself. Although *pathé* need to be eradicated, good feelings called *eupathies*—such as joy, watchfulness, and wishing—motivate us to live virtuously and are a natural consequence of a virtuous life.[24] Another positive *pathos* resulting from a life of virtue is *ataraxia*—namely a state of tranquility, a bodily and psychological freedom from disruptive *pathé*—which arises from a rational understanding and acceptance of that which we undergo.

The Stoic negative portrayal of *pathé* as irrational combined with the tendency of doctors in the Hippocratic tradition to link *pathé* with ill-health of the body guided Cicero's thoughts when he first chose the Latin word *morbus* (disease) as an appropriate translation for the Greek word *pathos*. In Cicero's words: "I might have rendered this literally and styled them [*pathé*] 'diseases,' but the word 'disease' would not suit all instances.... Let us then accept the word 'perturbation,' the very sound of which seems to denote something vicious and that these perturbations are not excited by any natural influence."[25] Just as unnatural disorders of the body cause disease and sickness within the body, so too, the *perturbations of the mind*—how Cicero defines *pathé* in Latin—cause the soul to be both diseased and sick. As a consequence of the perturbations [*pathé*] of the mind, there are produced, first, "diseases which the Stoics call *nosémata* ... then, sickness which they call *arrostemata*."[26] Following the Stoics, Cicero believed that there were cures to the perturbations of the mind; and although different perturbations demand different cures, simply holding the belief that they are unnatural, unnecessary, and vicious serves as a general cure for all *pathé*.[27] Cicero also insists that all perturbations of the mind are under our control if we exercise our wills.

In addition to Cicero's translation of *pathos* into *perturbatio* (perturbation), others translated *pathos* into the Latin as *passio* (passion), while still others translated pathé as *affectus* (affect; e.g., Seneca). While *pertubatio* always referred only to negative experiences, exemplified by a turbulent or frenzied mind, *affectus* and *passio* referred to positive or negative experiences.

Pathé: From Worldly Flesh to Heavenly Love

But with the rise of Christianity in the Roman world, *perturbio* and *passio* as types of *pathé* most commonly signified the movements of a human soul/psyche directed by the animalistic desires and lower appetites of the body, while *affectus* frequently meant the movements of human rationality and will toward the divine.[28] Giving into temptation and indulging in the lower passions and appetites of the body were conceived as acts of sin against God.[29] Similar to the Stoic narrative that describes *pathé* as a type of sickness in need of a cure, Christian philosophers and theologians viewed sins of the body and certain movements of the passions of the psyche/soul as forms of sickness and imperfections that likewise must be cured.[30]

In the works of Augustine and Aquinas, we find a reconstruction of the meaning and significance of the Latin cognates of *pathé* for the purpose of explaining Christian eschatology and—as Thomas Dixon has noted—to provide an alternative to the moral philosophy of Greek and Roman Stoics. In *The City of God*, Augustine uses the terms *pertubatio*, *passio*, and *affectus* to signify either lower sinful desires of the body or higher movements of the soul toward God. He also sometimes combines these terms to signify special movements of the soul.[31] Exemplary of the latter, he employs the terms "perturbations" and "passions" (*perturbation, passionum*), which combine the Stoic conceptualization of *pathé* as excessive impulses, weak opinions, and false judgments with Cicero's understanding of *pathé* as perturbations.[32]

Though he often adopts Cicero's understanding of *pathos* as *perturbatio* and is loyal to a few Stoic ideas, Augustine took great lengths to separate his biblically informed interpretation of *pathé* from those of the Stoics. Specifically, he took aim at the idea that *pathé* should—or even could—be eliminated (*apatheia*). Apatheia might be experienced in the "next life," but as a consequence of "original sin," *apatheia* is not attainable in this life.[33] The determining factor as to whether affections or passions are positive or negative is the direction of one's will (*voluntas*): "What is most important is the quality of one's will, because if the will is wrong, it will have wrong movements, but if it is right, they will be not only blameless but even praiseworthy."[34] In his own way, then, Augustine follows Aristotle's view that most *pathé* are neither good nor bad outside of the context in which they are experienced, i.e., *metriopatheia*. However, for Augustine, the movement of the will is blameless and praiseworthy if one's affections are directed toward the top of the Great Chain of Being: truth, goodness, and God; but they are inappropriate or wrong when the will is directed toward the bottom of this Great Chain: the body's lower appetites, passions, earthly desires, etc.[35]

Compared with Augustine, Aquinas offers a nuanced portrayal of the Christian version of the Great Chain of Being, placing "pure" activity at the top of this supposed order of nature and "pure" passivity at the very bottom of this conceptual grid. For Aquinas, God is pure activity—eternal, unchanging, and unmoved; following Aristotle, Aquinas identifies God as the Unmoved Mover and uncaused Cause of all things; God is neither moved nor caused. Matter without form is exemplary of "pure passivity," and is unable to actualize or move itself; it must be moved and caused by God. This cosmic portrait of the whole of existence shaped Aquinas's ideas about the different powers or faculties of the soul, some of which are available only to certain beings depending upon their location along the Great Chain of Being.[36] Of these different faculties, Aquinas focuses upon two of them to elucidate the passions and affects: the rational appetitive faculty (which is synonymous with the will) and the sensitive appetitive faculty.[37] Passions are powers of the sensitive appetitive faculty, which Aquinas divides into two kinds: the concupiscible and the irascible. Concupiscible passions, i.e., love and hatred, desire and aversion, and joy and sadness, relate to our sense of things as either good or evil; they cause either pleasure or pain, and are grasped in terms of movement and rest. The irascible passions are understood in terms of both movement and struggle; for these passions arise when we are faced with the difficulty and struggle of attaining good and avoiding evil. These types of passions include hope and despair, courage and fear, and anger (which has no contrary passion).

As acts common among both human and nonhuman animals, irrational passions are desires of the lower appetite and could lead one to sin. But, passions, in and of themselves, are neither good nor bad. But when they are moderated by the virtue of temperance and "subject to the command of reason and will, then moral good and evil are in them."[38] If actions arise because of rational judgment, will, and affection, these facets of the soul might contribute to the morality of our actions. But when passions cloud reason, it reduces the morality of actions. Passions, moreover, are often moved by our sense of some external event and the sensitive appetitive faculty itself is likewise moved by external causes; these are low on the cosmic order of the Great Chain of Being and are deviations from the nature of God as "pure" activity. Consequently, Aquinas claims passion and passivity to be fundamentally deficient and imperfect: "Now passion or passivity implies by its very nature some sort of deficiency ... Those creatures that come nearest to God, the first and completely perfect being, have little of potentiality and passivity in them."[39] The rational appetitive faculty, rational judgment, and exercise of the virtues, all resemble the perfect, immutable nature of God. When the rational appetitive faculty desires the things of God and the universal objects of good, one feels *affection* toward divine realities by means of "union with them by means of love."[40] According to Aquinas, then, love is an affect when it moves the soul toward God and is a passion when it gives rise to perturbations and upheavals of the soul.

Pathé and Modern Philosophy: From Mechanisms to Moral Psychology

Not unlike the way Christian premodern discourses of *pathé*/passions replaced, in part, those of the ancient Stoics, the tradition of modern philosophy supplanted the premodern Christian narrative of *pathé*, namely as movements away or toward God, with conceptualizations of *pathé* as functional components of the body or as functional descriptions of the body as it relates to the soul. For instance, René Descartes divides *pathé* into two fundamental types: *pathé* that are produced by the body and those that are produced within the soul alone.[41] Though Descartes sometimes refers to the first type of *pathé* as perceptions, he contends it would be "better to call them *emotions* of the soul, not only because this term may be applied to all the changes, which occur in the soul, but more particularly because, of all of the kinds of thought which the soul may have there are none that agitate and disturb it so strongly as the passions."[42]

Although the passions of the soul are motivating forces that incline the soul to want things for the purpose of preserving the physical body as well as to secure human happiness, they can also move us to perform vicious acts. Descartes names six fundamental passions: wonder, love, hatred, desire, joy, and sadness—all other passions are either composed from these or subsumed under them. In alignment with both Stoic and Christian perspectives, these *pathé* must be controlled by reason.[43] Similar to Aristotle's neutral view of *pathé*, passions for Descartes are neither good nor bad independent of the contextual experiences of them, though we must use our reason to exercise control over them. For Descartes, the faculty of the "thinking substance" must regulate, control, and monitor the passions; it must employ its "proper weapons" of "firm and determinate judgments," which guide our conduct, help us to act virtuously, and contribute to the experience of human happiness.[44]

Descartes also notes a second class of *pathé*, i.e., intellectual and internal emotions, that are distinct from the first type; he uses the term "emotions" not only to signify the passions of the soul caused by the body but also to describe those *pathé* that are caused only by the soul. Descartes uses the terms "intellectual emotions" and "internal emotions" to refer to those affects "produced in the soul only by the soul itself. In this they differ from its passions, which always depend on some movement of the animal spirits."[45] Though he isn't clear about the differences between these, it appears that "internal emotions" denote any *pathé* produced in the soul, while "intellectual emotions" are a specific type of internal emotions. Intellectual emotions differ from the aforementioned passions of the soul in that they are caused by rational, clear thoughts, rather than sensuous, confused thoughts.[46] This distinction between the "internal emotions" produced by the soul and the emotions/passions that were caused, maintained and strengthened by movements of and changes within the body was not unlike the Christian differentiation between the passions of the lower sense appetite of the body and the affections of the higher rational faculty of the soul and will. It also resembles, in part, the Stoic distinction between *pathé* and *eupathies*.[47] Unique to his own theory of the *pathé*, Descartes introduces the idea of an emotion; and his distinction between different types of emotions allowed him to explicate how these intellectual emotions, such as contentment of the mind and tranquility, arise from virtuous living and are the basis of all human happiness—a happiness that can withstand even the most violent and disruptive effects of our passions.[48]

Thomas Hobbes adopts a different mechanistic philosophy than Descartes, namely materialism: the perspective that only material bodies exist, and *everything is matter in motion.* The views of Stoic and Christian thinkers from Hobbes's perspective are utterly fanciful and even delusional, especially the tendency of thinkers within these traditions to embrace transcendental accounts of reality. Thus, he rejects many of the Stoic and Christian ideas, for example, the transcendent and governing *Logos* of the Stoics, as well as the Christian notions of sin, the "Fall," and an immaterial God.[49] In the same way that the whole of existence is matter in motion, Hobbes contends that human bodies are likewise matter in motion. We, as part of the material world, then, are nothing more than self-preserving machines motivated by a "perpetual and restless desire of power after power."[50] Rejecting the premodern's inclination to offer "metaphorical" explanations of *pathé* as passions, volitions, or motions of the soul, Hobbes contends that the powers existing within our bodies arise from the movements of the matter within us and have no other source.[51] Opposed to all of the previously mentioned philosophical perspectives, sense, as well as other human abilities such as imagination, speech, volition, and reason, etc., need not be received, mediated, guided, or explained by the motions or properties of a existent soul nor anything else conceived to be functioning separately from the movements of material bodies. For Hobbes, the same is true of the passions, each of which has its own motion.[52]

The basis of all *pathé* as passions is endeavor (i.e., *conatus*), and there are two motions of endeavor: appetite and aversion. Appetite is the motion of endeavor toward something desired, and aversion is the motion of endeavor away from something undesired. All passions are manifestations of our restless and unyielding striving for power, driven by these different motions of endeavor. Thus, opposed to the previous accounts, Hobbes contends that certain types of passions fundamentally have to do with power, the acknowledgment of power, and honor. This focus on power makes his theory of passions incredibly unique, for instead of dividing up human *pathé* for the purpose of outlining medical diseases (Hippocrates), describing the virtuous or happy life (Aristotle, Epicurus, and the Stoics), explaining the religious significance of the Great Chain of Being (Christian philosophers), or for demonstrating the superiority of the soul over the body (Descartes), Hobbes's narrative and multiple lists of the passions serve to elucidate the nature of power, political experience, and the political realm. This is noted in *Elements of Law* by recognizing Hobbes's distinction between *pathé*/passions as sensual pleasures directed at present objects and *pathé*/passions of the mind directed toward the future. Of these two, Hobbes is most concerned with future-oriented passions of the mind in relation to our ability to preserve our own lives, acquire social powers, and attain happiness. Given this, it should be no surprise that the first passion Hobbes lists in *Elements* is the passion of glory, which he conceives to be a future-oriented and imaginative desire for recognition of one's power and worth. This passion of glory as well as all other *pathé* as future-oriented passions of the mind are beliefs; they are the conceptions we have about the power we possess, how we might use it, and the way we should act.

Future-oriented passions of the mind as beliefs about how we might use our power instrumentally in society pose a serious problem for Hobbes. People have differing beliefs about the power they possess and how they should wield it; and when they act on these beliefs, social conflict often arises. During a time of war, in which according to Hobbes we return to a state of nature, conflict reigns, and there is no *common measure* or "right reason" by which every person could know what is good and what is bad, what one ought to do and not to do. Hobbes distrusts the abilities of individuals in the state of nature to be impartial in determining the common measure, for left to their own devices they will tend to favor themselves. Individual acts of reason that inform private judgments about conflicts cannot bridle passions of the mind; passions can only be bridled by other passions, particularly the passion of fear. Nevertheless, a sovereign power and the laws it creates can become social instruments of both reason and fear, each of which can be used to maintain the functionality of civil society and to avoid religious wars. And this is Hobbes's solution to the problem of the passions of the mind that contribute to our unchecked desire for power: the creation of the artificial monster of the *Leviathan* from which the common measure will be established by the sovereign, and the passions of the mind that lead to conflict will be kept in check.

In the works of Baruch Spinoza, we find another nuanced understanding of *pathé* echoing in part the premodern Christian distinction between *passio* and *affectus* (though informed by a different theological worldview) and resembling, though deviating philosophically from, Hobbes's act of connecting *pathé* with *conatus*. Spinoza completely rejects the Judeo-Christian—and any other— understanding of God as a being separate from the world, and instead defines God panentheistically as an "absolutely infinite being," a substance in the universe within which all other things exist.[53] This theological and monistic starting point makes Spinoza's theory of *pathé* incompatible with that of Descartes's, for it rejects Descartes's contention that there are two different sources *as substances* for our experience of *pathé*.

Though Spinoza evades falling into the trap of Cartesian dualistic thinking, he fails to avoid another powerful—similarly problematic—dualism that guides his view of *pathe*: the active/passive dualism that, as I have shown, guided Stoic thought. The general term Spinoza uses for all *pathé* is "affects" (or "affections"), adopting Seneca's Latin translation of the Greek word *pathos* into *affectus*. Following Seneca and being guided by one of the most common dualisms of ancient Stoicism shouldn't be too surprising; scholars commonly note how Stoicism shaped Spinoza's worldview. However, unlike for the Stoics, for Spinoza *pathé* as affects are neutral; they are neither positive nor negative outside of a particular context of experience. Affects are states within the body (e.g., desire, joy, sadness, etc.) by which the body's power to act is either increased or diminished, helped or coerced. In this way, Spinoza's narrative of the *pathos* is like Hobbes's view in the way that each links our experiences of *pathé* with endeavor or striving after power, i.e., *conatus*. We tend to strive toward things, Spinoza contended, that we believe will benefit us by increasing our power of acting and avoid those things that we believe will harm us by decreasing our power of acting.

Although *pathé* are neutral outside of how they either strengthen or weaken the body's power to act, Spinoza uses the active/passive dualism to divide *pathé* as affects into two types: *actions* and *passions*. Affects that are actions are positive because they empower us to act, while passions are negative when they weaken our power to act by *acting upon us*. Spinoza employs another dualism to elucidate the difference between these two types of affects, what we might call the adequacy/inadequacy dualism. He uses this dualism by employing it in his descriptions of both the ideas of the mind and the causes of things.[54] Regarding ideas of the mind, an adequate idea is a clear, distinct, and rational idea, while an inadequate idea is a confused and irrational idea. He applied this dualism to provide an understanding of the causes of things: a cause of something is adequate if its effect can be clearly and distinctly perceived through it, and it is partial or inadequate if its effect cannot be understood through it alone.[55] A mind's *actions* as affects arise from adequate ideas alone, and we act only when we are the adequate cause. The minds *passions* as affects occur when the mind is being dominated or manipulated by inadequate ideas alone, and we are acted upon when we are merely a partial or inadequate cause.

Spinoza employed this account of *pathé* for many of the same reasons the Stoics did. Within each philosophical worldview, the central problem to be solved is the experience of *pathé*, defined by the Stoics as false judgments, excessive impulses, and weak opinions, and by Spinoza as passions—types of affects—arising from confused ideas and partial causes. These negative experiences of *pathé* manipulate our wills and distort our reason; and we must exercise rational control over them to live well. For Spinoza, in particular, the exercise of reason and the experience of positive affects each have the potential to free us from the controlling power and bondage of negative passions. While Spinoza's understanding of *pathé* is quite unlike that of Descartes's or Hobbes's, each of these thinkers conceive the experience of *pathos* to be something negative, something opposed to reason and rationality, regardless of whether the source of these passions were the soul (Descartes), the political state (Hobbes), or rational affect (Spinoza).

With the writings of Adam Smith and David Hume, in particular, and the Scottish Enlightenment philosophers, in general, we find an abandonment of the tendency to locate *pathé* in relation to a mechanistic order; in favor of an understanding of *pathé* in relation to the structure of our moral psychologies. What is especially interesting about Smith's and Hume's accounts of *pathos* is the way they set our *disagreeable passions* against more refined or acceptable types of *pathé*, what they called *moral sentiments*. In this way, their thoughts concerning the meaning of *pathos*, though different than the Cartesian narrative that preceded theirs, followed a similar conceptual structure, one in which our *moral sentiments*, rather than our internal or intellectual emotions, were set in direct opposition to the least favorable form of *pathé*, the negative and unruly *passions*. Similar to medieval accounts, the philosophers of the Scottish Enlightenment also, on occasion, contrasted the passion with affect, and sometimes sentiment and affect were used interchangeably.

In addition to their introduction of the notion of moral sentiment as refined *pathé*, Hume and Smith introduced a new paradigm for understanding how *pathé* function within our bodies and how we can *feel with* the *pathé* of others. Quite opposed to the trends we have witnessed among the previous thinkers I have explored, Hume and Smith rejected the idea that reason alone has the power to control or direct *pathé*.[56] And whether referred to as calm and refined sentiments and affections or violent and disruptive passions, all *pathé* are identified by means of our faculty of moral judgment, which is rooted in our feelings of approbation or disapprobation. Thus, whether we are experiencing the *pathos* in question ourselves or see it expressed within another, we interpret it by means of our sense of it as something either pleasing (and thus approved by our senses) or displeasing (and disapproved by our senses—our feeling of it as bad or, at least, undesirable). But *pathé* are also interpreted by a companion faculty that facilitates our judgment, what Hume and Smith called *sympathy*.

According to Hume, sympathy is a mechanism by which we grasp the *pathé* of others by means of what I have called *empathic contagion*—an instantaneous and involuntarily "catching" of another's *pathé*; whereas for Smith, sympathy is an interpretive power of the experiences of ourselves and others by means of our imaginations, what I have called *empathic perspective-taking*. Smith's understanding of sympathy is widely conceived as being superior to Hume's for a few good reasons. First, Smith's version of sympathy incorporates and improves upon Hume's theory by subsuming, and thus including empathic contagion under the umbrella of the powers of sympathy.[57] Second, Smith's understanding of sympathy is more sensitive to context and thus more realistic as a description of how we are able—or not able—to sympathize with the experiences of others. Third, Smith's description of sympathy is broader and more pluralistic than Hume's, making it more akin to the many things we call empathy today; and relevant to my purposes, Smith's theory of sympathy incorporates all three relations of what I have called *relational empathy*. For instance, Smith included *empathic projection*, what Smith calls the action of "entering into," as a vital part of sympathy's functions, and he identified sympathy as *feeling with* others, as either necessary for or a direct component of *feeling for* others.[58] Independent of these noticeable benefits, both Hume and Smith rejected the untenable dualism of reason/*pathos* that has clearly been instrumental throughout this exploration of *pathos*. Unfortunately, this rejection has been ignored by many theorists of empathy today, so before we examine the value of any contemporary theory of empathy in relation to practice, we must first completely exorcize this and other ghostly dualisms that have haunted philosophy, confused theories of empathy, and disfigured experience itself.

Exorcizing the Ghostly Dualisms

This brief, and thus incomplete, historical exploration of the term *pathos*, its historically related or cognate terms, as well as the multiple ways these terms were shaped by different theories and worldviews, may be likened to taking a short stroll through a museum of philosophical ideas. Each new idea about *pathos*, as a painting of experience from a particular point of view, was used as a tool for the benefit of each philosopher who constructed it and the philosophy each theorist promoted. Interestingly, no one felt compelled to hold onto the meanings of the past, and neither should we, especially when certain meanings have distorted reality by introducing untenable dualisms, equating distinctions of the mind with rigid ontological dualisms.

The need for exorcizing the ghostly dualisms of the past is necessary in light of how they, as disfiguring ideas about experience, have shaped contemporary theories of empathy in the present. If history is a guiding light, it seems to be the case that dualisms of the past often reemerge, sometimes under a different name. This was the case with the reason/*pathos* dualism, as well as with the reemergence of the word "emotion," and the reason/emotion dualism that arose as a consequence of its historical popularity. Though introduced by Descartes in the seventeenth century, the scientific study of emotions didn't begin until much later, in the nineteenth century, after Darwin's truly groundbreaking work *The*

Expression of the Emotions in Man and Animals (1872). Though this work was a forerunner for discovering culturally universal experiences of emotions (e.g., the facial emotion of disgust), narratives of emotion vary, leading historians to note the complex and altogether ambiguous nature of this notion throughout the history of its use.[59] Nevertheless, the popularity of the word "emotion" replaced all previous understandings of *pathé*, and with the resurgence of this new term, the past was forgotten and the dualism of reason/*pathos*, which Hume and Smith had exorcized, reappeared in a new form; it was raised from the dead and given a new life with the appearance of a new dualism: the dualism of reason/emotion.

Even though there is little agreement concerning the number of human emotions today, philosophical and scientific explorations of emotional experiences are rooted in the observations, insights, and radical empiricism of William James. In his essay "What Is an Emotion?," James defines an emotion as "a feeling of bodily changes that arise within us after we perceive an exciting fact."[60] This went against how many psychologists of his time described the process by which an emotion arises within us—namely, that the "mental perception of some fact excites the mental affection called the emotion, and that this latter state of mind gives rise to the bodily expression."[61] Those who characterized emotions according to this common yet mistaken approach misunderstood the order of events that give rise to emotions. Though some contemporary scholars have interpreted some of the theories of *pathos* I have explored here to be theories concerning human emotion, this is misguided for at least two reasons. First, it is both mistaken and anachronistic to think that the words *pathos*, "passion," and "affect," as they were used within the traditions I have explicated, signify emotional experiences. Most scholars today agree that James's basic theory of the emotions is, for the most part, correct—*emotions are feelings of bodily changes*.[62] Irrespective of the fact that this concise and accurate description of the experience of an emotion didn't require an understanding of its relation to the experience of reason, psychological theories throughout the twentieth century have often felt the need to contrast our emotional experiences with our rational experiences. This has often resulted in the construction of dualisms and is exemplified in the contemporary dualism between "cognitive empathy," the feeling into and feeling with the mental states of others and "affective" or "emotional empathy," the perception of, and sometimes reaction to, the emotional experiences of others. This construction is rather disturbing, insomuch as it divides feelings and judgments into—fundamentally—emotional or cognitive experiences, without considering the pragmatic alternatives to thinking this way. Once experience is misrepresented, acceptance of this dualism creates further problems by making unclear distinctions between different processes inside of the body that are assumed to represent the experiences of "affective empathy" and "cognitive empathy." Conceiving empathy to be a pluralistic phenomenon and a historically rich term, these problems are averted when one rejects this dizzying distinction between the so-called affective and cognitive states, a dualism that is parasitic upon the dying—but apparently not yet dead—dualism of reason/*pathos*, i.e., reason/emotion.

Future understandings of empathy must avoid this trap of dualistic thinking and be more attuned to how dualisms are often smuggled into our descriptions of lived experience. One way to be diligent about the problem of dualisms is to recognize how and why dualisms have been constructed in the past and how, specifically, such dualisms are problematic in the present. The term dualism has a variety of uses in the history of philosophical thought, but basically a dualism is an idea that the fabric of reality, or some portion of it, is comprised of two fundamental things. For example, within many philosophical and religious traditions, reality is believed to consist of two fundamental and distinct parts: good and evil; within these same traditions, the body is often believed to have a fundamentally dual nature as well: a physical reality and spiritual or mental reality. The common thread that weaves these examples together as dualisms is the way each dualism is employed to describe, not simply two things in reality or two things that one perceives, but rather the inalterable fabric of an unchanging reality. From a pragmatic perspective, rather than informing us about an impermanent reality, dualistic thinking fundamentally distorts experience by ascribing properties or qualities to things that are either not inherent within the things themselves or that do not encapsulate the entirety and *relationality* of such things. Dualisms, then, often distort experiences by failing to include the qualitative and contextual feelings of our experiences, and how such feelings contribute to a variety of different outcomes. When it is recognized as something useful rather than a description of an inalterable and dualistic reality or some part of it, a distinction of, say, the mind and the body is quite different from a dualism, as it serves to elucidate our concepts and bring clarity to our words for a particular purpose.

With this understanding of dualistic thinking, a reexamination of part of the history of *pathos* and its related terms sheds additional insight into why a broad, pluralistic, and relational approach to understanding—and practicing—empathy may prove to be the most functional approach for understanding empathic experiences. What should be clear by now is that the social constructions of *pathé* I have described aimed to serve different needs according to different purposes. For example, for the Hippocratic school, the term *pathos* served the purpose of helping doctors to classify medical diseases; for Epicurean, Aristotelian, and Stoic philosophers, *pathos* was an idea that they used to describe their philosophies of happiness and/or virtue, albeit in different ways; Christian philosophers used the Latin translations of *pathos* to clarify their religious beliefs, ontological theories and, more generally, to satisfy their questions about eschatology; modern philosophers employed a number of terms derived from the Greek word *pathos* to explicate the mechanistic order of things; while thinkers within the sentimentalist tradition conceptualized the meaning of *pathos* and its related terms for the purpose of providing us with a better understanding of moral psychology.

Of these traditions, the Stoics were by far the most hypnotized by the habit of dualistic thinking. Their entire philosophy is literally littered with dualisms that distort rather than illuminate experience. All of reality for the Stoic is comprised of two fundamental realities *Logos*, i.e., Reason, God, Fate (which is also fundamentally male) and *hyle*, i.e., matter (which is described as a feminine reality). The masculine *Logos* is also fundamentally an active principle of the cosmos, which is ungenerated and indestructible, while the feminine matter is fundamentally passive and subject to destruction; it is disordered, chaotic, and irrational; it is moved, ordered, and guided by the rational, well-ordered, and unmoved *Logos*. These dualisms of *Logos*/matter, male/female, active/passive, indestructible/destructible, moved/unmoved, etc., were not separate dualisms that were used to describe independent cosmic realities, but rather they were employed to give an account of interrelated dualistic realities that when understood together were believed to unveil to us the very nature of reality itself. Emerging and supported by these cosmic dualisms, acts of human reason were conceived to be dualistic as well, specifically as manifestations of the active principle of the unmoved masculine *Logos*. Experiences of *pathé*, i.e., false judgments, weak opinions, and excessive impulses were expressions of the passive principle of the transient, feminine, material cosmos. Harmony with the *Logos* is rational, and disharmony with the *Logos* is irrational. Life guided by reason is virtuous, but when dominated by *pathé* it is vicious. Reason signifies control and strength, while *pathé* denotes weakness and even disease.

Though Christian philosophers and theologians tried to distance themselves from the Stoic understanding of *pathé*, which was something pejorative, they embraced the Stoic tendency to make dualistic claims about the nature of reality and the structure of experience. *Pathé* itself was conceived dualistically, either as passion or affect. The passion/affect dualism was further qualified by associating it with other clarifying dualisms, namely the dualisms of pure passivity/pure activity, nonbeing/being, flesh/spirit, temporal/eternal, earthly/divine, God and the Devil, etc. Pure passivity, nonbeing, and absence of the divine is located at the bottom of the Great Chain of Being, while God as pure activity, the unmoved source and mover of all things, is placed at the top. *Pathé* as passions are deficient and irrational; they are disturbing movements of our desires arising out of the lower appetites and directed to objects of sense within the temporal world—the bottom of this artificial chain of existing things. *Pathé* as affects are movements of our rational, appetitive will; they are, according to Aquinas, voluntary affectionate acts directed toward the goodness and love of God. Like the Stoic *Logos*, the Christian God is perfect and eternal, whereas the cosmos/creation is imperfect and impermanent. For each philosophy, the imperfection and transitory nature of the material world is problematic; human imperfection and temporality are likewise problematic—they must be overcome.

According to Descartes's dualistic approach, there are two types of *pathé*, or emotions: those that are generated primarily by the body's perceptions and those that arise from the soul alone. The creation of this dualism was made possible by a dualism he had already accepted— namely, the dualism of the body/soul, which itself was reliant upon a spatial/nonspatial dualism in which the body was deemed as a spatial dimension of experience and the soul was believed to be nonspatial. Descartes is often criticized for his employment of the reason/emotion dualism, but these types of criticisms are only valid when one thinks of Descartes's understanding of the emotions as those generated by the body's perception. Descartes's "intellectual or internal emotions," produced by the soul alone, were thought to be either in unison with or a consequence of the powers of the will and rationality of the soul/mind, and along with reason were thought fit to keep in check the other type of *pathé* (i.e., *émotion*, passions, perceptions) which arise from the body. Descartes's error was not simply that he didn't understand the role emotions played in rational thinking and socialized behavior (as noted by the contemporary neuroscientist Antonio Damasio),[63] but he was also hampered by his overly rationalistic tendencies and his lack of empiricism. Despite their myriad differences about *pathé*, Stoics philosophers, Christian theologians, and Cartesian modern philosophers never wavered from the idea that reason, whether it was conceived as the *Logos*, God, or as a faculty of the human soul, was superior to any other reality or experience, even if the contexts of a given situation proved otherwise. Also within each of these traditions, *pathé*—whether conceived as false judgments, weak opinions, excessive impulses, perturbations, sicknesses, diseases, an indulgence in the lower appetites of the body, emotions arising from the body and affecting the soul—must be controlled, regulated, or even eliminated by reason.[64] Virtuous living as well as genuine human happiness are not attainable without the dominance of human reason over *pathé*.

Dualistic thinking shouldn't be rejected simply because it makes definitive, yet false, claims about the nature of reality or some portion of it, but rather it ought to be rejected also because it often imprisons our understanding by forbidding our imaginations to entertain the complexity of dynamic, multifaceted, and contextual dimensions of lived experience. And though we can very easily separate reason from emotion *in thought*, reason and emotion blend, mix, and mingle within experience, and no amount of logic chopping or reflection can change this fact. Another fact: we also quite often experience reason and emotion simultaneously, as we note in times when, for instance, our experiences of elation, dismay, frustration, contentment, joy, are commonly co-experienced at the same moment we are reasoning. Take the following as two exemplary experiences of this truth: as we strive to bring clarity to some problem by offering a rational account of it, certain sentiments arise within us, and in the process of constructing a rational account of something, we often feel tension, distress, relief, clarity, tranquility, ambiguity, fear, pleasure, sufficiency, etc. Reason is never an isolated and distinct process within experience, and therefore it is not reasonable to think that it is one side of an unchanging ontological dualism. Reason only becomes isolated as we reflect upon it; it merely seems distinct as we consider its presence with different experiences. These seemingly obvious truths about the function of human reason largely evaded the perception of philosophers for thousands of years, that is, until William James explained why rationality is a type of sentiment or feeling.[65]

When philosophers exercise reason, says James, they do so for the purpose of attaining a sufficiently rational conception of things that they believe will both dispel and replace some irrational view. But then, once such a conception is attained, James asks, how do philosophers know that their conception is sufficiently rational and has evaded ignorance? His answer: the rationality is recognized by "certain subjective marks," for instance, by feelings of ease, peace, rest and by the felt transition from a state of perplexity to one of relief and pleasure. Therefore, rationality, in part, is the absence of the feeling of irrationality; it is a "feeling of sufficiency of the present moment, of its absoluteness—this absence of all need to explain it, account for it, or justify it," is what James called the *sentiment of rationality*.[66] These claims about feeling and reasoning are quite bold, yet if one were to disagree with them upon hearing them, would such a reaction be a purely rational response? Would it not include the subjective marks of feeling James described or, perhaps, an even stronger bodily sensation of discomfort or agitation, or maybe even a feeling of superiority or haughtiness?

The Stoic and Christian narratives that argued reason to be discrete power of the soul existing independently of and exerting control over pejorative *pathé*/passions, clearly did not take into account these truths concerning our experiences of reasoning. For the Stoics, experiences of *pathé* as false judgments, weak opinions, or excessive impulses were believed to either distort reason or to be manifestations of irrationality itself, but under no circumstances did the Stoics consider that reason and *pathos* could be experienced simultaneously, or that rationality itself could be a *pathos*. Similarly, according to the Christian worldview, experiences of *pathé*, whether understood as pejorative passions or positive affections, were always considered to be ontologically distinct from both reasoning and the intellect. Given the strong influences of these ancient and premodern philosophical traditions, how did it come to pass that James came to understand that reasoning is not as isolated and separate from other bodily processes as it was once believed? One correct answer to this question is that as the Christian premodern account became less convincing, the concept of *pathé* continued to change, it evolved, and took on a variety of nuanced meanings shaped by the ontological and metaphysical commitments within different philosophical traditions that followed premodern accounts—namely, the modern and mechanistic tradition of philosophy, the tradition of sentimentalism, and the traditions of understanding the *pathé* according to evolutionary theory. Philosophers within these various worldviews eventually opened the conceptual and linguistic spaces for James's account of *pathé* as emotions, that is, as feelings responding to physiological changes within the body.

James's groundbreaking revelation of the sentimental dimensions of rationality should have ended the use of the reason/emotion dualism and all other dualisms in the construction of empathic experience. Unfortunately, this has not been the case, as may be noted in the construction of the affective/cognitive dualism. Affective empathy and cognitive empathy, as a distinction rather than a dualism, has proven to be useful for recognizing different brain and neurological processes, but as a dualism these terms are conceived rigidly and often are parasitic on other dualisms. Future consideration of the meanings and values assigned to "empathy" must be wary of the distorting powers of dualistic thinking. The meaning of a word is its use, but from a pragmatic and pluralistic point of view, the meaning of a word or an idea becomes clear by the way it is used satisfactorily to describe lived experience. Relational empathy offers one way forward to avoid the traps of dualisms, but it can also assist us in understanding the fullness of lived experience by focusing our attention on the relations of experience and embracing the importance of different historical, semantic meanings of "empathy." It is vital, then, to understand the historical evidence for the three relations of feeling I have mentioned—feeling into, feeling with, and feeling for—before *relational empathy* can be considered as a candidate for describing the multiple experiences that people call "empathy."

3

Empathic Projection

On sufficiently clear mornings, the horizon invites us to admire the shifting and colorful lights of the sun's rays. Sometimes we enjoy these masterpieces of nature, suddenly, only for a few seconds, as other more pressing activities shift our attentions away from these slanted and scintillating dances of the sunlight.

During these unexpected yet inviting moments in which something appears to us and announces its beauty, we are able to *feel with* a portrait of grandeur and splendor without expelling much energy to interpret, grasp, and enjoy it. The beauty pounces upon us, and we immediately feel connected or unified with it. But not all things are so luminously inviting or can so easily capture our attention. Sometimes our encounters with objects of beauty, in fact, depend greatly upon the *acuity of our perception* as well as our ability to *observe carefully* what is presented before us. When we take the time to observe and *feel into*, for instance, the long process of a sunrise, our senses often need to be well attuned and patient so that we might bear witness to the panoply of transfiguring lights and shadows before us, where colors of yellow and orange paint the skies, clouds are bathed and illuminated in purple and pink, and the landscape is set aglow with fiery gold. This lengthy process of beholding the beautiful transformations of the sunrise requires that we both *feel into* it and that we perceive it with acuity in order to draw out the contours of its majestic attractiveness. As it is with the rising sun, so too it is the case with any object we perceive or observe with acuity for the purpose of grasping or feeling with it as an object.

Acts of acute perception and careful observation assist our ability to feel with or feel for things; and as such, these acts ought to be considered as skills that can be enhanced or nurtured through practice. Understanding complex objects (e.g., a work of art) seems to enlist such skills.

One could have an immediate feeling of the sublimity of a Kandinsky painting simply by looking at it for a moment or two, but to grasp the intricacies of it and to show concern about its significance as a work of art, most often demands acute perceptions and prolonged observations of it over time. The

Figure 3 Near Agora, Athens, Greece.

consistent practice of feeling into objects with skill and judicious perception can be called a habit. When one masters this practice or habit so that it procures its ends successfully and repeatedly, it could be a type of "second nature"; I will use the term *empathic projection* to signify the experiences of this relation of feeling into, whether it is experienced as the direct and immediate perception of something or a long process of carefully observing something over a period of time.

Even though we experience this type of empathy every day, discussion about it is rare. This is unfortunate for a variety of reasons. First, the English word "empathy" was derived from the German verb *sich hineinfühlenn* (feeling oneself into) and the German nouns *Einfühlung* (feeling into) and *Einfühlungsvermögen* (the capacity to feel into), each of which signifies this type of empathy. Second, I have good reasons for thinking that discussion about the experience of feeling into objects will elucidate the different types and relations of empathy mentioned in chapter 1, which is an important step for moving beyond thinking of empathy as merely a thing or an activity. Third, an inadequate grasp of this relation of feeling prevents us from understanding how a number of social skills (e.g., mindfulness, listening, observation, appreciating the habits of others, etc.) are manifestations of this relation. Fourth, this relation of feeling into is necessary for us to make informed judgments about our co-feeling or feeling with others and our environment. And these judgments—which are colored by our ability to perceive the dynamics of a certain experience—aid in our ability to feel for and act for others with care, concern, and compassion. Finally, the act of feeling into things is often directed toward the self as a mode of self-reflection or self-awareness, which in the literature is often referred to as self-empathy.[1] And a greater analysis of this phenomenon will be important to understand the practical use of the self/other and self/object distinctions when talking about empathy.

Although serious study of our acts of empathic projection as the relation of feeling into is rather uncommon today, careful and detailed examinations of its significance for our lives were extremely common from the late eighteenth century into the early twentieth century. During this time, theorists within three traditions of thought, namely romanticism, aesthetics, and psychology believed that the habitual practice of it could solve a number of intellectual, methodological, and practical problems. Some romanticists thought empathic projection could help improve the shortsighted methods of both science and history. Reflection upon the misgivings of scientific and historical methods inspired Counter-Enlightenment thinkers and romanticists to consider the value of the relation of feeling into objects as a technique of perception and reflection for reconnecting with the natural world and for understanding the radically different experiences, cultures, and histories of other people. This narrative, however, shifted in middle of nineteenth century, as theorists in aesthetics contended that empathic projection, as the act of feeling one's way into things, was instrumental for recognizing and admiring beautiful objects. With the rise of psychology in the late nineteenth and early twentieth centuries, which was in part facilitated by theories of aestheticism, we find yet another shift in which empathic projection was believed to be a skill that therapists needed to employ in order to gain knowledge of their patient's experiences.

One could argue, however, that the contemporary idea of empathic projection found its first modern application in the sentimentalist tradition of the Scottish Enlightenment, especially as it was articulated in the works of Adam Smith and his application of this idea in the discipline of moral psychology and his general understanding of sympathy.[2] Smith often speaks of sympathy as a fellow feeling (feeling with) with the passions of another after we have accurately entered into ("felt our way into") that person's experience, each of which is necessary for us to feel for others.[3] Smith's account of the relation of feeling into, however, falls short from a pluralistic point of view as it limits the possible objects of our acts of entering into to the experiences of people alone.[4]

Nevertheless, we find that a more pluralistic representation of the relation of feeling into emerged within the imaginative minds and colorful hearts of late-eighteenth-century-romantic poets and Counter-Enlightenment philosophers. These thinkers argued that the skill of empathic projection involves a process of encountering and trying to feel one's way into the dynamics of both animate and inanimate objects. For instance, by feeling into objects of nature, we are able to reconstruct a different narrative of our relationship to the natural world. During the Age of Enlightenment, rationalistic thinkers and rigid historians painted a rather bleak picture of the natural world and our relationship to it. These portraits, according to Counter-Enlightenment thinkers, severely limited our imaginations regarding what might be possible through acts of freedom; they also drained the mystery, awe, and wonder out of life itself, until the universe, in Roger Hausheer's words, was beginning to be seen "as a vast monolithic slab, cold, funeral and grey," in which people "were trapped like veins in marble."[5] Empathic projection, as an imaginative and transformative power of projecting ourselves into things, aimed to crack the marble by enlarging human freedom and reconstituting our relationship to the natural world.

The greatest bias of Enlightenment philosophers and historians was their unchecked devotion to the power of rationality and systematic thinking for shaping our moral senses and for engendering historical progress. This bias contributed to a more fundamental historical and cultural bias—a sense of superiority that seriously limited their ability to understand the radically different experiences of other cultures and their histories. This sense of superiority was undergirded and supported by physical and cultural anthropological "data," which painted a distorted picture of the physical, intellectual, and moral experiences of non-European peoples. This inaccurate xenophobic portrayal of the experiences and cultures of others contributed to larger and equally invalid unilinear theories of cultural development and historical progress. The core impulses of these biases inspired Counter-Enlightenment thinkers and romanticists to consider the value of the relation of feeling into and the usefulness of empathic projection as a technique of perception to understand the radically different experiences, cultures, and histories of others. The dawn of empathic projection as a manifestation of the relation of feeling into and as a type of empathy, arose, in part, as a reaction and an argument against these patterns of thinking and acting.

Romanticism, Empathic Projection, and the Counter-Enlightenment

As one of the Counter-Enlightenment thinkers, Herder suggested that our ability to "feel ourselves into" (*sich einfühlen*) objects of our perception and/or reflection is instrumental for mitigating our biases as they stand in relation to, for example, the experiences of others. In addition to the blind spots and failings of the Enlightenment's historical and cultural methods, Herder argued that his contemporaries' creation of "universal" moral imperatives (e.g., as articulated by Kant), which were based on abstract and biased conceptualizations of the "ideal" human, were incoherent, unproductive, and even harmful. Take, for example, the multiple formulations of Kant's categorical imperative. The ideality and universality of these formulations were founded upon what Kant sensed were unalterable, universal moral laws, which inform us of rational moral principles that ought to guide our actions. But, as many Counter-Enlightenment thinkers noticed, this moral theory didn't seem to apply to all people; for in Kant's anthropological writings and multiple articles on the subject of race, he contends that many non-European people weren't fully human. Herder's familiarity with these inconsistencies between Kant's ethical theory and his anthropological theory led him to be skeptical of the coherency and legitimacy of Kant's ideal moral theory as well as of all universal moral ideals and systems that were believed to be grounded in rational capacities. For Herder, reason plays an important role in ethics and morality, but it alone is not sufficient without understanding and utilizing the power of empathic projection, the act of "feeling one's way into" the different experiences of others.

It also became clear to Herder that many Enlightenment ideals and systems—and the language certain Enlightenment thinkers employed—did not allow one to give an adequate or fair account of the cultural, experiential, and moral differences of others. Herder rejects the rigid language that many Enlightenment theorists used to interpret nature and society, and he was simply unwilling to admit such rigid and definitive language into any serious discussions or evaluations of moral or cultural differences. Even moral evaluation itself, Herder warns, should occur only after we exercise sympathetic insight for others, which requires us to understand the similarities—as well as the experiential and perceptual dissimilarities—of those in cultures other than our own. This was what Kant and other Enlightenment thinkers simply missed: the process of feeling into an array of different experiences, circumstances, and relations is crucial for understanding the moral sensibilities of others, and it is only by feeling into the plurality and multiplicity of diverse experiences that moral discourses become clear. Without the habits or art of feeling into, then, philosophers and historians, who rely upon abstract, immutable moral systems and theories of progress, will always fail to grasp the moral experiences of others as well as the cultural and historical circumstances that inform such experiences.

But for Herder, empathic projection—the act of "feeling into" into objects, persons, and even relations themselves—is not simply a powerful technique for professional historians and socially minded philosophers. Mastery of this habit of action can help us to gain insight into how feeling into certain objects significantly influences our attempts to feel with others. Feeling with others might be recognized as a feeling of accord, unity, or resonance with the similar experiences of others in which we stand in agreement with them, but it may also signify discord, disunity, and dissonance with other people's ways of life within cultures other than our own. Quite unlike contemporary notions of empathy, then, where the goal of empathizing with others is often only to "match" the experiences of others in terms of and in line with our own, many of Herder's usages of empathy as the relation of feeling into aimed to identify and then to grasp (in a very incomplete manner) plural, incommensurable, yet equally valid truths found in the experiences of others. That is, we "feel into" the radically different experiences of "others" without having the aim or need to find room for such truths within one's own experiences, moral systems, or historical perspectives.[6] Herder's insistence that we ought to use empathic projection to understand sympathetically the experiences of other cultures or historical periods was formidable to the rise of empathy-based methodologies and techniques of anthropology and sociology in the twentieth century (e.g., in the works of Wilhelm Dilthey).[7]

The value of empathic projection, according to Herder, was not only important for grasping the moral sensibilities of others but also for interpreting a nation or culture's unique character. "Every nation," Herder claimed, "has its own inner center of happiness, as every sphere its own center of gravity."[8] But the abstract, uniform, and "rational" systems of the Enlightenment, Herder realized, have no means of penetrating the inner worlds of such centers. To feel into the unique and different experiences within these centers of happiness one must "feel oneself into [*sich hineinfühlen*] everything" including "the time, the place, the entire history" of a people.[9] The larger aim of this pluralistic understanding of the relation of feeling into was to provide an alternative approach for historians, so that empathy would become central in their attempts to understand the cultures, histories, and time periods of other civilizations. Herder hoped that such an empathically infused historical method would also elucidate the limits and follies of the rational and scientific methods of the Enlightenment used to construct hierarchical and unilinear theories of development and progress—activities that Herder believed to be exemplary of the biases and ignorance of his own civilization. But Herder's criticisms of these tendencies of thought were more than simply an intellectual assault on the Enlightenment tradition, they were also a call for us to adopt a poetic sensibility and relational metaphysics suitable for engaging with and interacting with others in a perpetually changing world.

Georg Friedrich Phillip von Hardenberg (1772–1801), most commonly known as the poet Novalis, shared Herder's antipathy of abstract philosophical systems, especially those that set limits on human freedom. The true philosophical system, Novalis believed, with a twist of the ironic, "must be freedom and infinitude, or, to express it pointedly, lack of a system brought under a system."[10] Novalis's dissatisfaction with abstract systems in general—and the transcendental idealism of Kant in particular—revolved around a few significant points of disagreement between romanticists, like Novalis and Herder, and the philosophy of rationalism, as exemplified in the philosophies of Fichte, Kant, etc. The main debate between these camps involved disagreements about the nature of the self—namely, to what degree is the self relatively fixed as an interpreting subject and which of the subject's interpretive faculties endow us with the ability to gain a correct understanding of the external world. For Kant, the so-called "transcendental ego" was a necessary condition and starting point that generated a unified, centered, and empirical self-consciousness. Without it, Kant claims, the lawfulness of the phenomenal world could never be established. In addition to this rational structure of the self as subject, nature itself must also be rational; otherwise, science is not possible, and scientific laws cannot be formulated.

Kant's narrative of the self as an interpreting subject rejected the possibility of a science of internal sensibility, i.e., psychology, and thus ignored the transformative power of empathic projection. Novalis, however, contended that this notion of selfhood ignored the qualitatively unique dimensions of the perceiving subject as well as the methods by which the self, by means of the process of feeling into, was transformed. Nevertheless, Novalis was impressed by Kant's narrative as well as Fichte's attempt to revise it in the *Wissenschaftslehre* (1794); but he also noticed that the theories of these and other rationalists failed to give an account of the processional, transformative, and dynamic nature of the self as it interacts with the external world. It should come as no surprise then that Novalis's dissatisfaction with both Kant and Fichte's representations of the self was largely due to their inability to include the process by which *sich hineinfühlenn* (empathic projection/the act of feeling oneself into) serves as an engine for perception that both drives and facilitates the process of self-transformation. The function of empathic projection for Novalis (as well as for Herder) is primarily ecstatic, serving to transform one's inner sensibilities, habits of perception—and even biases—by "coming out of one's self" for the purpose of observing and co-experiencing the perspectives or perceptions of others and their ways of living life.

One need not contemplate one's own experience for too long to realize the significance of Novalis's criticisms of Kant and Fichte's overly rigid descriptions of the self/subject. For experience shows us that selfhood is fundamentally relational, multidimensional, and in transition. Within a set of contextualized purposes and aims, accentuating the uniformity, stability, and continuity of the self proves to be useful, for instance, to establish laws about the natural world and our relationship to it; however, within other sets of contextualized aims and purposes, creative narratives about the unstable, fragmentary, and transitional dimensions of selfhood yields different types of truths about the qualitative dimensions of our experiences as well as the self. Kant's introduction of the transcendental ego failed to give an account of this dynamism of the self in transformation, and for this reason, he failed to convince Herder and Novalis that a singular and identical self could be established in the way Kant claimed it could be.

Both Herder and Novalis expressed discontent with a number of Enlightenment motifs, for instance: unilinear theories of historical development; assumptions about the moral and spiritual capacities of non-European peoples; characterizations of the superiority of Europeans; unsatisfactory portrayals of the subject of human freedom; the relationship of the human being to the world; an overemphasis on the rational and scientific dimensions of the natural world; and finally, the dualistic mentality that undergirded all of these theories. These motifs common to Enlightenment thinking were all substantiated by epistemological starting points that Herder and Novalis wholly rejected. In direct opposition to Kant, Novalis painted a plural portrait of the subject, the self, the "I," which he believed is useful for identifying how the activity of feeling into contributes to our ability to understand experience. What does it mean to possess knowledge of one's own experiences or those of others? Within the processional and ever-changing dance of the natural world, is it even possible to obtain self-knowledge much less a knowledge of others?

Novalis's personal experiences of ecstasy led him to believe that human beings do indeed gain certain forms of interpersonal knowledge through the process of stepping outside of themselves. This act is the first step by which we are able to realize the unity between our "selves" and everything we assume to be separate from us. Perhaps paradoxically, Novalis conceives of the self primarily as a "Thou"—what is inexhaustibly wholly other. Acts of empathic projection also serve to recognize and to accentuate radical difference. Novalis's narrative of selfhood rejects the rigidity inherent in dualistic thinking and challenges the coherency of dualisms themselves by illustrating how acts of empathic projection show us that both our experience and knowledge of the world is fundamentally relational.

Novalis's methods for relating this notion of selfhood are exemplified in his highly creative and unique literary works. For instance, in his novel *Heinrich von Ofterdingen*, the self becomes transfigured in and through a poetic process, where the "self-same" subject (protagonist) is simultaneously or alternatively multiple characters. *Die Lehrlinge zu Sais*, a work that Novalis never finished, narrates similarly fluid transformations of identities, while different voices express dissimilar ideas about nature and knowledge about nature. These poetic and playful portrayals of transforming selves describe how different perceptions and conceptualizations serve as functions of self-growth—a metaphorical, spiraling growth by means of the process of empathic projection and sensations of ecstasy. In opposition to the rather cold, dry bones, and overly analytic approach of Enlightenment science that emphasized the subject's role in gaining knowledge of nature in order to dominate and control it, Novalis's poetic creations emphasized an understanding of the multiple roles we adopt to feel into the plural, variegated, and spiritual dimensions of others and of nature.

Herder and Novalis's philosophical visions for empathic projection set the stage for further conceptualizations of it as an experience, and without their contributions, it is doubtful that the English word "empathy" would have been coined in the early twentieth century. Their criticisms of Enlightenment thinking were not criticisms of reason in and of itself, but rather how an overreliance on rational thought for gaining insight and knowledge about both the experiences of others and the natural world was severely limiting. For where the process of reasoning isolates, categorizes, and analyzes that which is made conceptually but not experientially distinct, empathic projection is a movement of body/mind consciousness that reveals to us the transformative, perspectival, and fluid dimensions of all things. Late-eighteenth-century romanticists described this movement and revelation as an act of thinking "spirit into objects," and this process often challenges the assumptions and biases of our distinctions. For as we feel into things, whether they are people, physical objects, relations, histories, or even ideas, we inject the energies and spirits of our understanding into them, and this act has a potency to also transform them as well as ourselves. And this is primarily why all systems, all rigid classificatory schemas, ultimately fail to give an account of the inventive and creative dimensions of our experiences.

Empathic Projection and Aesthetics

During the middle of nineteenth century, Hermann Lotze adopted Herder's and Novalis's understanding of empathy as empathic projection, namely their pluralistically minded philosophical view that explains how our senses and imaginations may enter into all forms by feeling into objects and their relations. According to Lotze:

> No form, is so resistant that our fancy cannot ... *place itself into it* ... Thus we are able, furthered by the help of our sensations, to understand the alien, silent form, too ... we ... penetrate into the peculiar vital feelings of those ... near to us, into the joyful flight of the singing bird or the charming motion of the gazelle ... the narrowly defined existence of the mollusk and the monotonous pleasure of its openings and closings; we ... extend ourselves ... into the slender forms of the trees whose thin branches the pleasure of graceful bending and swaying animates.[11]

But Lotze's interests in aesthetics coupled with his extensive background in medicine led him to understand this relation differently than his predecessors. For Lotze, empathic projection was described as a tool or technique useful for contemplating and understanding aesthetic objects, e.g., the structures of architectural works, the various forms of high art.[12] Lotze's ideas arose as a consequence of the historical shift regarding the meaning of the relation of feeling into to include the tendency to investigate bodily processes within the observer during acts of feeling into things. This turn to the inner workings of the body was stimulated by a number of scientific developments during the mid-nineteenth century. In particular, discoveries in ophthalmology and physiology encouraged thinkers like Lotze to incorporate the insights of these disciplines into his theory of empathic projection. As a consequence of these developments, two relatively disparate disciplines of thought, aesthetics and biology, were responsible for the tendency to conceptualize empathic projection—as the dynamic process of "feeling into" aesthetic objects—in the late nineteenth and early twentieth centuries.

This shift in understanding both the relation of feeling into and the act of empathic projection is recognized in the writings of one of G. W. F. Hegel's last and promising students, Friedrich Robert Vischer. Influenced by late-eighteenth-century romanticists and Hegel's phenomenological approach, Vischer argued that the (so-called) essential properties of objects in nature are in truth the projections of our own bodily perceptions, sensations, feelings, and thoughts. Our acts of empathic projection, our *feeling into* these inanimate objects of nature, imbue both life and soul into them. In a similar fashion, the architectural form, as a type of "symbolic art," is also injected with a life, a spirit or soul. Architecture, then, is a practice of aesthetics in which the architect animates matter by infusing it with "buoyant life" through the linear and planar suspension of its parts. Vischer's work initiated a new way of speaking about empathic projection, though it was his son, Robert, who, in his 1873 dissertation, *Über das Optische Formegefühl: Ein Beitrag zur Ästhetik*, coined the term *Einfühlung* after reading a section of Albert Scherner's book on the nature of dreams:

> Particularly valuable in an aesthetic sense is the section on "Die Symbolische Grundformation für die Leibreize" (Symbolic Basic Formation for Bodily Stimuli). Here it was shown how the body, in responding to certain stimuli in dreams, objectifies itself in spatial forms. Thus it unconsciously projects its own bodily form—and with this also the soul—into the form of the object. From this I derived the notion of what I call *Einfühlung*.[13]

Beyond analyses of dreaming, the younger Vischer defined empathic projection and envisioned its usefulness for aesthetics by drawing on a number of insights from physiology, especially optical science (e.g., the insights of Hermann von Helmholtz's *Handbook of Physiological Optics* as well as Helmholtz's invention of the ophthalmoscope in 1851). Based on changes in scientific disciplines, Vischer notes that a number of internal processes must be taken into account for grasping the dynamic, transactional, and transformative process of feeling into objects. Vischer's understanding of empathic projection, then, differs from romantic conceptualizations of it, in that for Vischer the act of projecting the self into an object of perception gives rise to a number of bodily processes, including, but not limited to, the muscular movement of the eyes, the reflexive sensations as responses to an observed object, a mental tracing of the object, a sense of resemblance between the object and the observer's mental states, a responsive and immediate feeling toward the object, and an association of ideas within the observer's mind. Similar to Vischer, Herder and Novalis equally thought that empathic projection has the potential to transform the self, but with both Lotze and Vischer the act of *Einfühlung* as well the process of change it evokes must be interpreted by means of a study of the observer's physical body. Related to and perhaps dissolving the Kant vs. Herder/Novalis debate concerning the self, Vischer suggested that multiple internal processes within the body during the act of feeling into objects both stabilize and destabilize the self. Robert Vischer's examinations of bodily processes as they relate to acts of feeling into objects were highly respected and embraced by the art historians of his time, but they also served as a creative impetus for a number of late-nineteenth-century theories.

The focus on the effects that the process of *Einfühlung* has upon the body was continued in the work and writings of Karl Groos, who made two significant claims concerning the psycho-physiological process of *Einfühlung* as well as its practical use. The first claim, articulated by Groos, asserted that *Einfühlung* was made possible by our natural ability to mimic internally or imitate the form, structure, and dynamism of external objects. The second claim, introduced by Lipps and later adopted by psychologists in the twentieth century, suggested that empathic projection was useful not only for aesthetic contemplation but also for gaining knowledge of other people's minds. Feeling oneself into the experiences of others for the purposes of understanding both the similarities and differences between oneself and others was certainly part of Herder's and Novalis's narratives of empathy, but it is with the rise of psychology in the twentieth century where we find both a scientific exploration of this process and the theoretical grounds by which understanding of the experiences of others was made possible by accessing different modes of our empathic senses by *feeling with* them (e.g., by means of empathic connection brought about through empathic mimicry, empathic inference, empathic perspective-taking, and empathic connection).

As an evolutionary psychologist, Groos conceptualized the process of inner mimicry or inner imitation based on his analysis of play as well as his general theory of childhood development. In *The Play of Man*, Groos notes that during play (or the state of illusion called dramatic play, i.e., "make-believe"), children derive pleasure both from the freedom and control they have over their bodies and over objects as well as from what Groos called the "play of inner imitation" or the "play of aesthetic enjoyment." (Adults experience similar pleasure by means of their ability to experience inner imitation during aesthetic participation.) Groos called this play of inner imitation *aesthetic sympathy*, of which the central dynamics are:

1a. The mind conceives of the experience of the other individual as if it were its own.
1b. We live through the psychic states which a lifeless object would experience if it possessed a mental life like our own.
2a. We inwardly participate in the movements of an external object.
2b. We also conceive of the motions which a body at rest might make if the powers which we attribute to it were actual (the fluidity of form).
3. We transfer the temper, which is the result of our own inward sympathy, to the object and speak of the solemnity of the sublime, the gaiety of beauty, etc.[14]

The play of inner imitation and aesthetic sympathy—what I and others today have called empathic mimicry—as internal symbolic reproductions of an object of perception—involves a two-part dynamic process, namely an interplay between two relations of feeling: *feeling into* and *feeling with*. The relation of feeling into expressed during perceptual acts of *Einfühlung* arises whenever we put ourselves into an object, and this act of projection is the means by which we often are able to attain "a sort of inward sympathy with it."[15] While observing an object, which for Groos is either a person or a thing, a number of very complex, inner psycho-physiological processes (e.g., postural sensations and light muscular innervation) facilitate our feeling with it, and *Einfühlung* is often the means by which we achieve the ends of both inner imitation and aesthetic sympathy. In other words, it is the act of empathic projection (*Einfühlung*) that commonly helps us to experience a feeling of pleasure, unity, connection, oneness, or feeling with the objects of our reflections.

Though the works of Groos contributed to this second discursive shift, it was the philosophical and psychological theories of Theodor Lipps that most significantly facilitated it. The works of Lipps functioned as a conceptual bridge between aesthetics and psychology in which the usefulness of *Einfühlung* as feeling into objects became instrumental for psychology and the practical, clinical, and therapeutic approaches of feeling into the experiences of others. Nevertheless, similar to Lotze's, the Vischers', and Groos's conceptualizations of *Einfühlung*, Lipps's described the relation of feeling into as empathic projection by which we feel ourselves into objects of art:

> The Doric column rises [literally rears itself up] as does every column ... This self-raising of the column is its "intrinsic activity." The word activity is used in the fullest sense of exertion, striving, expenditure of energy; at the same time expenditure as energy through which something is achieved. Such activity is not

without opposing activity or resistance, which must be overcome. This [resistance] is here occasioned by the weight ... But upon our observing the column and seeing it raise itself to a certain height above the ground, this [resistance] does not prevent the force which is directed against the weight from appearing to us as the actual activity; the force and not the weight will in our eyes seem to perform the act ... through which the column appears to gain its peculiar property.[16]

Lipps's description of *Einfühlung* both differs from and builds upon previously mentioned theories of this relation of feeling into. As illustrated in the above example of the Doric column, empathic projection as a mode of inner imitation involves the recognition of a force, tendency, or striving with the object (i.e., the rising of the column), as well as the resistance (i.e., the weight) that opposes it. Recognition of these counter-dynamics within objects vivifies them, and this can only be achieved when we "attribute to outer things our own feelings of force, our own feelings of striving or willing, our own activity or passivity."[17] Second, this inner imitation or motor mimicry is nonconscious, and it is not felt as a sensation within the body. This attribution of force, derived from one's own personal feelings, is neither an activity of merging oneself with the object of perception nor a subjective description of the object, defining (or adding to) the form, structure, and dynamism of it. The recognition of the counter-dynamics of a given object during the act of feeling oneself into it are recognized when we resonate with it and attribute our own senses and feelings to it based on similar activities of movement that we have experienced. For example, I attribute the rising movement of the column based upon my own experiences of rising (e.g., I arise from my bed whenever I wake from sleep). Whenever we interpret the dynamism of a perceived object in a positive, life-affirming manner, we conceive it to be beautiful, i.e., "positive empathy," or otherwise ugly, i.e., "negative empathy."[18] Positive empathy references those experiences in which we successfully and completely identify with—are unified with—the object of empathizing, and negative energy denotes all other experiences in which we fail to identify with or feel a certain unity with the object of our empathizing.

A third way in which Lipps builds upon, but mostly deviates from, the ideas of other theorists thus far explored is in the way in which he conceptualizes *Einfühlung* as a useful mode of conscious projection that is necessary for feeling with the *content of other people's minds*. Recall that for Groos, the play of inner imitation as the multidimensional process of aesthetic sympathy involved one's feeling into the experiences of other individuals as if they were one's own. Lipps elaborated upon this starting point by rejecting what he argued were unconvincing theories for explaining how we gain knowledge of other people's mental states (e.g., Mill's inference from analogy) and by elucidating the manner in which introspection helps us to grasp such states. According to Lipps, our knowledge of things begins with sense perception; self-knowledge requires reflective and inward acts of perception, and our ability to know others is derived from acts of *Einfühlung* or empathic projection.[19] But knowledge of others—for example, understanding their unique experiences, the inner workings of their minds, their emotional states, habits, and temperaments, etc.—depends, in part, upon how well we know ourselves and the differences between ourselves and others. Self-knowledge gained through introspection, perhaps most importantly, helps us to reveal our biases and blind spots, the limits of our perception as we practice *Einfühlung*, whether directed toward objects or the experiences of others or something else entirely. Lipps's most famous example, illustrating how we gain access to the experiences of others by means of a kinesthetic and/or psychological fusion/identification with them, is his description of an observer watching a tightrope walker. When you watch the tightrope walker venture across a high wire, you project your consciousness into her body and enter it as if it were your own body. With each precarious movement she encounters, and with each bodily expression she makes, your body internally reproduces it though the process of "inner imitation," and the perceptions of her bodily expressions are simultaneously and instinctively mirrored by your feelings and "kinesthetic strivings."[20]

Similar to Vischer, Herder, and Novalis, Lipps likewise thought that empathic projection has the potential to transform the self. But like both Lotze and Vischer, he asserted that the act of *Einfühlung* as well the process of change it evokes must be interpreted by means of studying the observer's physical body. Related to and perhaps dissolving the Kant vs. Herder/Novalis debate concerning the self, Robert Vischer suggested that multiple internal processes within the body during the act of feeling into architectural objects both stabilizes and destabilizes the self. The difference between these bodily processes is contingent on the static or dynamic nature of the object observed. As Robin Curtis and Richard George Elliott have noted, when confronted with a "static or fixed object it is a case of physiognomic *Einfühlung* or empathy of mood, which can bring about either an expansion of the self ... or else a constriction of the self. ... When empathy is felt toward a dynamic or apparently dynamic object, this is mimetic or active *Einfühlung*."[21]

Groos's focus on imitation and Lipps's emphasis on reading other people's minds engendered a major paradigmatic shift from thinking of empathy *centrally*, as a technique to *feel one's way into* inanimate objects, especially aesthetic objects, to a skill for *feeling in and with* the experiences of other human beings. From Herder to Lipps, the relation of *feeling with* was important, even essential; it just wasn't articulated to the degree that it was in a number of theories in the twentieth century. Feeling one's way into things had a final goal of, for instance, attaining sympathetic understanding (Herder), a feeling of unity with nature (Novalis), an internal resonance with or an inward mental tracing of aesthetic objects (Lotze, the Vischers), or a process of inner imitation with things or aesthetic sympathy (Groos and Lipps). These all denote some type of fusion or identification with one's object of perception or reflection. At the turn of the twentieth century, however, reflection upon the interplay between the relation of feeling into and the relation of feeling led many to equate *Einfühlung* with feeling with others. This began most prominently with Lipps, whose reflection upon the nature of this interplay became a topic of debate in the disciplines of phenomenology, sociology, and psychology.

The Skill of Feeling Into

To send ourselves out of ourselves, to think ourselves into the thoughts and feelings of beings in circumstances wholly and strangely different from our own ... who has achieved it?[22]

Samuel Taylor Coleridge

I am the poet of the body / And I am the poet of the soul / I go with the slaves of the earth equally with the masters / And I will stand between the masters and the slaves, / Entering into both so that both shall understand me alike.[23]

Walt Whitman

The relation of *feeling into* signifies the general mode or manner in which we *feel into* any object of perception or reflection. Accordingly, this relation is a general description of any particular experience in which two or more things are related to each other by a specific, contextualized act of feeling one's way into something. In the above quote by Walt Whitman, we find that the specific and contextualized act of this general relation was Whitman's intention to stand between the masters and the slaves and *enter into* both, so that both will understand him. Whitman's desire to enter imaginatively into the lived experiences of others was motivated by a related aspiration, namely that his poetry would be understood by anyone who might read it.

One could cite many other examples in which we experience this relation in our day-to-day lives. Though independent of the differences between experiences, it seems that while we sometimes experience the relation of *feeling into* quite suddenly and without intent, we also experience this relation consciously, willfully, and purposively, i.e., whenever we aim to become aware of the qualities and dynamics of an object. By stating that we occasionally experience this type of empathy suddenly and without intent, I mean that during these empathic experiences when we experience an immediate and instant awareness of an object, there is not a prolonged exercise of focused and careful observation. To illustrate the difference here, imagine you are walking through a forest and gazing upward you feel yourself into the golden and dancing lights adorning the very tops of the trees. As a consequence of this perception, you experience an immediate awareness of nature's ephemeral beauty. As an example of those times that require our careful observation, think about a detailed or complex object of perception (e.g., a work of art, a person's experience) of which you have no or little awareness. During these acts of empathic projection, you would need to employ focused perceptional skills and keen observation in order to gain awareness of the properties and dynamics of the object you are perceiving and/or contemplating.

Robert Vischer's theory of perception explains the difference between these quite well, as Gustav Jahoda has noted: Vischer "put forward an elaborate theory of different levels of perception, from simple unconscious taking in of visual stimuli to an intricate involvement of representational and imaginative functions."[24] Vischer's theory, then, provides an example of how the variety of experiences of empathic projection could be represented on a spectrum, ranging from the unconscious mental and visual absorption of an object to a complex and imaginative act of feeling into the qualities and dynamics of something complex. When romanticists and aestheticians spoke of the act—the skill—of feeling one's way into something, they were speaking of empathic projection somewhat akin to this intricate and difficult process of creative perception through prolonged and careful observation by means of the imagination's functions.

Despite their different conceptualizations of the relation of feeling into, each of the theorists I have covered here endorsed empathic projection *for the purpose of overcoming some problem*. Empathic projection, then, was conceived as a means through which the enhancement of our perceptual and observational abilities was instrumental for recognizing and appreciating different representations of objects and for resolving something problematic. For Herder, the main problem was the assumptions of the historians of the Enlightenment, whose historical methods were grounded in unilinear theories of human and cultural development.[25] Herder interpreted the skill of feeling one's way into objects as the solution to this and other problems. This is no simple task; for it involves a complex, imaginative—and severely painstaking—process of feeling into radically *different* ways of experiencing the world, the specific experiences of others, and the historical frameworks that inform one's interpretation of things (e.g., the mores, folklore, and language of a given ethnic culture). What was problematic for Novalis was the estrangement from nature that people of his time felt as a consequence of accepting overly rigid and stale portraits of nature grounded in mechanistic metaphysical theories. The solution to this problem required an alternative way of perceiving the natural world, a different mode of perceiving nature, by feeling into the beautiful and amiable contours of nature's unfoldings and by resisting the idea that the only legitimate understanding or viable interpretation of the natural world must be gained by means of scientific, often lifeless, portrayals of it.

When theorists of aestheticians and psychologists provided different understandings of the relation of feeling into, they, just as their predecessors did, defined empathic projection in light of the problems they were trying to solve. After Herder and Novalis, two dissimilar problems emerged. First, how might experiences of the relation of *feeling into* function as a perceptual aide for understanding, contemplating, and appreciating aesthetic objects? Second, what are the internal bodily sensations and interpretive processes that give us the power and perceptual apparatus to feel into the dynamics of other things? We find the former question answered in the works of the aestheticians I have mentioned here, and both the former and the latter questions answered in the works of Lotze, Groos, and Lipps. The problem for aestheticians was the inability to grasp the qualitative and aesthetic nature of the object perceived and contemplated, and the solution was to develop the ability of feeling one's way into the uniqueness and dynamism of the object. The act of *Einfühlung* as a solution was complex; it needed to be honed as a skill for understanding the dimensionality of objects and to envision, then materialize, new structures through an imaginative and creative process. Our perceptual and interpretive misgivings in the act of interpreting the complexity of objects was likewise problematic for Lotze, Groos, and Lipps, but for these thinkers, there existed a related problem concerning the body's inner capacities and processes that give rise to acts of empathic projection and allow us to feel with the experiences of others. From Herder to Lipps, empathic projection requires one to try to adopt a nonprejudicial attitude toward the object and to maintain an openness to the possibility of a completely new relationship to the object, even if such a new relationship resulted in a radical dissimilarity between the empathizer and object. The act of empathic projection, furthermore, was a solution to the philosophical problem of the nature of the self, offering a method of perception that transforms the self by means of enlarging one's interpretive powers, which in turn could potentially bring about a positive transformation of the self in which one's biases and shortsightedness are recognized, and certain limits of one's perceptions and interpretations of things are transcended.

William James recounted an experience that illuminates the difference between empathic perception as simple and direct perception and the type of empathic projection that functions as a vehicle for self-transformation. While traveling through the mountains of North Carolina, he noticed that there were a number of clearings among the valleys made for the purpose of creating farming and housing developments. At first glance, when James initially directly perceived and interpreted the significance of these developments, he was aghast with horror. Where tall, majestic, and glorious trees once stood, log cabins were being built, put together with ugly and unappealing clumps of clay. Where shadows and lights once played at the bottom of the forest floor, fields of corn were planted. All of the monstrous marks of the formation of early civilization, appeared to James as "a sort of ulcer," in which no form of construction—however graceful and pleasing—could replace the natural beauty they destroyed.

When James rode closer to these dreary, artificial, and embryonic places, he began to rethink his initial direct perception of the circumstances and began to sense that he was failing to grasp the inward significance of these developments:

> I instantly felt that I had been losing the whole inward significance of the situation. Because to me the clearing spoke of naught but denudation, I thought that to those whose sturdy arms and obedient axes had made them they could tell no other story. But, when they looked on the hideous stumps, what they thought of was personal victory. The chips, the girdled trees, and the vile split rails spoke of honest sweat, persistent toil, and final reward. The cabin was a warrant of safety for self and wife and babes. In short, the clearing, which to me was a mere ugly picture on the retina, was to them a symbol redolent with moral memories and sang a very paean of duty struggle, and success.

> I had been as blind to the peculiar ideality of their conditions as they certainly would also have been to the ideality of mine, had they had a peep at my strange indoor academic ways of life a Cambridge.[26]

By having this experience, James reconsidered his initial interpretation and direct perception of the situation and tapped into the skill of *Einfühlung* as empathic projection to reconsider his biases, reshape his perspective, and begin to consider the experiences of others from their point of view. Feeling into your environment, carefully observing it, and allowing your perceptual powers to be open to perceiving things differently, as this story explains, can be a powerful source for transforming the self and being open to the different perspectives of others.

From romanticism to aestheticism, different descriptions of the relation of feeling into as a mode of empathic projection explained different skills of observation by which we can more successfully feel with and/or feel for objects of our perception. Experiences of the relation of feeling with, whether described as a form of sympathetic understanding (Herder), a feeling of unity (Novalis), an internal resonance with or an inward mental tracing of aesthetic objects (Lotze, the Vischers), as well as the process of inner imitation/mimicry (Groos), all denote some form of sympathy, i.e., defined as some type of fusion or identification with one's object of perception. The Whitman quote mentioned at the beginning of this section also alludes to this twofold process, in that Whitman's action of *feeling or entering into* the experiences of others is performed for the purpose of having others feel with and gain a sympathetic understanding of Whitman's poetic intentions. Historically, this notion of sympathetic understanding has also been called empathy. In light of this and for pragmatic purposes, I have chosen to call this experience a type of empathy: a *sense* of being connected, united, in concord or in sync with another person or thing, which functions as one of the three relations of what I have coined *relational empathy*. Empathic projection, both as a type of the relation of feeling into and a different mode of perceiving and observing, is often an instrumental process that engenders within us a feeling of connection with the object of one's perception or reflection (empathic perspective-taking, empathic contagion, and empathic inference/accuracy).

Understanding the impact of the works I have covered here is extremely important, not only for embracing the variety of their understandings of empathic experience, but also for recognizing their influence upon theorists of empathy in the twentieth century. It was, in particular, the work of Lipps that set the course for the exploration of the experience of empathy in the twentieth century. The writings of Lipps, then, are representative of a major discursive shift between thinkers in the late eighteenth and nineteenth centuries, and psychologists, philosophers, and now, primatologists and neuroscientists in the twentieth and twenty-first centuries. For after Lipps, we find that the significance and usefulness of *Einfühlung* for contemplating aesthetic objects begins to wane; and eventually, as a consequence of the discourses of psychologists in the twentieth century, the use of empathic projection, and the practice of it for grasping or understanding inanimate objects, dwindles if not completely disappears. And as a consequence of the works of Lipps, emphasis upon the dynamics and importance of the relation of *feeling into* begins to give way to a focused examination of both the relation of *feeling with* and a new, English neologism, a surrogate term for *Einfühlung*, a name for an experience that has gained a popularity beyond what could have been imagined at its inception in the early twentieth century, a word called "empathy."

4

Empathic Connection

The rhythmic and soulful sounds resound within the dance hall. No one is sitting; everyone—with exuberant smiles and enlivened senses—is dancing and enjoying the moment. Flashing lights of blue, red, and green decorate the faces of the dancers as well as the uninhabited spaces of the brown wooden flooring. As Candice steps upon the dance floor, she feels the vibrations of the sounds reverberate throughout her body. As a new song begins, one of her favorites, she begins to dance as she *feels herself into* the beat. She feels united with the music and begins to both *feel into* and *feel with* the pleasant memories this particular song is evoking in her. As she scans the faces of the lively night scene, she recognizes her friend Hannah, who invited her to this venue. In sync with the rhythms, beats, and flow of the resounding sounds, Candice dances over to Hannah. Without exchanging words, Candice and Hannah begin to *feel with* the music and feel in sync with the movements and signals of each other's bodies.

As Candice is absorbing the vibrations and energies of Hannah's dancing skills, another friend Maurita also begins to dance, and Candice begins to feel into Maurita's dancing style. Candice senses immediately that Maurita's moves are not in accord with her own nor are they in sync with the music's melody and beat. The music changes, a new song fills the empty spaces of the night; a few dancers pause; they feel into the sound of the song, while attempting to recognize it. Candice doesn't recognize this new song and neither does Hannah, but Maurita does and now it seems as if she is an entirely different dancer, i.e., a good one. Meanwhile, Candice and Hannah are feeling into this new song, but it is unfamiliar to them and they struggle to be perfectly in sync with its flow. After a short time, they begin to anticipate some of the rhythms of it by feeling into, noticing, and feeling with the patterns within the song's melody. Within a very short time, all three friends are in sync with one another, feeling into and feeling with the ebb and flow of the song as well as the rhythmic movements of each other's bodies.

Figure 4 Tyson Coble, Gainesville, Florida.

In this short story, we find a few different examples in which the dancers experience the interplay of the relations of feeling into and feeling with. Recall, that this second type of empathy, feeling with, is experienced whenever we have a sense of being united, in agreement, or in sync with another person or thing (sometimes this feeling may not be consciously recognized). Today this relation is often described as an interpersonal phenomenon, but since we are taking historical variations of the meaning of empathy seriously, one can also experience it as a feeling of unity or connection with inanimate objects, for example, when one has a feeling of oneness or unity with a piece of music or, say, when one feels connected to the mission of a humanitarian cause. As an interpersonal experience, it is often referred to the act in which one believes that he or she understands and/or has taken the perspective of another person. Other times, it is thought to occur when someone feels the same emotion as another (such as disgust or joy), or when one feels a special positive connection with another person's temperament or personality, and as exemplified in the aforementioned short story, whenever one's bodily movement is in sync with that of another. With this description of three people dancing, we also find that the relations of feeling into and feeling with often intermingle within our experiences, and occasionally, they even occur at the same time. Theorists of empathic projection between the mid-eighteenth and late nineteenth centuries noted this interplay between feeling into and feeling with, identifying the former as a process of feeling into things or *Einfühlung* and the later as feeling with things or sympathy. Sympathy has been described as an experience of feeling with others, but it has also been used to describe the act of caring, showing concern, or having pity for others. In light of this, one shouldn't be too surprised that questions about the difference between empathy and sympathy are quite common today. Nevertheless, these words have histories, and understanding these histories are important for considering the value of contemporary discussions about them.

It is common knowledge that "sympathy" and "empathy" are derived from the Greek, but what is probably not quite so well known is that while "sympathy" was used frequently among the ancients, "empathy" was not. Also, although the original words for the English terms "empathy" and "sympathy" first appeared among the Greeks, "sympathy" took on many meanings within different languages over the last few thousand years; however, our contemporary understandings of "empathy"/*Einfühlung* really only go back a few hundred years to the Enlightenment. For a number of Greek and Roman philosophers, "sympathy" was frequently used to describe a similar, sometimes amiable, feeling between the psychological states of two of more people. Other times we find that it was described as something pejorative, as a nonrational and automatic "catching" of another's sensations, what I have called *empathic contagion*. We find an example of this in Plato's *Charmides*, in which Socrates claims Critias is experiencing sympathy (συμπάθεια) as an empathic contagion of ideas. Critias was under the false impression that he had arrived at the same intellectual impasse (*aporia*) as Socrates did concerning the nature of moderation. But while Socrates reached this impasse only after a long process of reasoning and doubting, Critias merely "caught" the beliefs and feelings of Socrates.[1] In the Hippocratic tradition, we find that sympathy also meant a "fellow feeling" between different parts of the body, e.g., the stomach and the head.[2] Similar to this usage, Plato used "sympathy" to denote a certain type of agreement or accord between different parts of the soul and even different parts of the city-state.[3] With these few examples, we find that the historical meanings of "sympathy," in part, resemble a number of contemporary understandings of "empathy" in that each term has been used to signify both people and inanimate objects.

The Stoics came up with an idea of sympathy that they called "cosmic sympathy."[4] "Cosmic sympathy" means that *the cosmos is in sympathy with itself*. This might sound strange, but what it means is simply that all things in the universe are interdependent, causally interconnected, and rational.[5] The cosmos operates and unfolds as a causal chain of relational events within which one part could affect, influence, excite, or change another part, even independent of the distance of time or space that might be between them. We find the first employments of the term *cosmic sympathy* among the early Greek Stoics, who contended that we act in accord and in sync with the unfolding rationality of the *Logos* by being in sympathy with its movements through acts of divination (e.g., astrology).[6] Divination in this sense, as defined by the Stoic Chrysippus, is the "power to understand, see and explain the signs, which the gods give to human beings."[7] Accordingly, a "real" diviner's ability to interpret the meanings of these signs arrives within the diviner as a sympathetic understanding of the coherency and well-ordered structure of the cosmos, its rational patterns, as well as the ordered movements of its parts. Perhaps, in part, as a consequence of Cicero's skepticism toward this usage, Roman Stoics downplayed the role of divination and other similar magical practices common among Greek Stoics. Instead, they emphasized the role that sympathy as "fellow feeling" plays in the construction of friendships, the building of community, and the formation of political alliances.[8] Nevertheless, the notion of cosmic sympathy maintained its popularity within Neoplatonic and Renaissance philosophical traditions up to the

Enlightenment, when thinkers such as Smith and Hume provided a humanistic interpretation of sympathy as an integral bodily experience that facilitates our moral psychologies.

The fact that "empathy" has never been colored by the magical, superstitious, and perhaps, pseudo-religious understandings that are associated with "sympathy," marks one significant historical difference between these two familiar terms. Another noteworthy difference lies in the linguistic structure and the possible significations of each word. Linguistically, the difference between "empathy" and "sympathy" is that they each have different prefixes. At first glance this may seem obvious and, therefore, unimportant. However, when one considers the different meanings of these prefixes—both as parts of "empathy" or "sympathy" as well as other words—noting this difference between them is informative. "Em" signifies "into," "upon," or "in."[9] The prefix "sym" takes on many more meanings than does the prefix for "empathy." For example, depending upon the context, "sym" denotes a variety of different things—for example, it has meant: unity, harmony, sameness, similarity, togetherness, and/or agreement between things.[10] The difference between the possible significations of these two prefixes is vital for grasping the difference between "empathy" and "sympathy." For whereas "empathy" can and has meant both a *feeling of similarity or difference* between an observer and an object, until the theories of Smith and Hume, "sympathy" has only signified a *feeling of sameness*, similarity, unity, etc., with something. "Empathy" is a more pluralistic term, then, which allows one to recognize both difference and sameness, both disagreement and agreement.

Today, "sympathy" is used to denote particular experiences of either the relation of *feeling with* or the relation of *feeling for*. As an experience of feeling with others, "sympathy" is often used to describe an experience in which one is affected by the condition of another and possesses to some degree a feeling similar to or corresponding with that person's experience. Quite often today, "sympathy" is used in this way to refer to feeling with the negative experiences of others, leading some scholars to define "sympathy" as only a "sensitivity to negative emotional involvements."[11] This is unfortunate as this excludes the multiple ways we experience "fellow feeling" with others. For as Adam Smith once noted, along with the negative experiences of others, such as their sorrow or pain, we also feel or sympathize with their positive feelings, such as intense joy.[12] In addition to these usages of "sympathy" as an experience of the relation of feeling, "sympathy" is also used to describe *feeling for* others, which is quite often described as a feeling of pity or feeling of concern for another. Oftentimes, this use of sympathy as feeling for denotes a feeling about the suffering of another without much action. Sympathy cards are exemplary of this, so too are common, sincere yet rather pragmatically powerless, phrases such as "I am sorry for your loss" and "I sympathize with her plight ... however."

Though I have no real stake in the outcome, I sense that once this rather strange history of the word "sympathy" is widely known and the current ineffectiveness of its usage is widely grasped, it will continue to be ineffective and thus less popular than the word "empathy."

From *Einfühlung* to Empathy: Phenomenology, Hermeneutics, and Sociology

The historical, linguistic, and semantic truths aforementioned are the reasons why this work is on the subject of empathy and not sympathy. Moreover, the plural and rich significations that have been assigned to the word "empathy," as well as the term *Einfühlung*—which both preceded it and gave rise to it—have provided justification for the multidimensional theory of relational empathy I am promoting. We found evidence of this pluralism from the linguistic and cultural pluralism of Herder to the interdisciplinary approaches of Lotze, Groos, and Lipps. Primarily with Lipps's contributions, we note the beginning of a major historical shift in which the objects of empathic projection changed from the forms of architectural structures or any other work of art to the content of other people's minds. In consideration of these contributions, Lipps is a world historical figure, by one way of interpreting him, in that his work is representative of a major discursive shift in the meaning and usefulness of *Einfühlung* (i.e., empathic projection). But there were numerous voices of dissent against the works of Lipps, mostly among phenomenologists and hermeneuticists whose criticisms and healthy skepticisms about Lipps's works invite us to consider the value of many of his claims, especially the claim that exercising the skill of *Einfühlung* could reveal the subjectivity of another person's mind.

Phenomenologists entered debates about empathy largely due to what they saw were glaring errors both in Lipps's theory of empathy as well as the previous accounts upon which he built his theory (e.g., accounts from Lotze and Groos). With these criticisms, phenomenological discourses about empathy focused on what would eventually be called the "problem of empathy."[13] But why did empathy suddenly become a problem? How was it that what seemed to be more of a skill than a problem, from Herder to Lipps, suddenly became a problem? And what did theorists think was so problematic about it?

Perhaps, most significantly, phenomenologists sensed that the notion of empathy was problematic in light of multiple meanings and usages associated with the term *Einfühlung* and as a consequence of this, it wasn't clear to them and other thinkers what precisely one meant when using it. Lipps used it to refer to both aesthetic objects and the *foreign* mental states of others. Though Lipps's influence was powerful and represented a shift in the discourse about empathy, the manner in which he and others defined "empathy" in multiple ways followed the historical patterns I've been emphasizing throughout this work—namely that "empathy" has always been conceived as a pluralistic notion and it stands for a number of interrelated experiences. But whereas I find this plurality to be beneficial and thus ripe for pragmatic reconstruction, phenomenologists found it troubling and interpreted this pluralism as a problem to solve. On the other end of the spectrum, it wasn't the ambiguity arising from the multiple meanings of "empathy" during the early twentieth century, but rather the ambiguity surrounding *specific* meanings of "empathy" that led phenomenologists to pause and to be critical of this popular idea. And Lipps, more than any other, was the target of this criticism.

Lipps's claim that acts of one can have *knowledge* of others though acts of *Einfühlung* was the central object of this criticism. In "Das wissen vom fremdem ichen," translated roughly as *the knowledge of foreigners*, Lipps made the claim that one can grasp, is able to feel with, another's mental states simply by living the dispositions, which I see manifested in the other, in me.[14] But how is it possible to perceive and apprehend the other, the experiences of another, the complete strangeness of another who is not me? Are not the inner experiences of others who are not me, in one way or another, strange to me—or at least hidden from me in some way? Does not the word "foreign" (*fremd*) signify something wholly other? And by its very definition does it not denote something that is inaccessible to my perception? Echoing the Novalis–Kant debate and at the heart of this phenomenological skepticism, there were a number of perplexing questions phenomenologists raised concerning Lipps's relationship between the self and others during acts of empathic projection. Lipps claimed that empathy, and therefore, the knowledge of another's ego (or consciousness), was made possible by two fundamental and innate instincts: (a) the instinct of imitation and (b) the instinct of the expression of life. This first instinct of imitation is known by reflecting upon experiences in which our inner mental states tend toward and are recognized as this second instinct, namely outward bodily expression.[15] For instance, if I feel inwardly afraid of something, this inner reality or sense tends to produce an outward expression, such as a frightened and fearful face. When I recognize any particular outward expressions of another, such as a frightened and fearful face, I then am able to imitate it, which arouses a similar experience of fear in me. Knowledge of others by means of empathy arises from understanding my inner and reproduced experience, which is then projected back into the other.

Edmund Husserl was skeptical of these claims for few reasons. First, it does not follow from Lipps's account of this process that I can have knowledge of another's mental states, for how do I *know* that what I am inwardly experiencing is representative of another's experience and not simply something I have imagined within my own psyche.[16] According to Husserl, we can't know whether empathy (as least as Lipps describes it) reveals the inner mental states of another because Lipps's philosophical understanding of the relation of feeling with others does not make it clear whether I am projecting my own self into an foreign body or if I am encountering foreign self through and within my own body. If the latter is the case, the question then for Husserl becomes: "how do I constitute someone else as the alter ego, as another ego (*Ich*), with its own 'centre' and 'pole' (*Ichpol*) of psychic experiences, affections and performances?"[17] This type of skepticism encouraged Edith Stein, one of Husserl's students, to create a phenomenology of empathy. Stein rejects Lipps's version of "empathy," which she argued limited the notion of consciousness to the natural instincts of the body without empirical evidence and put forth a false understanding of the relation between the self and another during acts of empathy. Recall that Lipps believed that during the act of empathy one's self experiences a fusion and complete identification with the other. Following Husserl's distinction between experiences that are grasped "primordially" and those that are grasped "nonprimordially," Stein claims that the concrete, unique, and immediately given experience of the empathizer while supposedly imitating and reproducing the outward expression of the other is fundamentally distinct from the concrete, unique, and immediately given experience of the other's subjectivity. Each person experiences her/his own ego primordially as an immediate perception and givenness arising from one's own unique and distinct ego consciousness, but each person does not have access to the other's primordial, bodily experience. For Stein, empathy as the experience of foreign consciousness "can only be a nonprimordial experience which announces a primordial one."[18]

In his work *The Nature of Sympathy*, the phenomenologist Max Scheler makes rigid conceptual distinctions between commonly confused and ambiguous terms about human feeling for the purpose of making clear the different phenomenological dimensions of the relation of feeling with—what he calls true "fellow-feeling" or sympathy. In accord with Husserl and Stein, Scheler is skeptical of Lipps's claims about the experience of *Einfühlung*, noting first that Lipps's association of *Einfühlung* with fellow feeling confuses two distinct phenomenological occurrences, one that merely contributes to fellow feeling and another that is actually the experience of fellow-feeling. Neither was Scheler content with Lipps's theory of imitation (empathic mimicry), which likewise must be distinguished from true fellow-feeling. Consequently, for Scheler, "neither 'projective empathy' (empathic projection) nor 'imitation' (empathic mimicry) is necessary to explain the primary component of fellow-feeling."[19] To grasp the true nature of our experiences of the relation of *feeling with* others, Scheler makes distinctions between four types of feeling: (i) immediate community of feeling, (ii) fellow feeling about something, (iii) emotional infection, and (iv) true emotional identification. An immediate community of feeling and a fellow feeling about something fail to meet Scheler's standards for "true" sympathy; and emotional infection, or what we have called *empathic contagion*, is merely a transference of a state of feeling according to Scheler's interpretation of it, and thus doesn't allow one to experience true sympathy with another. Like many of his predecessors, Scheler is highly critical of Lipps's theory of identification, especially Lipps's theory of emotional identification as recounted in his story of the acrobat, which puts forth a false idea of identification in which the conscious self of the individual watching the acrobat has fused with and has "sunk itself completely in that of the acrobat."[20] Experiences of "true" emotional identification for Scheler involve, as Dermot Moran has succinctly described them, a respect for "the other's individuality" and a recognition that "it is he or she who is having the experience," which "preserves the other's difference."[21] This facet of Scheler's account of sympathy, as a manifestation of the relation of feeling with, represents one of very few historical accounts of sympathy that doesn't fall into the common trap of describing sympathy simply as an experience of similarity or sameness between an observer and an object.

Husserl, Stein, and Scheler's skepticism regarding the possibility that one is able to both feel into and feel with the mental states and/or experiential subjectivity of another was novel though not entirely new. Generations before these thinkers, Friedrich Schleiermacher, whose theories of interpretation and translation were inspired by Herder's philosophy of language, considered the usefulness of "empathy" for interpreting texts. Interpretation, as hermeneutical inquiry into linguistic structures of texts and the psychological dispositions and intentions of authors, is for Schleiermacher an art and requires the implementation of what he called "grammatical interpretation" of the language as well as a "psychological understanding." This doctrine of psychological understanding states that for one to understand, grasp, and interpret accurately, say, an author's intentions, one must project and transport oneself into, feel with, and co-understand the author's mindset for the purpose of being able to place oneself on the same level of the author, thereby interpreting her/him correctly. During the rise of the social sciences in the early twentieth century, Schleiermacher's interpretive method of *Einfühlung* (which was adopted from Herder) was often compared, and sometimes conflated, with the method of *Verstehen*. *Verstehen* was a method used for grasping the significance of texts, historical events, and cultural forms as well as an important methodological tool that brought legitimacy to the social inquiry and differentiated the natural sciences from the social sciences.

Herder and Schleiermacher's hope that *Einfühlung* might be adopted as a method for assisting our interpretations of languages, texts, and cultures was revived in the works of Wilhelm Dilthey. Dilthey's early work on the idea of empathic projection was highly influenced by the romanticism of Schleiermacher and Herder, etc., and it too was akin to "psychologism," a term coined by logicians and phenomenologists to denote claims about psychological phenomena that were logically unsound and/or insufficiently rigorous from a scientific point of view. The works of Lipps were saddled with this title and Lipps defended his works against it. And though Lipps and Dilthey were remarkably different as thinkers, they each professed the importance of psychology for penetrating the inner life-worlds of others. But for Dilthey, especially in his later works, this does not happen, as Lipps believed, by way of empathic projection and empathic mimicry with the mental processes of *another person*. Neither is *feeling into* and *feeling with* another facilitated by introspection, as Lipps also believed. To penetrate the inner world of another, *to feel into and feel with the inner life-worlds of others*, we must employ a hermeneutic approach in which the objects of our interpretive gazes are not the fluctuating, psychic states of others as we interpret them and the weak powers of our perceptions. But rather, we must employ multiple sociological and analytical scientific methods in order to interpret the facts, signs, and cultural forms, which as expressions of psychic life and historical situatedness, provide for us the opportunity to penetrate the inner "life-world" of others. Dilthey's methods for doing this put him in a class by himself and would become foundational to the emergence of sociological methods throughout the twentieth century.[22]

In 1905, Sigmund Freud explored this interplay of feeling into and feeling with to understand how they function to produce laughter. When we hear a joke, we *feel into* the producer's psychic state and try to *feel with* it by comparing it with our own. Out of this process of feeling into another's mind and attempting to feel with or understand it by comparison, laughter is discharged.[23] Freud interprets this process to be essential in a number of other interpersonal interactions in which one's ability to feel into and feel with the contents of another's mind *accurately* is crucial for making a connection with that person. For instance, Freud thought that a teacher will never be able to educate a child without feeling into and feeling with the child's mind accurately.[24] Most importantly, the process of feeling into and feeling with another person's mind is necessary for the success of psychotherapy because it culminates in the experience of empathic connection. As a technique, empathy ought to be the central *modus operandi* of the therapist, who must be free from all forms of moralizing while empathizing with patients during therapy. The therapist must not be didactic and ought not to assign praise or blame to what the patient is experiencing or sharing.[25]

Freud's interest in the explanatory powers of these two relations was inspired by the reflections of Lipps, though he seemed to distance himself from Lipps's understanding of both the role of the self and the process of introspection during acts of empathizing with others. This disagreement echoes the debate about the self that Novalis and Kant introduced. On Lipps's side, the process of *Einfühlung* is a means to gain knowledge of another's mental or inner states that involves self-objectification of my "feeling" into a person's experience (feeling into) and is also an inward imitation of that person's expression (which involves the process of feeling into and feeling with). Whatever this "feeling" or internal quality of the self might be, this idea of the self as objectified into the other is entirely absent in Freud. Instead of thinking about the self in this way, Freud developed a bidirectional psychical field of mutual influence that involved certain speech patterns and listening practices, which in turn, helped psychoanalysts explore and interpret the patient's unconscious.[26] During this process the self of the therapist is not objectified, but rather is turned into a receptive vehicle for gaining an understanding of what the patient's unconscious is transmitting.[27] The therapist, then, *feels into* the patient's mind and general experience only in accordance with preset rules and directions the therapist follows for grasping the patient's inner psychic world.

Portrayals of empathy as a fusion or connection with another person's experiences among psychologists became prominent when the English word "empathy" was coined in 1909 by psychologist Edward Titchener (1867–1927), who fashioned this neologism based on *Einfühlung* and the Greek word *empatheia*. Titchener described empathy in three different ways, each of which portrays empathy as an immediate feeling with another. First, when we see another person act, for instance, humbly, we sometimes immediately feel with the person's kinesthetic experience. This happens immediately and without our intention. Titchener described this famously by stating, "Not only do I see gravity, modesty, and pride ... but I feel or act them out in the mind's muscle."[28] A second way Titchener describes empathy is by referring to his experiences of music in which he is able to *feel with* or grasp quickly and comprehensively the fitness of any given musical structure.[29] This second description of empathy is similar to how nineteenth-century aestheticians described *Einfühlung*, and likewise is directed toward an inanimate object rather than another person. In his third unique use of empathy, Titchener speaks of the interpersonal relationship between an experimenter and her/his subjects, one in which the experimenter must be in "full sympathy with his observers; he must think, by empathy, as they think, understand as they understand, speak in their language." These three types of empathy are quite different from one another. With the first, we immediately catch the experience of another by an unconscious act of empathic contagion. In the second, Titchener's sense of musical greatness is either in sync or not in sync, feeling with or not feeling with, a musical composition as he hears it. In the last example, though, it is clear that the experiencer must first be able to employ the skill of empathic mimicry with her/his observers and also feel with them by experiencing an empathic connection with them. The first two examples explain a type of instantaneous *feeling with* the experiences of others, while the last exemplifies a much more processional, back and forth, feeling into and feeling with others.

The Dominance of Psychology: Symbolic Interactionism, Animal Sciences, and Neuroscience

Despite phenomenological and hermeneutic criticisms of the methods of psychology, it was the discipline of psychology that "won the day" by conjuring up the most effective descriptions of the many experiences we call "empathy," defining them in such a way that they were pragmatic, and thereby, *influential*. There are a number of reasons why this came to pass. First, there was a general decline of interest in the subject of empathy in phenomenology and hermeneutics; and consequently, considerations of the value of empathy for treating patients during the early twentieth century had room to grow as the century unfolded. This is evident among theorists such as Carl Rogers and Heinz Kohut, who introduced new and popular ideas about empathy's effectiveness during therapy.[30] Second, George Herbert Mead's philosophical interests and insights into developmental psychology, what Herbert Blumer would later call "symbolic interactionalism," gave rise to a flurry of empirical research in social psychology and early childhood development.[31] Third, by the end of the century, primatology and neuroscience, as two offshoots or subdisciplines of psychology, were able to widen the scope of this empirical research by extending the experience of the relation of *feeling with* to nonhuman animals and by utilizing advanced technology to explore the structure and function of the nervous system. Finally, with the emergence of these new disciples, theories of biological evolution began to play a larger role in our understanding of empathic experience than it did earlier in the century.

Mead's contributions to the rise of empathy as the relation of *feeling with* emerged out of his philosophical interests in the self as a social process. Once again, the main theme of the Novalis vs. Kant debate returns. But instead of following the pattern of previous thinkers by conjuring up yet another artificial distinction between the self and others based upon an unempirical representation of the ego or "I," for instance, as we saw with Kant's transcendental ego or Husserl's primordial *Ich*, Mead turns to *experience* to explore how the self emerges during processes of socialization. Mead locates three stages in early childhood and describes how the abilities we learn during them contributes to the development of our sense of self. The first stage begins at age two or earlier when children learn to imitate and copy the behaviors of others. Although there is not yet a sense of self during this time, this stage is a necessary, or what Mead calls a preparatory, stage for self-understanding. Between the ages of two and six, children enter the play stage and learn how to adopt the role of someone they know, such as a parent or a doctor. Around the ages of seven and older, children learn what Mead calls the game stage. During this stage, children learn how to take up roles as they relate to the rules of the game and the roles others adopt during the game. Interestingly, we experience for the first time what I have called empathic mimicry during this first stage and empathic perspective-taking in both stages. Moreover, each of these stages make use of the interplay of the relations of feeling into and feeling with, albeit in childlike form. However, it is only during the complexity of this third stage that one is able to develop a *unified* sense of self for the first time by taking on the attitude of the "generalized other." Adopting the role of the generalized other doesn't mean that one is able to take the perspective of just one individual in the game, but that one is empowered to take on the perspectives of everyone in an organized social game.

The social-developmental processes of empathic mimicry and empathic perspective-taking that one experiences during early childhood continually operates to inform and reshape her/his understanding of the self as each interacts with others throughout a lifetime. As a child, one learns the rules of a particular game, which, unlike play, is organized and rule bound. But when one grows older, the "game" becomes a particular community or social group, which are bound by different rules. Taking on the attitudes of the generalized others in a social group or community means that one knows the attitude of every generalized other toward oneself and toward others in the group; it means that one is able to take up each individual's viewpoints on different aspects of society, the other's perspective on social problems; it means that at any time, one can know how she/he would respond in different situations *as any generalized other within the same community or social group*.[32] In adopting these myriad attitudes, we consistently employ the relations of feeling into and feeling with others, thus the interplay of these relations of experience are necessary for taking on the attitudes of all generalized others within all communities and social groups with which we engage. The social processes in which these two relations operate make it possible for us develop a unified self and are the vehicles by which the self is *transformed*. Mead elucidates two dimensions of the self and its transformative powers by making a distinction between the "me" and the "I," each of which represents different parts of the *self as a communal self*. The "me" represents the internalization of roles I derive from my interactions with generalized others by means of the symbolic processes that make this possible. But this is fundamentally different from the "I," which signifies a "creative response" to the symbolized structures of the "me," that is, the generalized others. With the creative responses of the "I," the self becomes transformed, and in relation to its community, it gains potency to transform and ameliorate it.

Beginning in the late twentieth century, biologists, primatologists, and neuroscientists began to widen the scope of Mead's empirical investigation, which in turn contributed to a widening of the meaning of "empathy." In biology and primatology, this came to pass by including nonhuman animals as objects of empirical observation. For a long time, that is, for most of our history, human beings have tried to separate themselves from "animals." With the rise (and sufficient understanding) of Darwinian evolutionary theory, this self-congratulatory categorization is as naïve as it is revealing, showing just how magnificent our hubris can be. Empirical conclusions in the biological sciences have been able to quell some of this conceit and set the stage for conducting scientific investigations into the possibility that empathy is experienced among nonhuman animal life. Skepticism concerning the possibility that this is possible in some way, for instance, that nonhuman animals can feel into and feel with the ambitions or intentions of other animals is rather fatuous in light of the fact that the animal's survival absolutely depends upon this ability. Accepting this as true, the question then becomes not whether animals can perceive accurately the objectives of other animals but rather how and to what extent different animal species are able to do this and if this ability constitutes an empathic experience, by any sense of the term.

Sometimes responding to a perceived threat or danger relies upon utilizing *empathic inference*. Historically, many have been skeptical of this claim, contending that what is perceived to be one animal empathizing or feeling with another is only a consequence of animal instinct arising out of personal distress rather than a feeling of unity with a member of its species. Today, however, many studies have confirmed that a number of animal species employ this type of empathy in that they are able to feel into and make calculated guesses about another animal's state and the safety of an environment. For example, oftentimes in unanticipated moments when an animal's survival is threatened, it grasps the presence of an existing threat, not by directly perceiving it, but by inferring and following the cues of a member of its species that signal the existence of the danger. Ravens more judiciously perform this type of empathy and make calculative judgments about the safety of possibly flying by dangerous animals that appear to be dead and thus a source of food. Other times, animals are able to grasp an existing threat simply by the immediate and automatic experience of *empathic contagion*, as an unconscious "catching" of and being in sync with another's experience. This is common among a number of species and is evident, for example, in what is called "yawn contagion," namely the act of yawning unintentionally immediately after someone nearby yawns. Empathic experiences in this sense are also evident in studies of pain contagion in mice, in which one mouse's experience of pain was intensified by witnessing pain in other mice. Empathy as *empathic mimicry* is also common among many species. Among chimps this is often expressed, De Waal notes, as imitation, that is, as a "reenactment of observed manipulations" by means of an unconscious process of body-mapping.[33] This phenomenon is witnessed when one chimp, while watching another perform a physical task, involuntarily mimics the actions and physical contortions of the observed chimp. In addition to this type of empathy, members of the same species commonly experience *empathic connection* with one another. Whales imitate the songs of other whales, and birds do the same with other birds; and for each of the species, it is clear that empathy, as the interplay of the relations of feeling into and feeling with, is the source of these unifying choirs. The experience of empathic connection is also evident in horses. When horses collectively pull a cart in unison, they experience empathic connection with members of their species by means of their ability to move in sync with the trotting of other horses, who are likewise "saddled" with this task. Though experiences of empathic inference, empathic contagion, empathic mimicry, and empathic connection are all evident among the social lives of different species, it is difficult to know for certain which nonhuman animals have the capacity to experience the more detailed and imaginative processes of *empathic perspective-taking*. Nevertheless, these five types of empathy involve the interplay of the relations of both *feeling into* and *feeling with*, in which *feeling into* can be noted as any experience from direct perception to careful and prolonged observation and *feeling with* is understood as anything from unconscious and/or automatic empathic contagion to mimicry and more complex imaginative experiences of perspective-taking.

Over the last few decades, as a consequence of our understanding of evolutionary biology and with the rise of advanced technologies, neuroscientists have added to the discourse about empathy as the relation of feeling with, offering us a view of the neurological systems of living species in ways that were previously unimaginable. And with this rise of neuroscientific research, we find a number of questions about empathy, from Groos to De Waal, were reintroduced and reexamined. Among neuroscientists, we find that the types of empathy as feeling with have been instrumental to their studies. Take, for example, the following definition of *empathic inference* by Danziger, Prkachin, and Willer: empathy is a "complex form of psychological inference that enables us to understand the personal experiences of another person through cognitive, evaluative and affective process."[34] With this definition, these neuroscientists deftly avoid falling into the trap of dualistic thinking by talking about cognitive vs. affective processes (which are real neurological processes) instead of splitting empathy into cognitive empathy and affective empathy, which is parasitic on the reason/emotion dualism. When it refers to the thoughts and feelings of others, empathic inference or mindreading can lead to what William Ickes and others have called *empathic accuracy*—"the ability to accurately infer the specific content of other people's thoughts and feelings."[35] Others, such as Claus Lamm and Jean Decety have preferred to examine the "neural substrate" of human empathy as *empathic perspective-talking*.[36] *Empathic mimicry* has also played a significant role in the discourses of neuroscience, whether it has been described as a necessary part of the "functional architecture of human empathy" or as the process of motor imitation during the process of empathy.[37] Perhaps, though, the most intriguing—and most controversial—contribution from neuroscience was the discovery of mirror neurons, which incorporates the understandings of empathy as *empathic mimicry, empathic contagion,* and *empathic connection*. Mirror neurons are specialized cells in the brain that are purported to "fire" not only when one performs a particular action but also when one watches or hears another perform the same action. The theory of mirror neurons was birthed, quite accidentally, during a study of a macaque monkey in Parma, Italy, where Italian scientists noted that certain neurons in the F5 region of the premotor cortex of the monkey fired both when it picked up a piece of food with its own hand as well as when it observed another pick up a piece of food.[38] In other investigations of mirror neurons following this study, scientists found that a number of auditory neurons also fire in the F5 region upon hearing the sound of an action. Though theorists and practitioners interested in empathy should continue to follow these developments regarding mirror neurons as well as all other types of mirroring processes,[39] it ought to be noted that some of the conclusions about the existence mirror neurons are not as empirical as many believe them to be, and for this reason thinkers such as Gregory Hickok view current theories and narratives about mirror neurons as rather mythological.[40]

The Skill of Feeling With

"Not only do we mimic those with whom we identify, But mimicry in turn strengthens the bond."[41]

Frans de Waal

The relation of *feeling with* signifies the mode or manner in which we feel with other persons or things by experiencing a sense of connection, unity, or concord with them. Accordingly, this relation is a general description of any particular experience in which two or more things are connected to each other by a specific, contextualized act of feeling unified, connected, or in concord with something. Depending upon the context, this might simply involve an experience in which we *feel with*, understand, or grasp, the thoughts or emotions of another. Or within a different context, we might experience this relation as a sense of being united with another person solely for the purpose of offering moral support to him/her. And still in another context and circumstance, I might *feel with* someone by identifying with this person in a very powerful way that deepens my emotional connection to him/her, builds a sense of trust between us, and perhaps, when my feeling and respect for this person grows, I might be inclined to mimic the honorable qualities of this person's character and, as a result, this *mimicry in turn strengthens the bond between us*. In this last instance we find that under the right conditions, certain concrete experiences of the relation of feeling with, for example, identifying strongly with others or mimicking them, can encourage or even give rise to experiences of the relation of feeling for, such as, feeling care for, building a bond with and establishing trust with another.

For pragmatic purposes, I sense that a number of conflicting definitions of "empathy as feeling with" in scholarship today (e.g., empathy as empathic perspective-taking, empathic accuracy, empathic contagion, empathic mimicry, and empathic connection) should be conceived as different—equally real—*modes of this general relation* rather than as competing ideas vying for the "true" or "correct" understanding of empathy. Second, the value of one of these types of empathy ought to be understood according to its function as recognized within and defined by one's understanding of the contexts in which it is experienced as well as by the actual or conceivable consequences of its use. In this way, the second relation functions very similarly to the first relation of feeling into in that each, as a general, broad, and pluralistic interpretation of different portions of experience, finds its value in how it is able to include rather than exclude rival definitions of "empathy" by means of embracing unique contexts and the felt consequences that flow from them. However, unlike the first relation, which in experience is always manifested by means of someone's intention, this second relation can be experienced both as conscious and unconscious feelings of the body. For example, I can be aware of the fact that I grasp and feel with the actions of another (empathic perspective-taking) but be unaware that I have unconsciously adopted the body language of a close friend (empathic mimicry). In the case of the former, my act of feeling with is confirmed by my cognitive awareness of it, while in the latter case, I unknowingly copied my friend's body language and adopted it as my own.

Among discourses about empathy today, acts of feeling with are understood in terms of their relation to other people's thoughts, emotions, experiences, etc. But based on the histories I have recounted, it is pragmatic to adopt the idea that the object can be anything, whether animate or inanimate. For the philosophers and theories mentioned in this chapter, what led to either skepticism or belief in the ability to feel with another person or thing was inextricably linked to the particular manner or process by which each thinker claimed one could know or not know the object of an empathic act. It follows from this, that it is the description of the *particular relation* between the "empathizer" and her/his object that ultimately contributed to a theorist's skepticism of or belief in our ability to feel with objects. Phenomenologists and hermeneuticists were skeptical that one can know, respectively, another's subjective ego consciousness or historical formations of another culture or time through a psychological process of identification. The process of "knowing" (in a logical and analytical sense of the word) the object of one's empathizing was not stated as a clear relation in the works of Lipps and others, and, in general, was not scientifically demonstrated. With Mead's contribution, as well as with the rise of biology, primatology, and neuroscience, we find a turn toward experience and the need for understanding empathy in light of observation and empirical research. With this historical shift toward experience, questions concerning the meaning or value of empathy are ongoing—they can never be completely and finally answered—and are subject to further empirical investigations. The difference between believing in and being skeptical about empathy as an experience of the relation of feeling with lies in the conceptual differences of the process of feeling with itself, one of which was deemed insufficiently logical, while the other was determined empirically and, to a large extent, understood symbolically.

It seems quite clear that the pragmatic difference between these two general approaches (i.e., skepticism vs. belief) for interpreting the value of the relation of feeling with, each of which relies on a fundamentally different conceptualization of the self than the other, lies also in the perceived adequacy or inadequacy of the consequences each approach produces. If one, skeptical about the possibility that he/she can feel with the experience of another, refrains from attempting to do so, justification of this decision can only to be found in the observable consequences of her/his restraint. Likewise, the act of feeling with, or believing that one is connected or in sync with another's experience, can only be judged empirically by the actions performed based on this belief and what they actually produce. Now, if this focus upon consequences is deemed to be a strong criterion for judging the value of our actions toward one another, then each option is nevertheless a manifestation of the relation of feeling with. This appears to be obviously true for one who acts upon his/her feeling with another, but is it also true for one who is skeptical and restrains from action? If one restrains one's action in lieu of his/her disbelief that she/he is able to grasp the other's experience, then this person's action of restraint flows from a feeling with the difference of and, perhaps, inaccessibility of the other's experience.

Each approach ought to be seen as a skill to be utilized in different circumstances for reaching different ends. Sometimes, it is practical for us to feel with the experiences of others, while other times it is best to admit that we cannot know or feel with another's experiences, some of which might be hidden from even our most astute observations. Exercising the skill of feeling with others, whether by recognizing similarities or differences with them, often both facilitates and enhances our closest relationships and serves as the tool by which we are able to build new and successful ones. In the context of an existing relationship, we recognize our feeling with others as something skillful when it produces a mutual sense of unity and connection *deemed to be necessary* for enjoying and strengthening the relationship. By "unity" or "connection" I do not mean that there exists a type of agreement necessarily, if by "agreement" one means thinking or sensing in exactly the same way as another does. A sense of feeling with, being unified or connected to another, could mean this, but it could also mean that there is *unity in disagreement* or a feeling of being connected to and understanding the differences between oneself and another.

Experiences of *feeling with* other persons or things is sometimes recognized as an instantaneous feeling with another person or thing, while in other circumstances, our experiences of feeling with comes by way of a lengthy, sometimes complex, process. We will call this first type *instantaneous empathy* and the second type *processional empathy*. An instantaneous experience of feeling with is recognized in those moments in which *Einfühlung* is exercised merely as a simple act of projection, an immediate noticing of the outstanding dynamics readily perceptible within the object observed. Think of an experience in which you instantly feel and are in sync with the general experience of another automatically, without even trying, e.g., when you see someone laughing voraciously or crying profusely, such instances provide for you an immediate and instantaneous grasp of and *feeling with* the other's experience. Examples of processional empathy, on the other hand, are recognized in those experiences in which feeling with the experience of another person is not so readily achieved; it is the difficult process of trying to understand and feel the emotions, thoughts, and experiences of others. Think of an experience in which you have had to inquire at length into the experience of someone in order to understand his/her perspective or think of those instances in which you have had to employ your imagination and infer what someone else might be experiencing in order to eventually feel and understand that person's point of view or general character. From a relational perspective, instantaneous empathy, as an experience of instantly and accurately feeling with others, requires little if any effort. In these instances, you immediately feel with the object of your perception or contemplation and there is no need to, for example, employ creative and strategic ways of perceiving the experience of others in order to grasp and feel with their experiences. In other words, the interplay of the relations of *feeling into* and *feeling with* plays no role in the emergence of our experiences of instantaneous empathy. During our experiences of processional empathy, however, this interplay of relations takes the lead role, and the manner in which this interplay unfolds (i.e., how well we exercise the skills of these relations such as mindfulness, empathic inference, imagine-other perspective, etc.) often determines the success or failure of our attempts to feel with and grasp the experience of others.

Developing the ability to *feel into* and *feel with* the experiences of others and the content of things is nothing less *than an art form*. And just in the same way that the significance and value of any work of art can only be recognized within the tradition from which it emerges, the art of relational empathy can only be justified as being significant or having value in the manner by which it arises out of a context of an embedded experience and is able to produce satisfactory consequences. I will refer to this interplay of relations as an art form by the term, *the art of affect attunement*.[42] By "affect" here, I mean the experience of being moved by an experience with another person and/or thing, and by "attunement" I mean the process by which we modify the manner in which we feel into and feel with the movements and experiences of other persons.[43] This sense of attunement as a modification of our empathic senses in experience helps us evade the consequences of mistakenly believing that we feel exactly with the experiences of others as well as, on a more philosophical level, allowing us to avoid falling into the misleading metaphors and/or false conceptual schemes of modernism, e.g., mirror metaphors that imply "sameness" and reject the reality of difference.[44] The interplay of the relations of feeling into and feeling with as the art of affect attunement is always a process (an unending process within life, which is always transitioning and in which all the relations of life are in flux) of reperceiving, reimagining, and reconstructing the relations between ourselves and others in order to produce satisfactory results.

Grasping the significance of the multiple and varied historical understandings of empathy throughout the twentieth century is crucial for reflecting upon contemporary disagreements about what constitutes an empathic experience. Today we find that most definitions of "empathy" do not give enough attention to the perceptual and observational processes by which we are able to, for instance, know what it is like to experience the world from the perspective of another or "to walk a mile in another's shoes." In other words, little emphasis has been placed on the need for understanding our experiences of the relation of feeling into things and as a consequence of this, I fear that our experiences of empathy, defined narrowly, lack a certain pragmatic potency. The broad approach to conceiving and defining "empathy" I have endorsed, however, allows us to include the majority of conflicting definitions of "empathy" constructed throughout history and find value for each within certain contextualized experiences. Without recognizing the historical transformations of the meaning of "empathy" we have noted from Herder to Kohut, from romanticism to neuroscience, from the relation of feeling into to the relation of feeling with, this conceptual pluralism that includes rival definitions of "empathy" would not have been possible. Neither would it be possible to detect the reasons why in the mid-twentieth century to the present day, we find another historical transformation in which the meaning of "empathy" began to be associated with the relation of feeling for, understood and described as an experience of concern, care, and compassion. This historical development contributed greatly to our contemporary confusion surrounding the meaning of "empathy," but which will, when understood as a third relation of empathic experience, actually dissolve a number of disputes about empathy that have arisen from this general confusion.

5

Empathic Care

Under a green sea of umbrella-shaped trees, myriad sounds echo throughout the Ituri Forest. And if you were to visit this sylvan scene, it wouldn't be long until you heard the loud chatter of monkeys overhead, the shrill trumpeting of elephants, and a host of other piercing and penetrating noises that would most likely set your nerves on edge. But if you listened long enough and were in the right place, you would also hear the mellifluous and soothing sounds of the Mbuti women as they sing lullabies to their infants; and you might also notice how these sweet sounds rise melodiously above the din of the forest, to the tops of the trees and beyond them, into the open expanse of the azure sky. Pregnant mothers of the Mbuti begin singing these lullabies to their infants even before they are born, reassuring them of the interdependence of all things, of the goodness of the forest, and of the support they will receive from others upon being born.

In addition to the lullabies of the Mbuti mothers as expressions and gestures of love, concern, and care for their children, you also would immediately notice that they employ the skills of empathy as *feeling into* and *feeling with* while singing to their children after they are born. You might also notice how one of the mothers would hold a male infant in her arms while searching for the source of his discomfort whenever he cried (feeling into); or maybe she would *feel into* the tone or seriousness of the crying itself. Maybe the mother would instantly grasp the reason for the infant's salty tears and *feel with* him and feel with the situation causing him difficulty. I am certain that you could imagine a few other ways the Mbuti mothers could both feel into and feel with the experiences of their infants. And if you were to live with the Mbuti people, as the anthropologist Colin Turnbull once did, you would notice several other contexts in which all the Mbuti people would make good use of our first two skills of empathy during their interactions with other members of their community.[1]

The experiences of the Mbuti women cast a light upon one of the major sources of not only our empathic skill by which we are able to feel for the

Figure 5 Hiking the Blue Ridge Mountains with C. D. Batson.

experiences of others (e.g., provide nurturing care to others), but also our empathic skills of feeling into and feeling with others. Cross-cultural research conducted within different disciplines continue to suggest that females generally possess a stronger capacity for empathy early on in life than do males. This is not to say that men are unable to develop these skills, but it appears that women have an advantage when it comes to empathizing with others. Females score higher on measures of empathy than males.[2] Also, adolescent girls have higher prosocial reasoning than boys when developmental states are considered.[3] At birth, female babies look longer at faces than male babies, suggesting that the interpretive glances by which we *feel into* the facial expressions of others is more pronounced in females than males. Young girls are far better readers of the emotions of others than young boys are; they are better at perspective-taking, and are in general more in tune with the modulations of other people's voices—three facts that suggest that females are more sufficiently equipped to *feel with* the experiences of others than males. Girls tend, on average, to feel greater remorse after causing harm to others, and conclusively appear to be able to *feel for* the experiences of others with greater care and concern than do boys during equal stages of childhood development.[4]

The convergence of the relations of feeling into, feeling with, and feeling for within one's experience is what I have called relational empathy, what I sense is the most inclusive and historically accurate perspective of those experiences we call "empathic." Sometimes in experience, however, it is evident that one or more of these relations are absent. For instance, within certain contexts of lived experience, the relation of feeling into can operate separately from feeling with, and each of these can operate separately from the relation of feeling for. In other courses of our experiences, it is likewise clear that one or more of these relations are missing and occasionally the absence of one of these relations can adversely affect the others. For instance, it seems to be required that I at least observe (feel into) another's pain to alleviate it (feel for). If I don't feel my way into the person's experience of pain, I might not adequately be able to grasp his/her experience and thus I might not be able to feel for or care for the person's pain as a result. That is, I would need to grasp the fact that another is indeed in pain by *feeling with* the condition of the person's state, if I will be able to care about it. Feeling into and feeling with the pain of others, then, seem to be necessary to feel for others.

But it is not the case that mastering the skills of feeling into and/or feeling with *causes* one to feel for that person in every context and circumstance. Take, for instance, the following example: imagine one day that one of the male members of the Mbuti tribe was attacked by someone from a rival tribe, he would certainly be able to feel into and feel with the invader's aims, intentions, and actions, but there is no reason to suspect that he would feel for, care for, or show concern for the invader or his aggressive, hostile actions. Or just think about the act of torturing another person. A torturer must *feel into* and *feel with* his victims' pain adequately in order to know the amount of pain he should apply, but clearly the torturer does not feel for his victims. These scenarios make it clear that one may have a contextualized experience of one or both of the first two relations of feeling without experiencing the third; however, it seems to be the case that this third relation of feeling, i.e., *feeling for*, requires at least one of the other two relations. Can one feel for, care or show concern for, another without acutely observing and/or grasping adequately the person's situation as well as her/his state of mind? This question cannot be answered in the abstract; only by having a sufficient grasp of the context within which caring for another arises can an answer appear. Nevertheless, reflection upon our lived experiences shows us that the presence or absence of one or more of these three modes influences our social interactions, albeit in different ways. When all three relations of feeling are present in mutually reciprocal and caring relationships or friendships, they seem to enhance the quality of our relationships with others by generating feelings of closeness and trust. Conversely, it seems to be the case that when one or more of these habits are absent within our relationships, miscommunication and misunderstanding often arises. Other times, beyond the mere presence or absence of one or more of these relations, it is the manner in which we express these as modes of empathic sensing that contributes to either positive or problematic relationships with others.

For the sake of clarity, by "feeling for" others as an expression of care I mean the act of showing concern for or expressing care for and not simply the sympathetic inner feelings we experience. If I possess warm wishes of care but do not have these feelings of benevolence affect my actions, it doesn't seem to be the case that I am providing recognizable care for another. But what if one's experience of these inner feelings leads to a socially recognized act of caring for another, do they then become a part of my extension of care to another, and thus can reasonably be called an experience of care giving? Or, what if I extend words of care and concern to another but then do nothing to demonstrate the meaningfulness and sincerity of such comforting words, ought this verbalization of care and concern be interpreted as care giving? If I were to move beyond simply feeling care and/or merely verbalizing my feelings of care and concern to another, I might do something concrete and act to improve a person's undesired state or situation. But what if my actions of care are perceived by this person as entirely unhelpful, would I then be justified in stating that I extended care to him or her? In lieu of the ambiguity that arises from asking these types of questions, what I am calling "empathic care" signifies any *act* of helping behavior that is undertook for the purpose of improving the well-being of another person, a group, or even objects (e.g., a philanthropic organization). Understood in this way, it is possible that acts of empathic care, which can range, for example, from an extension of kind words to a stranger to the devoted care of acting for the benefit of a friend throughout a lifetime, may not produce what one intends. Also, independent of the intention of the helper, such acts may not be recognized as helpful by the person who is the recipient of the so-called helping behavior.

Calling acts of helping behavior "empathic care" might seem unnecessary, or may even be a bit overly ambitious. After all, other words, such as "sympathy," "compassion," "benevolence," etc., seem to function just fine as names for acts of care giving, so what is the benefit of introducing empathy into the mix? Moreover, one could argue that since a number of common definitions of empathy don't signify acts of providing care for others, it is a stretch (if not a major distortion) to define empathy as an act of care giving. I suggest that accepting and employing this reasoning is costly—both conceptually and pragmatically. For in doing so one excludes the multiple meanings associated with the term "empathy," and by refusing to entertain and take seriously the various ways empathy has been understood historically and is commonly described colloquially as acts of concern or care for others, we exclude the possibility that these diverse articulations of empathy as care giving can be helpful, or even help clear up the ambiguity I just mentioned. A different way of looking at the relationship between empathy and care comes by way of noticing the fact that "empathy," however defined, always involves some sort of "concern" or "care" for an object; it is just a matter of determining what type of care and/or concern in involved in any given act of empathy and what one precisely means by the terms "concern" and "care." Another reason, then, for using the term "empathy" to describe the relation of feeling for and our acts of care toward others is that one would be hard-pressed to find a definition of "empathy" that does not, in some fashion, imply some sort of concern or care for the object of one's empathizing.

Social Psychology: Empathic Care and Empathic Concern

Returning to and reexamining the understandings of empathy and examining the use of the relation of feeling for in the mid-twentieth century to the present will justify the aforementioned claims. Remember that for Herder the main objects with which we ought to concern ourselves are the cultures, histories, perspectives, experiences, etc., of those quite different from us by feeling into them. This implies that we ought to care for and value different and perhaps irreconcilable viewpoints that do not align with our own. And it follows from this that Herder's insistence that one ought to practice *Einfühlung* is not simply a call to feel into and feel with or grasp the other's perspective, but also to *feel for* the other's perspective because doing so means that you are concerned about the limits of your own understanding and care about the other's perspectives and the radically different cultures and histories that give rise to them. Novalis likewise links the art of feeling into objects with the experience of caring for nature. Thus, for him, the act of empathic projection is simultaneously an act of being concerned about objects of nature and caring about what the act of feeling into and grasping the magnanimity of nature might bring, which was according to Novalis a poetic sense of identification or *feeling with* the natural world in order to counter prevailing understandings of nature as something completely separate from us and in need of our dominance. When those within the discipline of aesthetics adopted and redefined the meaning of the relation of feeling into for their own purposes, we find that even seemingly innocuous acts of feeling into artworks imply that one ought to care about his/her ability to interpret the works skillfully as well as the historical significance and greatness of the art itself. Even though empathy signified something quite different during the rise of psychology in the twentieth century, we find a prevailing and guiding idea that the habits of feeling into, feeling with, and feeling for objects served the major purpose of psychoanalysis—namely providing care for patients. Care and concern for another seems to be part and parcel of the meaning of the word "empathy," as it has been and is currently used in psychology to signify the experience of feeling with or gaining the perspective of a client or patient. Is it possible for a psychologist to *feel into* and *feel with* patients without *feeling for* them and having authentic concern for them, and acting with care primarily for their benefit? Certainly, it is possible, but I suspect most psychologists would think that something vital is lacking.

Another reason for believing that concern and care are part and parcel of the relation of feeling with lies in noting a historical expansion of the meaning of empathy that began in the middle of the twentieth century and has affected the direction of scholarship from that time until the present day. We can locate the beginning of this expansion of meaning in works and insights of the psychologist Carl Rogers. Early in his career, Rogers defined empathy as an accurate understanding of another, i.e., a *feeling with* others, that is, the perception of "the internal frame of reference of another with accuracy and with the emotional components and meanings which pertain thereto as if one were the person, but without ever losing the 'as if' condition."[5] Conceiving empathy in this way might seem at first glance to be only an experience of the relation of feeling with, i.e., empathic perspective-taking or empathic connection without empathic care. However, from Rogers's point of view, in order to feel with the patient, the therapist must also *feel into* the unique psychological states of the patient and *feel and care for* the patient in order to provide proper therapeutic care. For Rogers, then, empathy must include both empathic connection (feeling with) and empathic care (feeling for), as he noted in his 1975 article, *Empathy: An Unappreciated Way of Being*: "*It is impossible accurately to sense the perceptual world of another person unless you value that person and his world—unless you in some sense care.*"[6] And by the word "care" here, Rogers meant that one ought to act toward clients with empathic care; they must show deep concern for the well-being of their patients, listen intently and give value to what the patient says, and create the environmental conditions for the expression of concern and care toward the client. Rogers intentional inclusion of the relation of feeling for in his definition of "empathy" is insightful, for not only does this act express Roger's belief that empathy as feeling for others was necessary for his therapeutic practices, but that it is a vital dynamic for all caring and nurturing relationships between caregivers and their clients.

As Lipps represented a type of world historical figure, whose work and creativity seems to be an axial point upon which the objects of empathy as feeling into was shifted from aesthetic objects to the mental content of other people's minds, so too Rogers's emphasis upon empathy as the relation of feeling for brought about another significant shift in the historical narrative of empathy. And roughly a century after Lipps's contribution, we find that the concept of empathy was increasingly conjoined with—and even defined as—*the relation of feeling for*. This was encouraged, in part, by the habit of linking the notion of empathy not only with the relation of *feeling for*, but also by the manner in which definitions of "empathy" began to include the *reactions, responses*, and *helping behaviors* of empathizers. This linking of empathy with responsive, reactive, and helping behavior was a direct historical consequence of the rise of social scientific studies in which the experiences of empathy in *group settings* (especially during early childhood) were analyzed as scientific objects for the social psychologist as well as the psychologist.

Narratives about empathy among social psychologists began most prominently with the insights of George Herbert Mead. And though it might not have been Mead's intent, his understanding of the self as fundamentally relational and social contributed to the rise of the abovementioned numerous social scientific studies in which empathy was consistently linked with developmental change during early childhood. In addition to the influence of Rogers as a psychologist, then, it was the influence of social psychology that contributed to the emergence of the meaning of empathy as an experience of the relation of feeling for. No one has played a greater role in this semantic change than the psychologist C. D. Batson. Batson's works facilitated this historical transition of the meaning of empathy by linking "empathy" with a concern for and a reaction or response to the welfare of another person who appears to be in need. Batson coined the term "empathic concern" to denote this type of experience. Empathic concern, according to Batson, is "an other-oriented emotional response elicited by and congruent with the perceived welfare of a person in need."[7] Batson employs this notion of empathy (as empathic concern and as an experience of the relation of feeling for others) for the purpose of analyzing the differences between experiences of egoism and altruism and the degree to which each of these motivates us to help others who we perceive to be in need. Helping behavior that is egoistically motivated is directed toward the end state goal of increasing the helper's own welfare and diminishing one's feelings of distress, while altruistic acts are directed toward the end goal state of increasing the other's welfare and reducing another person's distress.[8]

To illustrate the difference here consider the following: Imagine a middle-aged man is traveling by plane and is attempting to sleep during the flight. Unfortunately for him, a newborn infant is crying incessantly, and this is disturbing his ability to fall asleep. To remedy the situation, maybe he would feel into and acutely perceive the infant's experience and perhaps this would allow him to feel with and grasp the source of the baby's discomfort. He might then respond with a proper emotion to soothe the infant and might even help the parents calm the infant's tearful uneasiness. Though it is possible that this act is motivated by his own desire to sleep as well as out of genuine concern and care for the infant and its parents, it might be motivated simply by his own interests in catching some sleep. If this were the case, this passenger's act of feeling for the infant would be self-regarding and egoistic rather than altruistic, i.e., it would be directed toward the end state goal of increasing his welfare and diminishing his feelings of distress. However, if his motivation to act was directed toward the end goal state of increasing the other's welfare and reducing another person's distress, his motivation would be altruistic.

Batson devised several ingenious scientific studies to test his hypothesis, what he calls the empathy-altruism hypothesis, to test the roles egoistic or altruistic motivation plays in helping behavior. Helping others sometimes produces a few consequences that benefit us. For instance, by responding to the needs of another, we sometimes relieve ourselves of the distress we feel at seeing him/her in need. Other times, we avoid feelings of guilt and shame by helping others; and on still other occasions, we receive praise from others and gain a sense of pride from acting on another's behalf. Batson's empirical investigations have demonstrated that these three reactions to a person in need do not provoke the same motivation as do one's feelings of empathic concern. Empathic concern for another, according to Batson's empathy-altruism hypothesis produces altruistic *motivation*, while these other three reactions are largely egoistically driven. Empathic concern produces the motivation to act for the benefit of others rather than ourselves. This does not mean that empathic concern leads to altruistic acts, nor does it mean that empathic concern and the altruistic motivation it produces is necessarily a morally good thing. Sometimes, as Batson and his team of researchers have shown, even empathy-induced acts of altruism are unfair, immoral, and unjust.[9]

Quite different from other theorists of empathy, Batson is more philosophically careful about the ambiguity surrounding existing and multiple meanings of empathy and recognizes the multiple and different meanings ascribed to the term "empathy." For instance, in one of his many famous works, Batson lists eight different experiences that have been called empathy, namely:

1. Knowledge of another's internal state, including his or her thoughts and feelings
2. Adopting the posture or matching the neural response of an observed other
3. Coming to feel as another person feels
4. Intuiting or projecting oneself into another's situation
5. Imagining how another is thinking and feeling
6. Imagining how one would think and feel in the other's place
7. Feeling distress at witnessing another person's suffering
8. Feeling for another person who is suffering[10]

Though each of these overlap in our experiences, we can easily recognize these types of empathy and their utilization of one or more of the relations of feeling into, feeling with, and feeling for. For instance, number 4 denotes a concrete experience of the relation of *feeling into*, described as projective empathy in the writings of Herder, Novalis, Lotze, the Vischers, Groos, and Lipps. Numbers 1–3 signify a variety of different experiences of the relation of *feeling with* and sometimes the interplay of the relations of *feeling into* and *feeling with*. Specifically, number 1 was promulgated by Lipps, which was subsequently doubted by phenomenologists and hermeneuticists, then demonstrated by Mead to be a contributory factor to the emergence of the social self. More recently, Ickes and others have recognized this first type as empathic accuracy, which comes by way of empathic inference. De Waal has recognized numbers 2 and 3 among human and nonhuman animals, while neuroscientists have located these types of empathy as processes within the body, that is, variations of empathic contagion and empathic mimicry (e.g., motor imitation and mirror neurons). Numbers 5 and 6 are experiences of both the interplay of the relation of *feeling into* and *feeling with* and empathic perspective-taking, each of which are often referred to as types of empathy. Empathy types 7 and 8 are experiences of the relation of *feeling for*, from Carl Rogers to the present day, and sometimes the relations of *feeling into* and *feeling with* are cooperative within these expressions of feeling for in experience.

The writings of Martin Hoffman also contributed to this discursive shift in which descriptions of empathy as the relation of feeling for has enriched the meaning of empathy that was previously and most predominantly understood as an experience of the relation of feeling with (or what Batson calls "feeling as"). Hoffman's definition of "empathy" also includes a *reaction to the another's condition or circumstance* as well as a feeling of *concern for* the well-being of that person. Accordingly, Hoffman defines "empathy" as "the spark of human concern for others and the glue that makes social life possible"; as well as an "affective response more appropriate to another's situation rather than one's own."[11] Similar to Batson and Hoffman, Eisenberg and Fabes define empathy as a response, namely an *affective response* that stems from the apprehension or comprehension of another's emotional state or condition.[12] This understanding of empathy includes both the relations of *feeling into* and *feeling with*.[13] For to *apprehend* one's experience, one must both feel into and feel with the person's emotional state or condition. But it also includes one's response that stems from these relations, and this inclusion of an affective response—an action toward the object of one's empathizing—is remarkably different from simply apprehending or comprehending the experience of another. For a "response," whether as helping behavior or simply an emotional reaction to the conditional state of that person without action, signifies an experience of being moved by another's situation in such a way that one's body is reacting to the other person's state out of concern for the person's experience. Empathy as an affective response based on grasping another's emotional state correctly necessitates that one is experiencing concern for the circumstance of that person.

In Simon Baron-Cohen's work *Science of Evil*, we find another definition of "empathy," a two-part definition, composed of not only the relations of feeling into and feeling with but also the relation of feeling for. He put forth this understanding of empathy for the purpose of creating a spectrum of empathic experiences, so that we may understand why some people have more empathy than others and why a few people are completely devoid of empathy or have what Baron-Cohen calls "zero degrees of empathy." Accordingly, empathy is evident "when we suspend our single-minded focus of attention and instead adopt a double-minded focus of attention." A single-minded focus means we are thinking only about our thoughts and reflections, while a double-minded focus denotes that we are thinking about another's mind at the same time we are thinking about our own. This definition alone, though, is insufficient, for it is missing an understanding of the full process and content of what we experience during empathy. So, Baron-Cohen adds a second and necessary part to his definition: "Empathy is our ability to identify what someone else is thinking or feeling and to *respond* to their thoughts and feelings with an appropriate emotion."[14] As was the case with Eisenberg and Fabes, Baron-Cohen includes an action, an affective response, a feeling for the person, and not simply a taking in of the experience.

Empathic Care: Neuroscience and Evolutionary Psychology

Evolutionary biologists were conspicuously absent from these conversations about empathy and human sociality from the beginning to the middle of the twentieth century for a few understandable reasons. First Darwin's ideas about evolution as natural selection were distorted by others who devised theories of human nature that were founded on ruthless competition and struggle alone, rather than on cooperation and helping behavior. There were several historical reasons for this. Natural selection became associated with Spencer's notion of the "survival of the fittest." Darwin liked this phrase originally, but eventually it began to signify something quite different from what he meant by it, namely it began to be used as a title for social theories of evolution and historical development—rather than for the process of *variational* evolution—and it was further supported by a false notion of biological inheritance propounded by Sir Francis Galton (Darwin's cousin). This false theory of inheritance was used as "scientific evidence" for the theory and practice of Social Darwinism and other misguided, oppressive, and highly conservative social-political theories.[15] Out of these theories, arose another mythological construction of human sociality, called the "myth of rugged individualism." This myth lauded the idea of the free and unencumbered individual who was able to achieve total self-sufficiency without assistance from an outside source, especially state or government assistance. These myths continued to be foundational throughout the twentieth century and they are one reason why it took biologists so long to contribute to narratives of empathy as the relation of feeling for and nurturing acts of human and nonhuman sociality. Petr Kropotkin, who was relatively unnoticed during his time, offered a counternarrative to these ideologies in 1902 in his work *Mutual Aid*, in which he views a communal principle at work during the process of evolution—namely the principle of cooperative behavior. Darwin's struggle for existence was, also, in truth, the cooperative struggle of masses of organisms against hostile and threatening environments. Among numerous species, mutual aid as feeling for and extending care to others is recognized in the social helping behavior of food sharing, which as a reciprocal act is crucial for the survival of a species. Many other examples have been noted—for example, one study has shown that empathic care, as an act of prosocial helping behavior, is evident even in rats.[16]

Over the last few decades, there has arisen a completely different social narrative of Darwinian evolutionary biology, which incorporates empathy as the relation of *feeling for* into a new paradigm of both human and nonhuman sociality, *while not ignoring the role social competition and struggle play in the formation of the social structures of different species*. Frans de Waal maintains this delicate balance between accentuating both cooperative and competitive tendencies among human and other animal species in all his writings on empathy. Like the definitions of empathy put forth by Batson, Eisenberg and Fabes, Hoffman, and Baron-Cohen, De Waal links empathic behaviors in human and nonhuman animals with *acts of reacting and responding* to others as well as to acts of helping behavior. Though De Waal uses the word "response" in some of his descriptions of empathic behavior, it is important to recognize that his and Preston's definition of "empathy" was not formulated in light of the subject's response, but rather upon a "process model," which "makes empathy a superordinate category that includes all subclasses of phenomena that share the same mechanism. This includes emotional contagion, sympathy, cognitive empathy, helping behavior, and so on."[17] Recall, Preston and De Waal's definition of "empathy" is pluralistic and broad and as such it is part of the debate of whether it is best to provide a broad or narrow understanding of empathy for practical reasons.[18] Preston and De Waal's broad understanding of empathy is based on scientific observations that demonstrate empathy to be "a phylogenetically continuous phenomenon" as well as upon the fact that "all empathic processes rely on a general perception-action design of the nervous system that . . . is adaptive for myriad reasons, and exists across species."[19]

In *The Age of Empathy*, De Waal symbolizes this evolutionary development of empathy as a multilayered phenomenon with the image of a Russian doll, a.k.a., a Matryoshka doll, a set of wooden dolls of decreasing size placed one inside the other. At the core of the Russian doll, the smallest doll represents the development of the automatic process of *empathic contagion* as well as the capacity to match another's state; and around this core, other large dolls signify more sophisticated empathic abilities such as concern for others, consolation, perspective-taking, and targeted helping.[20] With this metaphor we find empathy to be described both as experiences of the relations of *feeling with* (i.e., contagion, state matching, perspective-taking) and *feeling for* others (i.e., concern for others, consolation, targeted helping). The relation of feeling into is also significant in De Waal's vision of the evolution of empathic development, where he and Preston identify the act of "attended perception" as part of the empathic process and further state that with the "perception-action model of empathy, there is no empathy that is not *projection*, since you always use your own representation to understand the state of another."[21] Moreover, De Waal is one of a few scholars today who has recognized the importance of Lipps (especially his understanding of the relation of feeling into) and considers his works to be vital for understanding the "nature of empathy."[22]

Neuroscientific studies have shown that experiences of feeling with others have been correlated with subsequent experiences of feeling for others, and our ability to feel with the experience of another can affect our desire to feel for others. For example, one's ability to perceive accurately another's experience of distress has been shown to prompt or encourage helping behavior.[23] Moreover, empathic accuracy of another person's fear generates empathic concern,[24] while the inability to feel with and recognize another's fear seems to affect our abilities for feel for or show compassion for others. It does not follow from these findings, however, that empathic accuracy or empathic perspective-taking *are necessary* to feel for the well-being of others and to act compassionately for their benefit.

In addition to these contributions, a few neuroscientists of the early twenty-first century have defined empathy as the interplay of the relations of *feeling into* and *feeling with* with the relation of *feeling for*, or even just the interplay of the relations of *feeling with* and *feeling for*. Neuroscientists, it seems, despite the high-tech and scientific technological advances they have enjoyed, have not been able to escape the pattern of imprecision and ambiguity concerning the meaning of empathy that we have recognized throughout multiple histories. For example, defining "empathy" primarily as an experience of the interplay of the relations of feeling into and feeling with, neuroscientists Danziger, Prkachin, and Willer have defined "empathy" as "a complex form of psychological inference that enables us to understand the personal experiences of another person though cognitive, evaluative, and affective processes."[25] Recall that empathic inference is an act of reading or inferring the contents of another person's mind, and inference requires us to carefully, sometimes consistently, *feel into* the experiences of another, while trying to guess (infer at feeling with) what that person might be thinking. When we guess correctly what others are thinking, we experience empathic accuracy and feel with them (or believe that we do). In his article on the neurodevelopment of empathy in humans, the neuroscientist Jean Decety defines "empathy" similarly, that is, as "the ability to recognize the emotions and feelings of others."[26] Elsewhere, though, in the introduction to his edited work, *Empathy: From Bench to Bedside* (2002), Decety defines empathy as "the natural *capacity* to share, understand, and *respond with care* to the affective states of others."[27] Or, in relational terms, "empathy" is an experience of both the relations of feeling with and feeling for. One is capable of *feeling with* (i.e., sharing and understanding) another's state, and able to *feel for* (i.e., respond with care) the affective states of others. And in order to do these things well, it requires that one observes and identifies these states correctly, or, in other words, that one *feels into* them with perceptual acuity so that one's sharing and understanding of another's states informs the manner in which he/she responds with appropriate care.

Jean Knox's investigation in 2014 explores how the notion of empathy is used among both psychologists and neuroscientists today. In this highly intuitive and perspicacious article, Knox draws from Singer and Lamm's insights, who note that within neuroscientific discourses two forms (i.e., relations) of empathy are recognized in the therapeutic relationship—namely, the forms of *feeling with* and *feeling for*.[28] For Singer and Lamm, "feeling with" others occurs when an observer's emotions reflect affective sharing, and "feeling for" others arises whenever the observer's emotions are inherently other-oriented and so give rise to compassion, sympathy, and empathic concern. In the context of thinking about the therapeutic relationship between a doctor and a patient, Knox defines "feeling for" the patient as what she calls "empathic concern," namely "a benign, thoughtful altruistic concern for the patient's suffering and desire to help him or her to find relief through understanding."[29] "Feeling with," as Knox conceives it resembles what we have called empathic contagion, or in her words, feeling with "is essentially . . . an implicit, automatic unconscious and often bodily response, rather than a conscious thoughtful process."[30]

Several scholars have acknowledged this trend of thought in which the relation of feeling for has generally replaced the notion of empathy as the relation of *feeling with* during the twentieth century. For instance, in *The Better Angels of Our Natures*, Steven Pinker notes it as a semantic change, claiming that the popularity of empathy over the last few decades coincided with this change in the meaning of empathy. "The meteoric rise of empathy coincided with its taking on a new meaning, one that is close to 'sympathy' or 'compassion.'"[31] Pinker is well aware of the multiple and conflicting meanings of empathy and lists numerous types of empathy throughout this work, e.g., empathic projection, empathic inference and accuracy, empathic contagion, and empathic perspective-taking.[32] However, this new understanding of empathy as sympathy or compassion, Pinker suggests, has been combined with the notion of empathy as perspective-taking; and as a consequence of this conceptual collision, many people hold the belief that "beneficence toward other people *depends* on pretending to be them, feeling what they are feeling, walking a mile in thein their moccasins, taking their vantage point, or seeing the world through their eyes."[33] In relational terms, Pinker is claiming here that many people today commonly recite a trite narrative about the experience of empathy in which a false sense of feeling with others is necessary for one to feel and care for others. Of course, whether not beneficence depends upon empathic perspective-taking, or any other type of empathy, can only be judged by understanding the context in which it is experienced. But again, it is certainly not the case that empathic perspective-taking is *necessary* for being kind and compassionate to others in all instances. Both young children and certain autistic children do not possess sophisticated perspective-taking abilities; nevertheless, they demonstrate basic compassion in response to the distress of others.[34]

From the middle of the twentieth century to the present day, empathy has been commonly understood as the relation of *feeling for*, recognized in acts of care, concern, helping behavior, compassion, etc. And whether or not one wishes to admit that all forms of empathy involve some type of caring or concern/interest for something, it is clear that conceptualizing empathy as feeling for others began with studies of early childhood development, which were always framed in relation to the ability of children to feel and understand another's pain and examined by noting their *reactions and responses*. With Batson's insightful and highly influential works, and many empirical works before him, the parameters of social scientific studies of feeling for others expanded and began to include both adult humans and nonhuman animals. These scientific approaches of social psychology combined with Rogerian therapeutic approaches, in which care for the patient was vital for understanding the patient's perspective, contributed to the rise of thinking of empathy as an experience of the relation of feeling for. Later contributions from biologists, primatologists, cognitive psychologists, and neuroscientists picked up on and continued this trend.

Deviating from the histories of empathy as *feeling into* and *feeling with*, it is within this history of describing empathy as the relation of *feeling for* where we find a pattern of thinking in which the objects of one's empathizing are primarily the experiences of another's pain or suffering. This common focus on the negative, or otherwise undesirable, states of others has profoundly shaped—and limited—the meaning of empathic care in that the extension of concern, care, sympathy, compassion, and helpfulness toward others have been all understood in terms of the actions of an empowered, stronger person toward a disempowered, weaker person. Emphasis upon this power relation both form and limit the parameters of moral discourse by clothing positive interactions between persons, such as prosociality or helping behavior, in the terms of such dynamics of power, which in turn disinvites conversations about the multiple ways acts of extending concern, care, sympathy, compassion, and helpfulness to others aren't expressions of this particular power relation. This pattern of association, which has become popular as a consequence of psychology's dominance over the meaning of empathy, has been proven to be useful for illuminating a variety of different experiences, though at the same time, it is also responsible for narrowing the parameters of empathic experience by excluding those acts for caring for others in which this power relation between the stronger and the weaker is absent. Take, for example, instances in which we feel and care for the flourishing of another and act for the benefit of that person by helping to enrich this positive experience. The study of empathy as feeling for others has focused, almost entirely, on the negative and disempowering experiences of others rather than on the extraordinary, beautiful, and radiant qualities of their experiences. But the future need not repeat the past; there is no pragmatic reason for us to mirror the trends of the past and no practical purpose to prevent the expansion of this meaning of empathy to include, e.g., an experience of *symhedonia*, i.e., feeling for another person's good fortune.

These multiple narratives of empathy of the relation of feeling for, along with the numerous accounts of empathy as both the relation of feeling into and feeling with, provide substantial reasons why one ought to take seriously the current debate concerning whether we ought to adopt a broad or narrow understanding of empathy. There is no pragmatic reason for accepting either side of this debate outside of the felt consequences of accepting and adopting one viewpoint over the other; however, the conceptual richness of these multiple historical and varied accounts offers us a larger pool of ideas and practices about empathic behavior. And embracing this multiplicity might mark the first step by which we might draw from this well of intellectual productivity and apply the insights of these creative thinkers to solve myriad social and practical problems that otherwise would neither be addressed nor resolved, and thus might remain interminable.

The Skill of Feeling For

"In the beginning was the Power!"
Thus should it stand: yet, while the line I trace.
A something warns me, once more to efface.
The spirit aids! From anxious scruples freed,
I write, "In the beginning was the Deed!"[35]

Goethe

The relation of *feeling for* signifies the mode or manner in which we feel for other persons or things by showing concern and acting with care, compassion, or kindness toward them. Accordingly, this relation is a general description of all our experiences in which an individual is connected to persons or things by specific, contextualized acts of feeling concern or acting and providing care, kindness, compassion, etc., for them. Depending upon the context, this might involve, for example, feelings of concern about another's state of mind who is going through a trying and difficult situation after the death of a close friend or—as an act based on concern—and by extending care to such a person by doing something primarily for her or his benefit. Or within a different set of contexts, we might experience this relation of feeling for as a reaction or response to the site of an injured stranger and a desire to help such a person. Or, an experience of feeling for might be directed toward an object in way that avoids the aforementioned power relations of the strong and weak. Feeling for others in this way might also involve feeling for the joy of another and actions that aim to enhance and intensify it. Or, in relation to empathic care toward objects, feeling for something in this way, might involve the act of helping the success of a noble social cause by volunteering for them or even by writing a check to support the organization that encourages people to act toward others with empathic care.

Realistically, everything isn't as rosy and clear cut as these few examples suggest; caring for others is far more complex. Feelings of care, concern, etc., are often not necessary to help others—for instance, we could help another unintentionally or indirectly without having or being motivated by a feeling of care or concern. Also, experience shows us that caring for the well-being of others sometimes comes about only by feeling for and caring about *oneself* first and one's ability to nurture one's habits of care giving *that will empower* his/her ability to care for others. Take the example of the artist who wants to create works of art that will last and be enjoyed long after her death. Such a desire will never come to pass unless she has the hours of privacy and seclusion from others in order to make such a masterpiece. She must care for her art, and this might involve neglecting opportunities to extend care to those around her as she creates works of art out of her care for those who will be moved by her art. Self-care, then, is often vital for caring for others, but it is also true that an overemphasis of self-care can prevent us from caring for others. Even so-called "selfless" acts are also (simultaneously) acts of not caring, for when one's energies are directed at benefiting the lives of some, this necessarily excludes the opportunity to direct one's care toward others. Thus, every choice to care for another involves, in a real and significant way, the choice not to care about someone or something else. It follows from this that all acts of care involve some type of sacrifice.

This way of thinking about care in relation to sacrifice is important because it dissolves a rather popular, often regurgitated, myth that *all acts of care* are, in truth, only acts of selfishness in which our extension of care to others provides positive feelings for us and, as this myth goes, the goal of such acts aim merely to benefit ourselves. This interpretation profoundly mischaracterizes those actions of care, kindness, and compassion in *which the caregiver sacrifices what he or she would rather do in order to act for the well-being of another*. Extensions of care in this sense involve the sacrifice of one's own will, desire, and preferences for the purpose of benefiting another and are not exemplary of selfishness; they are, however, *self-regarding* acts (all acts are self-regarding), and although it might be the case that such self-regarding acts benefit the caregiver, who might receive good or have positive feelings about her/his actions, this is not the same as selfishness. Selfishness is exemplified in feelings, words, and actions aimed primarily to benefit oneself alone, especially at the expense or general disregard of another person's well-being. This can be recognized quite easily in an experience of a person who only speaks of the issues, problems, thoughts, worries, prospects, goals, etc., of her/his life, often without inquiring into the well-being with whom such a person is conversing. A habitually selfish person also often acts in calculated and deliberate ways that take into consideration only what will maximize his/her life, rather than the lives of others.

A number of conditions within experience influence—and often limit—our acts of empathic care, sometimes even independent of our will to extend it to others. Circumstances often shape our ability to show concern or care for persons or things. For example, empathic care requires limited resources such as time, energy, opportunity—even financial recourses—and these dynamics shape the parameters of the circumstance in which we find ourselves in a given context, sometimes preventing us from expressing the care we desire to extend to others. Think about the simple act of driving in a car. If you accidentally cut someone off in traffic, you might wish to have a gentle talk explaining the error of your ways, but the situation in which you find yourself, confined to a car and traveling upon a road that is made for moving and not stopping, isn't conducive for this. No matter how noble your desire to show care for the driver, your situation severely limits your ability to extend care to another because your car, in effect, depersonalizes you and significantly hampers your intentions, however noble they might be. The distance between ourselves and others, whether it is experienced as a feeling of distance in time, in space, or both, significantly influences our capacities to feel for another and act, in some way, for their benefit. Philosophers have noted the manner in which our nearness to or distance from others in time and space oftentimes radically debilitates our actions of care, benevolence, and helpfulness toward others.[36] But one need only turn to one's own experiences to recognize how this dynamic of our lives affects our feeling and acting for the benefit of others.

The distinctions we make between members of in-groups and out-groups also radically affects our motivation to care for and help others. We often experience, what has been called, "enhanced empathy" toward those with whom we experience a positive bias and perceive as members of an in-group; and conversely, it has been demonstrated that we often behave unjustly toward those we consider to be members of a somewhat undesirable out-group.[37] Numerous studies have demonstrated how this in-group vs. out-group distinction shapes and limits our experiences of extending empathic care to others. *In general,* "we" tend to experience self-other merging and identification with others more readily when they are members of an in-group (e.g., friends and family members) and tend to feel empathy for the physical pain of those within an in-group vs. those who we identify as being part of an out-group.[38] We also tend to respond or react with empathic care to those within an in-group, feel motivated to help them when they are in distress, and also seem to have a greater willingness to provide financial—even costly—assistance to them when compared with our willingness to help members of an out-group in a similar, dire situation.[39] *But specifically,* when this distinction is used to identify racial in-groups and out-groups, studies have repeatedly painted a rather bleak picture in regards to our ability to extend the same sort of empathic care, concern, and helping behavior to members of other ethnicities/races. And oftentimes, experiences of these in-groups racial/ethnic biases are not consciously recognized as such.[40] Knowledge of these very real, yet limiting, circumstances and dynamics of our lives is important, for it helps us to make practical judgments about our concern for others and how we might judiciously extend acts of empathic care in such a way that make a positive difference in the lives of others.

In-group and out-group behavioral tendencies represent just a small part of a larger problem called *familiarity or selectivity bias* in which individuals extend care to those with whom they are familiar, while excluding others, largely for reasons of simplicity, safety, and security. When considering empathic care as a type of skill, then, it is vital to consider what we include and exclude as objects of our care and *for what purposes* we do this. How we define and practice "empathy" significantly shapes these purposes; thus, similar to the trends of thinking during the nineteenth century, the pluralistic approach I am endorsing regarding the objects of our empathic care here would include any particular object(s), whether animate or inanimate. This is important to keep in mind even if one is adamant about reserving empathic care as an act that is directed toward humans rather than nonhuman animals. For it is one thing to show concern and care for another living being but quite another to show concern and care for another living being *in relation to* objects, whether animate or inanimate, that shape that person's circumstance, as well as the manner by which one is connected to him or her in lived experienced. Embracing and grasping this plurality of experience, in which multiple and interrelated objects shape circumstances, can only, it seems, enhance one's ability to gain a lucid awareness of his/her own individual habits of caregiving as well as a contextualized understanding of empathic care in general. Thinking of empathic care in this pluralistic manner might also provide a more realistic portrait of the demands of serious and devoted empathic care as well as accentuate the need for well-ordered and functional institutions and organizations to provide empathic care where individual human efforts fail, whether due to the effects of in-group/out-group mentalities or some other dysfunctional behavioral tendencies.

Despite the above limitations and other similar failings of empathic care, one of the benefits of adopting the conceptual framework of *relational empathy*, lies in how it, as a conceptual and practical tool, can help to transform the habits and behavioral tendencies that contribute to one's failure to provide empathic care. Relational empathy, as I have described it, occurs when the modes of *feeling into*, *feeling with*, and *feeling for* come together in one's experience toward an object or objects. Subsumed under one or more of these general, and largely abstract, relations, one can place every understanding and definition of empathy as descriptions of lived, contextualized experiences in which one empathizes with others. When all three of these relations are present in one's encounter with objects, we can say that his/her experience of empathy involves some mode of empathic projection, empathic connection, and empathic care, and when an act of such relational empathy serves its most general purpose and intention, we can say that one has perceived acutely (feeling into) and grasped accurately (feeling with) something and has acted to care for (feeling for) the well-being of it. If we think of the acts of treating other persons with respect, listening carefully to them, and explaining things carefully to others, these all would similarly require that we perceive acutely (feeling into), grasp accurately (feeling with) and care passionately about (feeling for) the well-being of another person or situation.

But just as it is the case that either the relation of feeling into or the relation of feeling with can operate independently of the other two and thus function to serve some purpose, it is also true that empathic care, as a third relation or type of empathy, sometimes functions without the need to exercise empathic projection and empathic connection. For instance, I can feel into the perspective of another without feeling with that person's perspective or caring about it. Similarly, I can feel with or grasp another's emotional state without caring for the person's well-being, as this might be the result of my inability to perceive acutely the gravity of the person's feeling and/or the seriousness of the situation that brought about such a state. The same is true of our experiences of the relation of feeling for. If I were to see a three-year-old child walking in the middle of a busy street during rush hour, I would probably not need to put into action the skills of empathic projection nor would I need to strain in an attempt to understand either the child's experience or circumstance, for the end goal of grasping these are already immediately realized without any effort. I instantly perceive that the child is in need—I grasp the gravity of the situation—and act out of care for the benefit of the child without having to exercise the art of feeling into or feeling with his predicament.

Relational empathy and all other conceptualizations of empathy are identical to one another in one important way: they are all social constructs that aim not only to describe experience but to change the quality of our lived experiences. The value of any given notion of empathy, then, lies not in "being right" in some silo of truth apart from and unrelated to our lived experiences, but rather *by what the notion does*—the manner in which, for example, it shapes habits, decreases the suffering of sentient beings, or contributes to the flourishing of our lives. In addition to assisting one to improve his/her habits of empathic care, relational empathy does, or will do, four other important things. First, it includes and embraces conflicting definitions of empathy; and consequently, it has the potential to dissolve mere verbal disputes about what empathy is. Second, it directs recurring questions about empathy (e.g., Is empathy moral? Can empathy be developed?) away from abstract speculations about the "nature" of empathy and instead directs our attentions toward the variety, contexts, and consequences of different lived experiences. Third, it serves as a conceptual framework for recognizing *specific experiences* that might be subsumed under one or more of these general relations,[41] and for collecting and analyzing data for the purpose of improving the structure and functionality of institutions and organizations. And finally, relational empathy, as a pluralistic and pragmatic approach, will in the future serve as a vehicle for hope in action and affords us the opportunity to widen the windows of our perception, challenge our biases, and helps us to practice what pragmatists such as Dewey, Hook, and Stuhr have called "democracy as a way of life."[42]

6

Is Empathy Moral?

Depending upon the context, words can be very slippery, vague, evasive. As T. S. Eliot once noted, they strain, crack, break, and bend; and when they are exceedingly imprecise, they often fail to relate the complex depths of our feelings and senses.[1] Sometimes words fail us because of own ineptitude, often brought on by a lack of desire to listen empathically and attentively to others; while other times, one's mood, current situation in life, or even a lack of caution about the multiple meanings of words, can be the fount of our inability to communicate sufficiently what we feel. There are many other reasons why language fails us, but often enough, words fail us simply because *experience outstrips language*—namely, there is always something more to be said about our experiences than our words, however precise and eloquent they might be. Take, for example, what we call an *ineffable experience*. What paltry words could adequately describe the feelings arising within us while witnessing the beauty and grace of an afternoon fog flowing and floating over a still and glassy green sea? Or further into the depths, what frail utterance could explicate a profound feeling of love one has for another, a powerful and unbreakable love for which one would sacrifice everything just for the beloved to experience its life-giving force? Words are often miserably inadequate to convey precisely what we feel, and on occasion, they even distort and cheapen these and other similarly sublime and ineffable experiences.

James and the Dissolution of Verbal and Metaphysical Disputes

Perhaps the desire for an experience of sublimity or ineffability was what motivated the philosopher William James to join a few friends on a mountain camping trip in 1907. Whether or not this was the case, in his work *What Pragmatism Means*, James recounts an event on this trip that illustrates a method

Figure 6 Clouds of Northern Georgia, with Praphat Xavier Fernandes.

of resolving certain metaphysical and verbal disputes. At some time during this wilderness adventure, James took a pleasurable walk in the forest, and upon his return, he found the other members of his camping party in the midst of a ferocious metaphysical dispute about a squirrel, a man, and their simultaneous movements around a tree. Here is the story:

> Imagine a squirrel clinging to the bark on one side of a tree and a man standing on the ground on the opposite side of it. Where the man stands, he cannot see the squirrel, so he ... tries to get sight of the squirrel by moving rapidly round the tree, but no matter how fast he goes, the squirrel moves as fast in the opposite direction, and always keeps the tree between himself and the man, so that never a glimpse of him [the squirrel] is caught. The resultant metaphysical problem now is this: does the man go around the squirrel or not?"[2]

The man certainly went around the tree (at least once, the full 360 degrees), but James and his friends wanted to know: *Did the man go around the squirrel*?

When I have posed this question to my students over the years, their answers resemble those of James's camping party—half of them say "yes" and half of them say "no." James's answer, in part, *rejected the question itself* by directing our focus toward the multiple meanings and usages of words and how they function within different dimensions of reality to provide plural truths about experience.

The "reality" of what happened, says James, is entirely contingent upon what *you practically mean by "going round" the squirrel*. The man does indeed go around the squirrel, if by "going round" you mean, that the man passed

> from the north of him to the east, then to the south, then to the west, and then to the north of him again, obviously the man does go round him, for he occupies these successive positions. But if on the contrary you mean being first in front of him, then on the right of him, then behind him, then on his left, and finally in front again, it is quite as obvious that the man fails to go round him.[3]

Clearly, to "go around," then, does not have a single meaning—and many words are like this, they are imbued with plural meanings. As we have seen from our historical account, neither does the word "empathy" have a single and definitive meaning. From a pragmatic perspective, measuring the value of one meaning of a word as well as the other significations we assign to it begins by making clear distinctions between different usages of it, then considering the consequences or conceivable consequences in doing so. When successful, this pragmatic method often dissolves needless verbal disputes about the meanings of words and shifts our focus toward the recognizable practical differences of speaking, thinking, and acting in one way rather than another. James believed that making similar useful distinctions in relation to different contexts of experience would help us dissolve other unnecessary metaphysical and verbal disputes. But there is an even greater pragmatic point here about a pluralistic understanding of language and its ability to broaden our understanding of experience: there is no set vocabulary that gives meaning to words nor is language a fixed and structured system of rules that govern our usages of words.[4] Words change over time, however slightly, and when different contexts of experience emerge in time, our newly arriving feelings, sensations, and thoughts are not always easily encapsulated by any existing word. Words are productive tools; words do things, they perform, and when they fail to perform adequately, when they fail to denote precisely what we practically mean, we either color words with different shades of meaning and signification or we create new words for the purpose of generating clarity.

Infusing our words and theories with a sufficient amount of clarity so that we will avoid falling into unnecessary and useless metaphysical and verbal disputes only marks the beginning of making language work for us. For one then must, as James once said, "bring out of each word its practical cash-value and set to work in your stream of experience."[5] Establishing clarity and avoiding disputes about the meaning of words or the soundness of our theories, rather than providing for us a final solution to conceptual or semantic problems, always indicates a "program for more work" that requires us to consider what purpose such clarity serves, what consequences they might produce, and how existing and problematic realities might be changed.[6]

Having offered a pluralistic theory for understanding "empathy" I have called relational empathy, the program for more work here is to explain how a pluralistic and relational pragmatic approach will function to help us to find pragmatic answers and solutions to three outstanding questions about empathy that are asked most frequently today: Is empathy moral? Can empathy be developed? And how might empathy facilitate democratic engagement? For each of these questions, though, an understanding of relational empathy requires us to take seriously the ambiguity surrounding the other key notions of these three queries, such as "moral," "developed," and "democratic." Let's begin with empathy and morality.

Many unresolved questions about empathy today are questions concerning the morality of empathy. But these questions are difficult to answer, for not only do people mean different things by the word "empathy," but they also disagree about the meaning of what constitutes and/or justifies good, bad, right, or wrong actions and behavior. Analogously to James's insights about the meaning of "going round," there is also widespread disagreement about the meaning of "morality" and how it differs from "ethics." Adding to these conceptual and practical issues, theorists of empathy define and understand *morality* in terms that are grounded upon radically *different theoretical foundations* and are drawn from the academic disciplines or general moral worldviews to which they are loyal. These commitments, in turn, shape how theorists, and laypeople, both define and analyze the *moral value of empathy*. A consequence of this is that a scholar's devotion toward one moral theory over others directs him/her to speak of certain types of empathic experience while excluding others. It *seems* that these truths lead us to the conclusion that each definition of empathy as a description of our embodied feelings and actions must stand on its own and can only be judged by its relevance to contextualized circumstances, how they have resolved or intend to resolve existing problems, as well as one's satisfaction of consequences arising from their attempts.

Portraits of Morality

"Ethics" and "morality" are often used interchangeably, most notably as terms to denote subjects of studying, for instance, right and wrong behavior, good and bad actions.⁷ "Ethics" is derived from two Greek words *ēthikós*, which meant "relating to one's character," as well as *ēthós*, which chiefly meant an individual's habits or character, but also "customs" or "mores," i.e., the general character of a people. Your character is produced by habits or what you repeatedly do, and when you repeatedly do things well, you are thought to be *doing well consistently or flourishing in life*, which for the Greeks meant that you were "good-spirited" or happy. "Morality" is cognate with "mores," and began as a word when Cicero chose *moralis* as the Latin equivalent for *ethikos*.

The study of ethics and morality is complex. It is not exactly rocket science, of course, because as we all know, understanding and practicing ethics is much more difficult than any science in which there are definite, final answers to most questions that are represented as established, yet fallible, facts.

In contemporary parlance, "ethics" is commonly defined as a branch of philosophy involving serious reflection upon the moral nature of goodness and the establishment and usefulness of moral principles. It is also conceived as the moral principles that are believed to govern and guide a person's behavior or the conducting of an activity. A principle is a generally accepted moral standard, code, or rule for good behavior and when we live by a good moral principle, when it guides our decisions and governs our behavior the principle is believed to help us produce good actions. To say that moral principles govern a person's behavior or the conducting of an activity, of course, means that they rule over our behavior and are used as standards to follow when we conduct an activity. What the meaning of morality here suggests is that moral principles are a very important part of the study of ethics and the development of ethical behavior. Thus, to say that a person has or lacks good *moral principles* or that a person's behavior is either principled or unprincipled is to say that the moral principles that person holds matches up and guides her/his behavior. Yet another way we speak about the moral and ethical is simply to name things as good, whether reasons for doing so are accurate or inaccurate, and when we think and feel something to be good.

Many have claimed that we need to establish a secure and absolute foundation that rids us of the complexity of making tough moral decisions, while others attempt to banish the complexity by claiming that all ethical positions are simply expressions of our opinions. Adopting one of these two positions, perhaps, might provide psychological relief from having to think about the complexity of making tough moral choices, but quite often neither option helps us make well-informed and judicious decisions whenever we are confronted with a *complex* ethical dilemma. The ethical philosophy that claims we need to adopt the right moral principles that will govern and guide our behavior so that we act rightly is a version of the first option here; unfortunately, there isn't much empirical evidence that supports the idea that the holding of moral principles affects us in this way. For we sometimes use vague and abstract moral principles to justify the actions we favor, and this happens often in moments when we are under pressure to justify what we have done (especially when we fear that we have acted wrongly) as well as when we do not have enough time—or simply do not take the time—to consider how the principles we hold should guide our choices. Thus, situational pressures often effect our moral judgments independently of how fervently we hold onto and cherish our moral principles. Indeed, over the last few decades, a few descriptive and empirically minded approaches have dismantled the coherency of a particular theoretical claim about moral behavior, namely *that moral actions and behavior are strongly guided by valuing the correct ethical principles, standards, and laws*; and therefore, our actions and behavior *ought* to value these correct, stable, and unchanging ethical principles, standards, or laws for making good moral judgments.

The Ineffectiveness of Values and Principles

How are moral principles established and what legitimizes them? Though ethical traditions have devised different meanings of the term *correct ethical principles*, there is a common twofold process that we recognize throughout the history of philosophy by which they are often established and legitimized. First, one "discovers" the metaphysical, ontological, and natural order of reality; then second, one draws the correct ethical principles that both mirror this reality and are naturally derived from it. To be good or behave rightly, then, one must *act in accordance and alignment with the established and correct moral principles, which reflect the harmony, order, and nature of reality*. If one holds and abides by the correct moral principles, standards, laws, etc., then good behavior is likely to follow. Concomitantly, if one desires to know what the differences are between good and bad actions or behavior, then one only need to see how well, if at all, they align with and follow the correct moral principles that are drawn from and, in one way or another, mirror the external reality. All actions, therefore, ought to be judged by their ability or lack thereof to conform to good, rational moral principles. Without denying the fact that this assortment of ideas, beliefs, and moral actions have called different things, I am going to follow C. D. Batson's lead here and call this theoretical and normative approach *principlism*.[8]

We find the influence of principlism upon philosophical and religious thought since the Axial Age, a stretch of time that gave birth across the globe to similar ethical systems, each of which established certain principles, standards, or laws that were believed to guide and govern behavior.[9] Now, these principles were not adopted simply because they were sensed or reasoned as good or right, but rather because they were thought to mirror an external metaphysical, ontological, and transcendental order. One must first, therefore, discover the existing order of the cosmos, and then and only then, can one establish the correct principles to live well and align one's actions with that perceived reality. Among so-called "non-Western" philosophical and religious traditions, we find this pattern in Taoism, Confucianism, and Buddhism (just to name a few) within which certain ontological and metaphysical realities and teachings (e.g., the Way, Samsara, the nature of the "self") must first be known before one can live a good life.

Among ancient Greek philosophers, we also find this pattern. For instance, according to Plato, one must first come to understand that this world is a pale, less real copy of eternal Forms before one is able to live virtuously by reasoning correctly about the good life. The external and unchanging nature of the Forms justifies the moral principles by which one ought to abide. For Aristotle, the cosmos must be grasped as teleological before one can establish the correct moral principles (e.g., the doctrine of the mean) that will both govern and guide moral behavior. For the Stoic, the natural and governing order of the cosmos, the *Logos*, needs to be grasped before one can adopt the correct moral principle of *apatheia* that is necessary to live virtuously. Epicurus followed this same pattern, but for him one needs first to come to know that the universe is atoms and the void, then and only then can one seek after the good life that mirrors this material reality in which pleasure, i.e., the absence of pain, is the highest moral good.

For most, but not all of these ethical theories, reality was conceived hierarchically, composed of a lower realm within which we experience and interpret reality, e.g., the realm of illusion (Maya), ignorance, a separation, a Fall, etc., and a higher or transcendent reality such as Nirvana, the Forms, unity with God, and heaven. Relative to this order, moral principles and ethical norms within these traditions were established and derived from the higher realm and were seen as blueprints for aligning one's behavior with the structure of the higher realms as well as, one might say, with the clues or directions for escaping the ignorance and falsity of the lower realms.

Philosophical and religious narratives during the Middle Ages did not waver from this basic conceptual structure for distinguishing the good from the bad, or the right from the wrong. But for monotheistic religions of this era, the source of truth for determining the external metaphysical, ontological, and natural order was chiefly *the text* of the given tradition, which was believed to be revealed by God. Correct ethical principles, standards, and laws were then interpreted and drawn from folklore and the texts, albeit in different ways, which established different traditions of the monotheistic religion in questions. Moral authority for making judgments about the good/bad, right/wrong were determined by the religious authorities of these traditions and the rituals and practices they established based on their interpretations of the text. With the rise of modern philosophy, the authority of these religious texts and traditions, especially those of Christianity, were challenged and *partially* abandoned in favor of a different source for determining the ethical principles that if followed would lead to good actions and behavior: *human reason*. During the early modern period, we find this pattern within the philosophies of Descartes and Spinoza, each of which expressed the importance of reason for controlling unruly *pathé*. During the late period, we find a devotion to principlism like no other in the works of Immanuel Kant.

With the moral philosophy of Kant, the contexts and consequences of our experiences are entirely ignored; they are even berated as irrelevant ideas that distort our understanding of the nature of morality, the rationality of the categorical imperative, and the moral law within us. Kant's belief in the power of principles and standards and their ability to shape our actions and behavior cast quite a spell over the philosophical study of morality, during his time and up to the present day. Even several political and philosophical theories since Kant, which have aimed to draw a necessary connection between rational moral principles and justice, have passively accepted Kant's basic idea that it is necessary to establish a rational account of the role standards and principles play in our moral judgments. Without such an account, the use of political power to establish the sociopolitical conditions believed to produce moral goodness and justice could not be legitimized.

The Shortcomings of Principlism

Independent of whether one, or more—or none—of these portraits of morality identified moral principles that seem right, social scientific evidence has demonstrated repeatedly that principlism as I have defined it as a moral and normative theory, does not consistently *function* when followed to govern and guide our actions and behavior when we experience situational pressures. Thus, merely holding a moral principle, independent of whether it is deemed "right" by some governing power or authority or even agreed by all to be beneficial or "good," doesn't necessarily lead to the good behavior that the principle promotes. In whatever form it takes, principlism, as a normative ethical theory for interpreting and evaluating the moral dimensions of our actions and behaviors, is a defunct and dysfunctional ethical theory filled with misinformation about the relation between holding or believing in moral principles, standards, laws and the actual content of our embodied and contextual moral actions, behaviors, and experiences. In addition to the fact that social scientific evidence repeatedly demonstrates the failures of principlism, one should be skeptical of principlism because moral principles are by their very nature abstract, vague, and therefore subject to differing interpretations as well as rationalization.

Imagine two people who are developing a friendship decide to have lunch together one Sunday afternoon. One of the sources of their emerging friendship is their shared belief that their lives ought to be guided by the moral principle "Live empathically." As they are about to order their meals, one of them, who is vegan, asks the waiter about the contents of one of their meal options. Once this first friend orders her meal, the other friend, who is neither vegan nor vegetarian, orders a steak. As this happens, the vegan chastises her friend and begins to think that her new friend lack's integrity. But by doing this, she embarrasses her friend, who, with a tinge of remorse but an even greater feeling of being an object of unwarranted cruelty, begins to feel deeply harmed and begins to reflect upon the vegan's integrity. Each believes the other's behavior to be directly opposed to the moral principle that each accepts as morally right and good. Each believes the other lacks integrity.

Experiences, like this one, in which we witness how the same moral principle can give rise to a wholly different interpretation of its meaning and application than one's own, puts us in a position to explain and justify our actions to make them seem to be in accord with the *principled behavior* we endorse. Principles are often prone to such rationalization whenever more pressing or relevant needs and desires, rather than our accepted moral principles, direct and guide our behavior. This arises, in part, because the abstract moral principles, standards, and "laws," we hold are often functionally irrelevant with the unique contexts of different, and perhaps new, experiences, circumstances, and situations in which we make moral judgments and decisions. And because of this, the principles that do not fit or align with the varieties of our experiences, no matter how crimson they glow in our hearts, become irrelevant to our experience in light of their ineffectiveness. In these circumstances, the meanings of our principles are often "redefined" to make them align with the ethical needs of a given time so that they produce the habits of behavior that will serve emerging moral needs and concerns.

Moral geniuses or visionaries often do this to awaken a moral consciousness and to counter or fight against the injustices of one's day. Independent of these considerations, it does not follow from principlism's inability to be an effective ethical theory that principles themselves are unimportant. Functional principles, when stipulated as general claims about how we ought to act or behave, assist our ability to understand both similar and dissimilar moral experiences and are often resources for questioning problematic moral claims and making sound judgments about our own and other's actions and behavior. But functional principles can also become dangerous when their ineffectiveness is ignored, when it is believed that their "truth" cannot be challenged and are thus not subject to critique.

Recognizing principlism's shortcomings is an important step before evaluating moral claims and arguments about empathy. For since principlism fails as a sound theoretical, ethical, and normative approach for analyzing morality, in general, and empathy, in particular, what normative theory ought to take its place?

The most significant voice of dissent against principlism—and even normative theories— was that of William James, who wrote a too often ignored and underrated essay on moral philosophy called *The Moral Philosopher and the Moral Life*. James's central claim in the work is that "there is no such thing as an ethical philosophy *dogmatically* made up in advance."[10] But there are, of course; as most ethical theories are chockfull of dogmatic moral ideals, principles, and standards that are established for the purpose of governing and guiding our behavior and assisting us in differentiating between good and bad moral judgments. But how can moral ideals, principles, or standards, as abstract and free-floating ideas about goodness, truly be called good outside of their participation in life, outside and somehow transcendent to a conscious experience that feels it to be good? For James, they can't: "nothing can be good or right, except so far as some consciousness feels it to be good."[11] Nothing can be grasped as right or wrong in advance of experience, antecedent to the contextualized and relational experience in which it either functions or fails to produce moral satisfaction. As it goes then with any moral philosophy and every moral claim, the following moral hypothesis, and interpretations of the moral value of empathy, would be based upon the context of a given experience and the consequences it produces.

For Empathy: Empathy Is Moral

Empathy is very often considered to be a positive, all-together good, and helpful ability that heightens the power of our moral aptitude, assists our moral development, and has the potential to bring about significant, powerful, and melioristic social change. Of course, not everyone who promotes these prospects for empathy define "empathy" in the same way, which clearly is a problem. For instance, "empathy," defined as an experience of the interplay of feeling into and feeling with, has been recognized as instrumental to the psychologist's goal of achieving therapeutic results for her/his patients.[12] Understood as an experience of feeling with and grasping the contents of another's mind, empathy has been praised as being necessary for prosocial development in children as well as the connective "glue" of the social world, and this empathic connection with others, it is claimed, is the foundation for producing our desire to help others rather than hurting them.[13] As a combination of the relations I have introduced, this way of thinking about empathy's prowess has been lauded as a successful tool for conflict mediation,[14] demonstrated to be useful for counteracting violent behavior,[15] and noted as an "important determinant of moral behavior."[16] According to Jamil Zaki in his insightful work called *The War for Kindness*, an important role for empathy is empathic care and an experience of feeling for others to "inspire kindness: our tendency to help each other, even at a cost to ourselves."[17] In a similar conceptual vein, Batson's notion of empathic concern, as an experience of feeling for another, is a motivational force for producing altruistic behavior.[18] For Baron-Cohen, empathy as feeling with and for others by *responding* to them with the appropriate emotions functions as a "universal solvent" to solve any and all problems.[19] Baron-Cohen's motivation for writing his well-known book *The Science of Evil* was to convince us of the necessity and overall goodness of empathy as a practice:

> Empathy is one of the most valuable resources in our world. Erosion of empathy is an important global issue related to the health of our communities, be they small (like families) or big (like nations). Families can be torn apart by brothers who can no longer talk to each other, or couples who have developed an awful mistrust of each other, or a child and parent who misunderstand each other's intentions. Without empathy we risk the breakdown of relationships, we become capable of hurting others, and we can cause conflict, increase community cohesion, and dissolve another person's pain.[20]

The philosopher Michael Slote also sees empathy as a positive force in much the same way as Baron-Cohen does. But taking his cue from Hume and the moral sentimentalist tradition, Slote defines empathy by contrasting it with sympathy. "Empathy," says Slote, "involves having the feelings of another (involuntarily) aroused in ourselves, as when we see another person in pain."[21] Hume (who used the term "sympathy" for what Slote here calls "empathy") described this phenomenon as both the experience of another person's feeling(s) *infused* into us and a type of *contagion* between what one person feels and another feels. Defined in this way, empathy is a manifestation of the relation of feeling with another by means of an experience of *empathic contagion*. Sympathy, for Slote, is feeling for another person—for example, when we feel for someone in pain. A conclusion one can draw from this distinction is that we can experience empathy (or feeling with another) without sympathy (feeling for another) and sympathy without empathy.[22] Empathy, says Slote, is the "cement of the moral universe" for it helps to create, something like, moral approval and disapproval, which are crucial for helping us to understand what moral judgments and utterances mean as well as how we make judgments of moral claims.[23] Still following Hume's general account of sympathy, Slote defines empathy also as a *mechanism* that allows our moral approval and disapproval "to focus on moral agents rather than on the consequences of their actions,"[24] and suggests that this account of moral approval and disapproval does not presuppose moral judgment.

Slote's understanding of empathy is a mode of what I have called *empathic contagion*, namely an automatic, involuntarily, and unconscious "catching" of the feelings or beliefs of others. We experience empathic contagion as well as empathic mimicry with many other species, especially and primarily those species that have experienced similar social and existential situations and challenges that required them to develop similar evolutionary traits, which facilitated acts of helping behavior and the ability of the species to survive collectively. Along with the automatic neurological processes that have endowed us with empathic contagion, the early experiences on our evolutionary journey as a species also helped to generate the skills of empathic mimicry and empathic inference by which our ancient ancestors were able to recognize the pains and concerns of others as well as the need for them to be well nourished.

Would there have been any hope for the survival of our species if our ancestors could not infer—could not guess—what others were experiencing, such as accurately intuiting another person's feelings of hunger that led to acts of food sharing and mutual aid? According to De Waal, these dimensions of empathy as well as other more highly developed imaginative abilities, such as those of empathic perspective-taking are by *nature good* as they are unique evolutionarily building blocks that enable us to act in a morally good and compassionate way toward others.[25] And beyond simply grasping, intuiting, or knowing the perspectives others, De Waal notes, the inborn capacity of empathy as feeling with, by which we are able to "connect to and understand others and make their situation our own," greatly enriches our thinking and "can only be to any society's advantage."[26]

Other scholars likewise promote empathy as a crucial dynamic of positive social interactions and even as a source for bringing about melioristic, revolutionary social change. For instance, Hoffman contends that a person's *prosocial moral structure* is "a network of empathic effects, cognitive representations, and motives,"[27] which includes the internalization of socially learned moral rules, principles, behavioral norms, a general sense of right and wrong, the consequences of behaving badly, and a grasp of how one's previous acts have hurt or helped others, have caused self-blame or guilt. Hoffman predicts that this understanding of the moral strengths of empathy as an affective response to another's situation other than one's own "is likely to promote prosocial behavior and discourage aggression in cultures guided by caring and most justice principles."[28]

The sheer popularity of the moral potential of empathy has also contributed to the belief that empathic sensibilities serve as a guiding power to solve or even eliminate outstanding social problems throughout the world. The sentiment resonates with Roman Krznaric who has recognized empathy as "the watchword of a new generation of activists campaigning on issues such as economic inequality, disability rights, climate change, and gender justice."[29] Krznaric sees these historical developments as an opportunity for us all to join these and other empathy-inspired movements and leave an indelible mark on the world. Moving beyond this, Jeremy Rifkin entertains an even grander historical perspective about empathy in which empathic concern—as an aid to the well-being and survival of humanity—grows in direct proportion to the destructive effects of physical entropy. Our ability to feel for others and act upon our senses of empathic care and concern for them is a positive force in the world that stands and works against these entropic effects as well as the self-serving and materialistic concerns of humankind. The force, power, and cultivation of empathy has the revolutionary potential to transform a world in crisis and thus bring about global social meliorism.[30] Vilayanur Ramachandran has made an even more ambitious claim that the discovery of mirror neurons "will do for psychology what DNA did for biology," for they are the source of our abilities to imitate, emulate, and *feel with* others, and this helps us to appreciate cultural diversity.[31]

Against Empathy: Empathy Is Immoral

Irrespective of these positive portrayals of empathy as a moral good, one should keep in mind that claims about the moral goodness of empathy are made *by means of reflecting upon the felt consequences of having or sharing in empathic experiences, however defined.* Empathy, then, is determined to be "good" because of what it is believed to do, not because it is in line with a given moral principle or is in accord with an accepted moral standard.

By focusing upon different contexts of experience and recognizing different consequences of empathic experience, some theorists have pointed out a "darker" side of empathy, noting that in certain situations it can be used to procure malevolent ends. Accordingly, "empathy" has served as a tool one uses to get what one wants, to manipulate others, and to realize nefarious ends. Take, for example, the ability of a torturer to feel and to understand the experiences of the tortured. The torturer must "feel into" the pain and suffering of the tortured and "feel with" or gain his/her perspective in order to know how much pain should be applied in order to achieve some desired end—which is usually to extract vital information. Clearly, the application of too much pain might not generate this desired result, while not applying enough pain won't work either. The torturer must use a few different empathic techniques to find the right balance to achieve the desired end. Without the relation of *feeling for*, exemplified by definitions of empathy that are understood only as an experience of the relations of *feeling into, feeling with*, or both, empathy will always stand the chance of being perceived as immoral depending upon the circumstance.

As it was the case for those who viewed empathy under a positive moral light, the way in which anti-empathy theorists define "empathy" shapes the initial starting points of their investigation. For instance, anthropologists Nils Bubandt and Rane Willerslev define "empathy" generally as the relation of *feeling into* and *feeling with*, and specifically as "the first-person imaginative projection, at once emotional and cognitive, of oneself into the perspective or situation of another."[32] Using this definition as the basis for their research, they noted during their fieldwork in Siberia and Indonesia that this type of empathy isn't always used to bring about social cohesion, compassion, and altruism, as some have claimed. Rather, it is used both as an immoral tool to trick and deceive others during hunting and to exaggerate and radicalize the alterity of the other during acts of political violence. Empathy as feeling into the other, they claim, is distinct from both the relations of feeling with (sympathy) and feeling for (compassion) in that empathic projection, as they define it, allows one to understand the other vicariously, both without losing one's own identity and without caring for the well-being of the other.[33] This results in an insistence of one's own identity, the promotion of one's aims and aspirations over another, and the dehumanization of—and sometimes, an attempt to destroy—the other. This cross-cultural, anthropological investigation into the morality of empathic projection illuminates an important fact about our experiences of empathy, however they may be defined, namely that the goodness or badness, rightness or wrongness of empathic experiences are discerned by grasping the experiential and cultural contexts in which they are expressed and by making moral judgments about the actual, or conceivable, felt consequences that have arisen or might arise from them.

Reflection upon the differing and unique contexts of an empathic experience, what one indeed means by "empathic experience," and the consequences that arise from the experience, seems to be the consistent approach for determining the morality of empathy and the deciding factors that make one inclined to promote or demote empathy—to be "for" or "against" it.

Jesse Prinz, a philosopher loyal to the same sentimentalist tradition as Slote, defines "empathy" as "a kind of vicarious emotion: it's feeling what one takes another person to be feeling. And the 'taking' here can be a matter of automatic contagion or the result of a complicated exercise of the imagination."[34] This clear and concise definition of "empathy" is similar to that given by Bubandt and Willerslev, in that empathy is an act that involves some process of grasping or gaining the felt experience of another, though Prinz's definition is more pluralistic by the way it includes empathic contagion, or what he calls automatic contagion, which does not require one to project oneself imaginatively into the experiences of another. Prinz is likewise skeptical of the manner by which many proclaim empathy to be fundamentally good and socially beneficial. Indeed, he completely rejects the idea that empathy is necessary for morality. Prinz's "anti-empathy" tendencies, like all theorists examined thus far, is guided by the manner by which he defines "empathy" and how different contextualized experiences of this type of empathy operate instrumentally to bring about unjust and immoral consequences. For instance, studies have indicated that empathy as the act of feeling what one takes another to be feeling may lead to preferential treatment by means of empathically induced acts of altruism that are nevertheless unfair, immoral, and unjust.[35] And even when empathy operates to stimulate feelings of compassion or acts of kindness, we often have more empathy for the suffering and pain of those similar to us.[36]

In his work *Against Empathy*, Paul Bloom delivers an argument against a specific understanding of empathy and makes the case for what he calls "rational compassion." Bloom defines empathy as "the act of feeling what you believe other people feel—experiencing what they experience" and elsewhere as "the act of coming to experience the world as you think someone else does."[37] Bloom claims that most psychologists and philosophers use the term "empathy" in this way (a claim that is patently false, given the theorists and ideas of empathy we have explored). Bloom says that he is not against certain types of empathy, such as the act of "understanding other people, getting inside their heads and figuring out what they are thinking," or what Bloom calls cognitive empathy, which he thinks is "morally neutral."[38] Nor is he against empathy that refers to "everything that is morally good—compassion, warmth, understanding, caring, and so on."[39] But our moral decisions as well as our moral actions are often influenced by experiences of the type of empathy Bloom stands against.

Empathy, then, as both the act of feeling and experiencing what you believe other people to feel and experience as well as the act of coming to experience the world as you think someone else does, is a poor moral guide and, in the end, makes the world a far worse place: "It grounds foolish judgments and often motivates indifference and cruelty. It can lead to irrational and unfair political decisions, it can corrode certain important relationships, such as between a doctor and a patient, and make us worse at being friends, parents, husbands, and wives."[40] This type of empathy is also prone to bias; it is parochial and "focuses you on certain people at the expense of others; and it . . . distorts our moral and policy decisions in ways that causes suffering instead of relieving it." [41] We feel empathy in this sense with those who treat us fairly or cooperate with us, and we tend not to have empathy in this way for those who cheat us or are in competition with us. We have empathy for friends and family members over strangers and empathize more readily with members of our in-group than an out-group.

Irrespective of these negative portrayals of empathy as a moral experience, one should keep in mind that claims about the moral goodness of empathy are made primarily by *considering the felt consequences of having or sharing in empathic experiences, however defined*. Empathy, then, is determined to be "good" because of what it is believed to do—the consequences it produces—not because it is in line with a given moral principle or is in accord with an accepted moral standard.

It isn't the least bit controversial to state that these perspectives concerning the morality of empathy—whether empathy is perceived as either good or bad—are wholly contingent upon how each theorist *defines* "empathy," how each operationalizes empathic actions as certain *contextualized* practices, and what each thinker has determined are the significant *consequences* of these actions and practices. The morality of empathy, then, is inescapably front-loaded by how it is defined, by its *relations* to selected experiences understood within one context rather than another, as well as by the actual or conceivable consequences of it as an action.

One of the apparent failings of adopting narrow conceptualizations of empathy is that it seems, at least upon an initial examination, that a vast ambiguity concerning the nature of empathy abounds because of narrow approaches; and consequently, there doesn't seem to be a common thread that weaves together disparate narratives about the moral value of empathy as experience—since different definitions of "empathy" relate to different experiences. This, however, simply isn't the case, as I have just shown by examining the differences between those who consider empathy to be either morally good or morally suspect. For upon this further examination, there has appeared to be at least two common tendencies that are foundational to the narratives of the moral value of empathic experience. First, each thinker I have explored here interprets empathy to be either morally good or bad based upon the *context* in which an experience of "empathy" occurs; and second, each conceptualization of empathy is judged good or not in consideration of the consequences the experience of empathy produces.

I have resisted defining "empathy" narrowly by offering a pluralistic and broad notion of relational empathy that aims to include rather than exclude disparate historical voices about the empathic experience. One benefit of doing this is to show that there have been several different experiences that people have called empathic and that investigations into the nature and value of these experiences were conducted for the purpose of establishing empathy as a *solution to some outstanding problem*, whether that problem was conceived as, for example, historical biases (Herder), overly scientific interpretations of nature (Novalis), the inability to perceive the contents of other people's minds (Lipps, Mead, Rogers), a lack of prosociality, helping behavior, or concern for others (Hoffman, De Waal, Batson) or something else entirely.

Another benefit to thinking about empathy pluralistically and pragmatically when it comes to questions about the morality of empathy is that this pluralistic and broad account, as an interpretive starting point for exploring narrow accounts, has yielded the truth that moral assessments of empathy are pragmatic—i.e., the main criteria for making moral judgments about the value of empathic experiences rely exclusively upon the *contexts* in which they are experienced and the *consequences* they produce. This is as fascinating as it is paradoxical, not simply because one wouldn't expect there to be such a surfeit of moral theories resembling the ethical approaches of American pragmatists, but also because the moral approaches for interpreting the goodness or badness of empathy *deviate significantly from what most people mean and have meant by calling things and actions as "moral" or "ethical,"* which as two terms are often used interchangeably to qualify what is believed or identified to be good or correct, to describe things as pleasurable, correct, upright, satisfactory, and desirable.

Relational Empathy and the Moral Sanity of Relativism

When it comes to questions about the morality of empathy, *it is all relative, that is, it is all relational.* This claim might cause some to shriek in horror; after all, the word, "relativism" is often perceived to be a pejorative and philosophically naïve viewpoint, which is often recognized by the following claim: the truth values of all perspectives are relative to differences in perceptions, languages, belief systems, experiences, etc., and it is not possible for one to interpret and judge these differences from some objective viewpoint. Based on this common interpretation and way of defining and understanding "relativism," relativists are titles reserved for adolescent theorists who hold the position that morality, truth, etc., are all contingent upon your perspective. This so-called philosophical position is often characterized and summarized by the following phrases: "If it works for you, it can't be wrong," or "truth is a matter of perspective," or "morality is all about how we perceive things: if I perceive something in one way it's good for me, if you perceive it in another manner, it is simply good for you." Richard Rorty once characterized this imaginary position as "the view that every belief on a certain topic, or perhaps about any topic, is as good as every other." And further pointed out that, "*No one holds this view.* Except for the occasional cooperative freshman, one cannot find anybody who says that two incompatible opinions on an important topic are equally good."[42] Let's call this view that Rorty rightly rejects as an imaginary position, *traditional relativism*, and the view I am endorsing for understanding the variety of moral senses regarding our empathic experience, *relational relativism*.

Even though it is evident that relativism as "traditional relativism" isn't a position one holds, there are historical reasons why it became a philosophical problem. We can note this problem among the ancients, but its characterization in the last one hundred years or so arose as a historical response to what were perceived as the problems of "psychologism" and "irrationalism." Regarding the former, phenomenologists and analytical philosophers of the early twentieth century believed that so-called promoters of psychologism (remember Lipps?) were not taking into account established logical truths when they explained variations in human psychology, and to counter this they linked relativism with psychologism in order to discount the validity of each.[43] The apparent danger of relativism was also promulgated by philosophers who equated the philosophical position of relativism with both irrationalism and social-cognitive anarchy.[44] If one is inclined to compare traditional relativism with, say, absolutism, one would be hard-pressed to say that that the former has wrought as much damage as the latter.[45]

James defined "relativism" as relational relativism and linked it to the method of radical empiricism, which is grounded in the pragmatic notion of truth. Truth in this sense is a relation between an idea and its object(s), and the truth or falsity of any relation is contingent upon an *agreement* between an idea and a given object of thought. Nearly every theory of truth includes, in one way or another, this notion of a relation between an idea, thought, or claim and something external to it with which it is supposed to agree, and *moral truths do not depart from this formula*. But the truth of a given claim for James relates to the contexts of the relations within experiences, and all truth claims begin with a given relation or set of relations that stand ready to be either "short-circuited or traversed at full length."[46] The relation known as truth, according to James, "like all relations, has it fundamentum, namely, the matrix of experiential circumstance, psychological as well as physical, in which the correlated terms are found embedded."[47] Translation: All truths are drawn from the situations, circumstances, and contexts within experience and are therefore *relationally* relativistic; they must be grasped as *historical* claims subject to falsification in light of their coherence with further *experience*.

Independent of one's epistemological loyalties (and biases), it should be clear that embracing relativism—as relationalism—provides us with an interpretive framework to judge the goodness or badness, or rightness or wrongness, of any experience we call "empathic" relative to the *contexts* of a circumstance and situation as well the actual and/or conceivable *consequences* that have arisen or might arise from such an experience. Clearly with such an approach there will be disagreement and discord; this a good thing, for it is necessary for robust and healthy democratic exchanges. Thinking of relativism in this way also provides for us a more realistic and plural approach for grasping the moral significance of our *personal* experiences of empathy, however defined, which likewise cannot be satisfactorily moral *prior to the felt experiences within a given context and the consequences that arise from it*. It follows from this that there can never be a final word about the morality of empathy (just as there can be no final word about ethics, morality, and experience itself), since future experience may provide for us the gift of a more enhanced perception and a better understanding of the multiple effects of a contextualized empathic experience.

The central difference between those who embrace relationalism and radical empiricism and those who adopt any other foundation for understanding morality, e.g., principlism, lies in the fact that the former approach refuses the attempt to "go above experience" to establish a perspective for all times and places, which would subsequently provide us with an interpretive framework to make noncontextual judgments about our actions and behaviors. This difference is crucial for distinguishing between the multiple approaches for examining the various meanings of "empathy," for it forces us to turn to the variations and multiplicities within *historical contexts* to define empathy and to consider the actual and/or *conceivable consequences of behavior* for determining the practical and moral value of empathic experiences.

Adoption of the moral theory I am promoting for interpreting empathy would require we leave behind all claims that imply that variations of and variety in experience are unimportant for making moral judgments. This requires the abandonment of the majority of ethical, mostly elitist, systems and moral theories in which established moral norms and codes of conduct operate as so-called "universal" moral truths. These universal moral truths, in turn, are thought to be foundational for establishing the correct moral principles, standards, and laws that aim to provide a singular, rational, and abstract account of good behaviors and moral actions. A radically empirical approach is antithetical to any such account of morality, especially one in which its supporters refuse to entertain contrary ideas about good and bad, or right and wrong behaviors and actions simply because they are recalcitrant to the moral ideals, beliefs, and principles they deify.

Relational Empathy: Context, Consequences, and Morality

Since we can't have a vantage point outside and above experience, a relational and radically empirical approach sheds the greatest light upon the questions concerning the moral value(s) of empathic experiences. For the moral value of empathy, however defined, is always relative to the context in which it is experienced and the consequences arising from it—*and one cannot accurately conceive of a circumstance in which this is untrue*. Consider for your approval of this fact experiences of the relation of feeling into. What would it mean to say that the projection of my senses into an object of either perception or reflection is morally praiseworthy? What is the moral value of someone, say, in a park who is projecting her/his feelings and thoughts into tree as its multicolored leaves seem to be vibrating as they are rustled by powerful winds? Only the context of such an experience and the consequences produced by it qualify the act itself as either good or bad. Furthermore, what determines the morality of, say, one's ability to mimic or successfully emulate another's habits of behavior, or adopt another's perspective? Or what is the source of the feeling of goodness or rightness when one feels connected to or united with someone or something? Only the context of such an experience and the consequences produced by such an act qualifies the act as good or bad. Highly gifted individuals called *empaths* can feel with the emotional states of others by "catching" their psychological states or moods without even attempting to do so. What if the empath can't control this tendency, are we justified in calling it *good* if it makes the empath consistently feel disappointed in her/his ability to control this propensity? And what might be the moral value of other dimensions of empathic experience, such as empathic inference, empathic concern, and empathic care? If I act with empathic care—authentic care that is motivated to increase the well-being of another person's life—but, due to the relational context of the act itself and the consequences it produces, I inadvertently make that person's life far worse, how could I legitimately claim that my action has moral worth? The answers to these questions about the morality of empathy are—and will always be—shaped by the context and consequences of our actions. Thus, the practice of relational empathy, as a contextualized practice of feeling into, feeling with, and feeling for other persons and things has no moral worth outside of the consequences it produces, which itself can only be understood in relation to the context of it as an experience. Without an understanding and assessment of the context and consequences, empathy is amoral and only becomes moral as it is grasped contextually and is judged in terms of the consequences it either produces or might produce.

The insight and understanding gained by means of our investigations should, in turn, provide us good reasons for defending different ideals and beliefs about the moral dimensions of experience, i.e., why we acted in one way or another and how we ought to habitually act. When our theories, ideals, beliefs, and actions—as instruments—fail to change the conditions of experience satisfactorily, they become mere artifacts, irrelevant to the emerging problems and ethical concerns within life-in-transition. However, whenever the use of these instruments satisfies our and other's aims and purposes, we say that they are functional; they are working and producing the type of change that efficiently address or solve problems. *The value and goodness of the change itself always stands ready to be contested and/or reconstructed.* And independent of the functionality, usefulness, and consequences of our theories, ideals, beliefs, and actions, the persistent act of challenging the legitimacy of our starting points—which is one exceptional thing philosophers do—kindles a light to illuminate the path of future inquiry.

To adopt either a narrow or broad approach for both conceiving of and defining "empathy" involves a choice between two radically disparate starting points that will structure the inquiry in dissimilar ways. Different inquiries forge different paths of investigation, and thus produce different, however nuanced, understandings of experience. I have adopted a broad, plural, and pragmatic approach that is inclined toward the inclusive. It directs us toward the expansive, transformative, and multifarious nature of experience. It helps us to shift our incomplete understandings of experience by providing us with a pluralistic mindset and temperament sensitive and responsive to the transitions and transformations of life. But even the most pluralistically minded account of experience places limits on our understanding by excluding dimensions of it—this is a necessary consequence of all our interpretive gazes; but by adopting a pragmatic-pluralistic account of experience, we might become emboldened and try to expand the limits of our perspectives while recognizing and reflecting upon our biases, whether they be biases concerning morality, in general, or the morality of empathy, in particular.

7

Can Empathy Be Developed?

As the winged apple seed glides and falls and finds a home to sprout and flower into a fruit-bearing tree, so too do we by the power of our actions initiate the possibility of becoming something different from—something greater than— what we currently are. For our actions, whether with or without intent, whether conscious or unconscious, whether propelled by good or ill fortune, are *agents and instruments of transformation* and have the power both to nurture the skills we possess as well as to bring about *better* conditions in the world.

This second claim that our actions are able to engender more favorable circumstances is readily acceptable to our ears as a true claim about experience in general; however, when we speak of specific cases, when we locate and isolate particular instances wherein our actions seem to facilitate a *change* from one state to another, disagreement often arises concerning the qualitative nature of the transformation in question, i.e., whether the change is something positive or negative, good or bad, right or wrong. In this way, all claims about human development are moral claims as well; in a similar fashion, all claims about empathic development are also moral claims concerning how different ways of developing this or that dimension of empathic behavior is perceived as good or bad, right or wrong.

During the golden age of ancient Greece, a wealthy young man named Meno asked the philosopher Socrates whether virtue arises from nature, teaching, practice, or something else entirely.[1] For many of us today, the word "virtue" is rarely used; but when it is, it often refers to either an admirable quality of another person's *moral character* or to someone's actions we perceive to be morally good. Among the ancient Greeks, virtue referred to these praiseworthy moral dimensions of experience as well, but it also signified something far broader, namely, and most notably for our purposes here, virtue meant greatness or excellence *(arete)* during an activity or arising from an activity.

Socrates was certainly well acquainted with this general meaning of virtue as it was often employed in antiquity to describe the quality of human activities as

Figure 7 Springtime in Knoxville, Tennessee.

well as the things produced by action;[2] nevertheless, Socrates responded to Meno's question by claiming that he did not know what virtue was and wasn't certain if he knew anyone who did. After inferring that Meno likewise didn't know the nature of virtue, Socrates refused to answer Meno's question until he stipulated a clear definition of "virtue," reasoning an enquiry into the nature of virtue ending with a firm understanding of it must proceed any discussion about its origin.

Meno offered several different definitions of "virtue" to placate the philosopher's demand, all of which Socrates deemed unacceptable as *mere instances* of virtue rather than a single definition of what virtue is *in and of itself*, independent of any example of it. After Meno's multiple failures to define virtue in this way, Socrates finally concedes, begrudgingly, to answer Meno's question by stating that if virtue were a type of knowledge, it could be taught or acquired, but since he nor anyone he knew were teachers of virtue, Socrates held that virtue cannot be taught. Moreover, since the many things we call "virtuous" are defined inconsistently, experienced variously, and do not share a common nature, neither does virtue arise from nature. From these claims, Socrates concludes virtue to be something akin to a divine gift, similar to way poets acquire the gift of inspiration, that we are unable to understand or define sufficiently.

Socrates's request to produce a definition of an idea independent of any concrete example of it is representative of a common trend throughout the history of philosophy. This approach for understanding experience is often referred to as a "whole-to-parts" approach for attaining knowledge of a given thing, whether that thing be a concept such as justice, a skill like empathy, or even the nature of reality. As a method for understanding things, this approach begins by conceptualizing what are believed to be the invariant and universal properties of a given thing, the unifying characteristics between different things of the same class, and then by establishing a definition based on these actions for the purpose of generating knowledge and increasing our understanding of the world.[3]

Socrates conversation with Meno is valuable in that it helps us to recognize that we often don't have a clear meaning of the things we say and his refusal to claim knowledge of that which he doesn't know is exemplary of profound wisdom. But his demand for a definition of virtue—apart from a particular instantiation of it—is representative of a "whole" to "parts" approach for understanding things as well as an ahistorical method for uncovering the meaning of different experiences.[4] William James noticed the problems when philosophers cling to abstractions in this ahistorical manner—even when this way of understanding things becomes unintelligible. For by thinking one's abstractions to be objectively and irrefutably "real" without noting how they have become unintelligible and without comprehending how they are altered qualitatively within experience, one does not see the pressing need to redescend into the world of pure experience in which the meanings of the abstracted ideas have changed. When intellectuals cling to their abstractions, drawn out of the varying contexts and circumstances—concrete levels of existence—they fail to finish the function of thought itself, says James, which is to reinsert the conclusions of thought "into some particular point of the immediate stream of life."[5] This unfinished process quite readily occurs when intellectuals not only cling to their abstractions but also when they cling to abstractions that operate within a system of classification. Systems of classifications themselves and the social semiotic systems to which they relate, for James "depend on our temporary purposes. For certain purposes it is convenient to take things in one set of relations, for other purposes in another set."[6]

One way of interpreting Socrates's repeated refusals of Meno's definitions of virtue is to view them as a deep longing within Socrates to understand things only by means of this whole-to-parts method, and Socrates's failure to do this successfully seems to leave him in a state of resignation, skepticism, or some form of quietism, from which nothing can be said, and nothing can be done, and this demonstrates that whole-to-part approaches are wholly dysfunctional and that coming to understand anything with clarity can only come about by means of a parts-to-whole approach in which the uniqueness of particulars and the contexts of our experiences are taken seriously for pragmatic reasons. Of course, this requires the adoption of a "parts-to-whole" approach in which our descriptions and definitions of things have value and are operative so long as they are sufficiently intelligible to function as tools for solving problems.

Pragmatists begin first with the multiple relations of things and between things, and then construct a whole, i.e., a general conception, definition, and description of things for the purpose of putting different ideas about them to work. The "whole" once constructed and operative as a conveyor of the meaning of something, though, is never believed to be the final representation of it, for the representation of the idea in relation to the object defined is subject to change—and often does—when either different circumstances and/or new experiences lead us to realize that our previous thoughts about something have become less intelligible because of changing circumstances, unique conditions, and a plurality of new facts and perspectives.

My construction of the idea of relational empathy is an example of putting to work a part-to-whole approach in that the establishment of the relations of feeling into, feeling with, and feeling for—as wholes—have been drawn from parts, i.e., definitions of empathy throughout history. Relational empathy, which as a fallibilistic and pragmatic unified theory constructed for the purpose of social meliorism, can only be deemed valuable or good in consideration of what it produces. Throughout this exploration of different meanings and practices of empathy, we have also found that most theories of empathic experience throughout history have been whole-to-parts considerations in which the whole of what empathy is thought to be or could be was conceived and articulated by admitting certain relations or parts of experiences at the expense and exclusion of others. And one way but not the only way this current investigation of empathy differs from its predecessors is that it takes seriously the historical differences concerning the parts, relations, or dimensions of those previously constructed notions of empathy for inclusive reasons and practical purposes. No whole, no idea, ideal, or working theory, can ever be final, they must be torn down and deconstructed when dysfunctional, then eventually reconstructed, if experience uncovers that such a task may be instrumental for solving problems.

Developing Empathy and Nature vs. Nurture Questions

Meno's questions about virtue were explicitly about its origin, namely concerning whether *virtue* arises from some innate and natural capacity or whether it is acquired, developed, and nurtured. Attempts to understand and practice empathy have often followed this pattern of thought in that that study of empathy is marked by different narratives about its origin and shaped by nature versus nurture questions about its possible development.

Questions about the origin and development of empathy are different, of course, from those about virtue/excellence, for while the former deals with the origin or development of different forms of empathic *behavior*, the latter are concerned with the origin or development of the apparent *quality* (i.e., excellence) of things, activities, and behavior, including but not limited to empathic behaviors.

Nature vs. nurture questions about the origin or development of empathy occasionally arise from the same malady of the mind I have noted throughout this work, namely the belief that certain conceptual distinctions, while sensible if used heuristically, are thought to be part of an impermanent structure of reality—that is, when these distinctions are perceived *to be ontological dualisms, when they are believed to be coherent and discrete representations of distinct experiences opposing one another in the same way that they appear to be distinct and separate in thought.*

Questions concerning the possible development of empathy are often parasitic upon the nature/nurture dualism and this is demonstrable whenever theorists and scholars, loyal to the methodological commitments of their disciplines, describe empathy *primarily* but not solely as either an innate, biological capacity or a learned and socialized behavior. We have seen this trend throughout this work wherein the methodological commitments of biologists and neuroscientists, for example, lead them to think of empathy, for the most part, as a natural capacity, while the commitments of psychologists and sociologists encourage them to view empathy as an interpersonal and behavioral experience. Expertise and specialization, then, while necessary for the establishment of sound empirical studies and legitimate scientific claims, often function to perpetuate the nature/nature dualism quite clandestinely.

The pragmatic response to the nature/nurture dualism—or any dualism—is first to reject it outright after demonstrating how it distorts both experience and reality.[7] Once rejected, the terms of the former dualism turned distinction, now freed from their conceptual prison, are available to be used fluidly and relationally to illuminate some context of experience that the dualism once obfuscated. Beyond enlarging the possibility for clarity, these acts open the discussive space for dissolving the artificial philosophical problems the dualism once served as they illuminate the social problems that the employment of the dualism has previously concealed. With the perennial "problems" of philosophy dissolved and pressing social problems exposed, the pragmatist then turns to the art of making known and reconstructing the cultural and social conditions that have allowed the problems to persist.

This practice is, however, never entirely unencumbered, for like all empirical investigations it begins with the selection and inclusion of certain relations of lived experience with the cost of excluding others. This is unavoidable, but it is not problematic so long as it is understood that conclusions drawn are provisional and that all theories drawn from empirical studies are *fallible*—they are subject to further visions and revisions, modification, or even falsification.[8] Though scientists who study empathic development are loyal to this notion of fallibilism (gifted to us by the American pragmatists), the nature/nurture dualism often guides the interpretive framework of the scientific community nevertheless.

But perhaps what is even more interesting in relation to the question of empathy's possible development is that this nature/nurture dualism has greatly influenced the perspectives of nonscientists regarding whether empathy can be taught or learned. Nonscientists are often inclined to interpret empathic experience as having its origin in either natural dispositions or the process of nurturing one's habits and character. In his work *The War for Kindness*, Jamil Zaki creates a useful distinction for recognizing those members of the public, i.e., nonscientists, who hold that empathy is either rooted in nature or in our ability to nurture it as a skill.

On the one hand, notes Zaki, there are *fixists*. Fixists hold the belief that empathy is an immovable and innate capacity to *feel into*, *feel with*, and *feel for* others for the purpose of acting kindly toward them. Fixists also interpret empathy to be an automatic, reflexive, and instantaneous trait, requiring very little if any effort, much less skill.[9] In contrast, there are mobilists. Mobilists, according to Zaki's characterization, for the most part, come down on the nurture side. The pragmatist's response to this distinction is to assign value to it based on how it functions heuristically to illuminate the differences between those who hold different mindsets about the origin of empathy. Zaki's empirical studies, concerning people's beliefs and mindsets, put to work a practical distinction that elucidates the lived differences between the perspectives of people who hold contrary beliefs about the origin of empathy; thus, by means of his heuristic distinction between the mobilist and fixist he steers clear of falling into dualistic thinking.

In addition to rejecting them outright, another pragmatic response to dualisms—and especially the nature/nurture dualism—is to consider the functional value of accepting either side of a given dualism/distinction as an answer to a proposed question, such as the question we have proposed here: Does our ability to experience empathy, however defined, arise from some innate capacity or from the establishment of certain habits? This pragmatic response helps us to note not only the simplicity and general fecklessness for understanding experience dualistically, but also how, on occasion, experience itself shows us that the division represented in the dualism in question fails to provide a path forward for personal and interpersonal growth and transformation.

This approach, in which we try to determine how accepting either side of a dualism/distinction as an answer to an outstanding question, is an act of applying Peirce's pragmatic maxim, which again directs us to "Consider what effects, that might conceivably have practical bearings, we conceive the object of our conception to have. Then, our conception of these effects is the whole of our conception of the object."[10] Relevant to the focus of this chapter, the object of our conception is either side of an existing dualism that serves as an answer to the question of the origin of empathic experience, and the effects of either answer/conception represents the whole of the answer's instrumental value. Descending from the obfuscating heights of this abstract description, either side of the dualism, i.e., nature of nature, radiates clarity only when we can determine what effects might be produced by holding either viewpoint. And it is clear, that if you believe that empathy can't be developed, then chances are you won't even try. But if you believe that empathy can or even might be able to be developed—and you exercise your will toward this end—then your first step is to grasp the habits that have led to or might conceivably lead to empathic behavior.

Habits, Relational Empathy, and Directing Transformation

In consideration of the fact that the effects of an inborn, innate, fixed capacity to empathize cannot be clearly mapped out with any certainty, any discussion about or directive concerning empathic development must begin and end—then begin again—with the formation of habits and the conceivable power we might derive from them for the purpose of changing the way we exist in the world.

Philosophers have contributed more profound thoughts about the importance of habits for our lives than this truism denotes. And it seems to be the case that the philosophers who have accentuated the importance of habit formation are also empirically oriented and pragmatically minded theorists. For example, Aristotle's focus on the observable forms and substance of things coupled with his rejection of the immaterial, eternal Forms that Plato endorsed is representative of this trend, and this turn to empiricism spilled over into his ethical and political theory. At the heart of this empirical turn lies the idea of habit formation as well as a philosophy of life that interprets our power to form good habits as the foundation of all ethical and political activity. "Ethics," recall, is derived from two Greek words *ēthikós*, which meant for the philosophers of the ancient world, "relating to one's character," as well as *ēthós*, which chiefly meant an individual's habits or character, but also "customs" or "mores," i.e., the general character of a people. Thus, for Aristotle, we are what we repeatedly do; and by extension of this truth, relevant to this current investigation, we become empathic by repeatedly acting and behaving empathically. The idea here is that your character (*ēthós*)— which is the most consistent representation of your being—is produced by habits or what you repeatedly do, and when you repeatedly do things well, you are thought to be *doing well consistently* or *flourishing in life*, which, for Aristotle, meant that you were "good-spirited" or happy.

Being "happy" in life, in this context, does not denote a mere feeling of contentment or peace nor is it a sense of pleasure; rather, happiness for Aristotle is found in the activity of doing well and flourishing at a particular activity in life or the whole of life itself. One, therefore, could be good-spirited, flourishing, and even happy during the activity of behaving empathically when one flourishes at empathizing. According to Aristotle, when certain habits become part and parcel of one's daily routine and the constituent parts of one's character leads one to flourish greatly and do exceptionally well in each activity or even in the whole of life, that person is thought to be excellent. Taking Aristotle's insights seriously, one task for us here would be to consider how relational empathy can be developed by means of forming the right habits that lead to a satisfactory transformation of our empathic actions or empathic behavior so that these changes contribute to the goal of flourishing.

David Hume is another philosopher whose writings on habit were seminal and quite relevant to questions concerning how relational empathy can be developed. Often when we reflect upon our "habits," independent of whether we consider them to be good or bad for us, we think of our specific actions (such as the habit of jogging, or our general actions, such as one's financial or spending habits) but rarely do we consider the functional value of our mental habits and the modes and patterns of our thoughts. According to Hume, the actions of our behavior, as they are displayed in our manners, are clearly exemplary of those actions we call habitual; but so too are our mental habits and Hume sees certain habits of the mind as instrumental to the ways we think and reason. Hume's famous example of the billiard balls demonstrates how powerful our habits are.[11] Hume reasons that when you see billiard ball A hit billiard ball B, then see billiard ball B move, you aren't observing an act of causation, that is, you aren't seeing *billiard ball A* cause *billiard ball B* to move; rather, you are inferring a relation between two events based on the habit of seeing, thinking, and reasoning. The takeaway from this for us, relevant to the question of developing relational empathy, is simply that our mental habits provide for us powerful associations by which we can interpret and make inferences about our experiences.

What one can take away from the Aristotelian and Humean accounts of habit is that all types of habit formation, whether they be habits of the mind or habits of our behavior, are the driving forces that produce consequences and thus help us to transform our lives for better or for worse. And although Aristotle and Hume were not card-carrying pragmatists, most contemporary pragmatists consider them to be important forerunners to pragmatism. The most significant difference between these two empirically minded thinkers and the philosophers of American pragmatism is that the latter built their empirical philosophies atop of their theories of relations in such a way so that the relations between things and *contextual dynamics of the relations themselves* shape both the observations and the conclusions drawn from them, and thus the qualitative nature of the transformation they produce.

Two philosophers of the American tradition of pragmatism, C. S. Peirce and William James took the notion of habit and the attending art of habit formation to another level by empathizing the importance of both belief and relations and the manner in which each is formative to our actions. Following Hume, Peirce bridges the mere apparent gap between thought and action by locating our habits not only in our actions or behavior but also in our *thoughts, especially the thoughts that contribute to the establishment of our beliefs*. Indeed, according to Peirce, the very essence of a belief is the establishment of a habit, which is itself a *rule for action*, and "different beliefs are distinguished by different modes of action to which they give rise."[12] The establishment of a belief in, for instance, the relevance, potency, and transformative capabilities of relational empathy is necessary for developing the daily practice of feeling into, feeling with, and feeling for an object of one's perception or reflection. This belief alone, of course, isn't satisfactory, for without the belief we would not possess the will to act and behave empathically. But Peirce's emphasis on the habit of belief adds another layer to the insights of his pragmatic maxim that directs us to consider what effects we conceive the object of our conception—our ideas or habits of belief—to have. The habit of belief, as an idea or a collection of ideas, is for Peirce inseparable from the actions of our behavior, for "the whole function of thought is to produce habits of action," for at the root of every distinction of thought is what we believe to be tangible and conceivably practical.[13] The experience of different existential relations, it follows, will engender different habits, and habits as the expressions of these existential relations are established by our beliefs—as habits—which constitute the rules for action that facilitate the process of transformation arising from the cultivation of new habits of behavior.[14]

William James, who by now should be recognized as the main hero of this work on relational empathy, dedicated a whole chapter in his *Psychology: Briefer Course* to the acquisition of habits in which he claimed that "an acquired habit, from the physiological point of view, is nothing but a new pathway of discharge formed in the brain."[15] This way of perceiving habit formation, which locates our habits within the physiological processes of our bodies, was the first serious work to consider the notion of the plasticity of the brain and how, through the strength and effort of our will, *we are able to forge new pathways in our brains and thus create the habits of mind and body that are necessary for positive transformations*. James's understanding of habits was seminal, for it laid the foundation for and greatly shaped the methodological approaches of contemporary neuroscience as well as reshaped the philosophical approaches to consciousness. Regarding the latter, James revolutionized philosophical speculations about "consciousness" by specifying that consciousness exists only as a function and what contemporary neuroscientists have discovered is that the formulation of new habits can alter the way consciousness functions.

Understanding James's approach gives everyone who wishes to change his/her behavior a literal blueprint for positive character transformation and for enhancing one's skills to empathize. Habits simplify our actions, according to James, and make them more precise and relatively effortless while diminishing fatigue.[16] Although habits themselves make our experiences less arduous, abandoning old habits and establishing new ones isn't so easy. Considering this truth, James puts forth a few maxims for making certain a new habit becomes entrenched in one's experience. If you have ever sprained your ankle, then you know that until your ankle heals completely the tendon of your ankle is susceptible to being reinjured. Analogously, as the tendon has a greater chance of bending the same way when an ankle has been sprained, the physical flow of neurochemicals within the brain can tend to follow the same pattern or groove when a habit is ingrained. Since changing one's habits requires one to change the neurochemical pattern or groove, James suggests that whenever we wish to produce a new habit, we should take care to "launch ourselves with as strong and decided an initiative as possible . . . and never suffer an exception to occur till the new habit is securely rooted in your life."[17] A good way but not the only way to make certain the new habit becomes a part of your consistent routines and elemental to your character is to seize every opportunity to act in line with your new habit and to associate a positive emotional connection to the repetition of the habit. James thought we were a "bundle of habits"; therefore, our ability to forms habits is crucial for recognizing who we are and what we will become.[18]

The general take among contemporary neuroscientists does not diverge too far from what Peirce and James had to say about habits over one hundred years ago. One's habits of belief, as Peirce noted, are crucial for stimulating development, and our brains, James argued, are plastic, and we have the capacity to change the wiring of our brains and thus develop new habits that lead to positive transformation. In his popular work *The Power of Habit*, Charles Duhigg reaffirms these facts but also illustrates how we can develop new habits. Indebted to James's insights about habits and the plasticity of the brain, Duhigg understands habit formation as a three-step loop within the brain. The first step involves a cue; the second step is the routine of habit performed; and the third is the consequence or reward derived from the habit. Duhigg uses this tripartite model to build upon James's insights regarding the creation of new habits by noting that to break old habits, one must identify one's bad habits; and to create a new habit, one needs to assemble a cue, a routine, and reward. Just like Aristotle, James, and so many others before him, Duhigg notes that to make the habit successful one must possess the will for positive transformation by cultivating new cravings, which as cues will engender new routines and habits that will produce the desired consequences. Again, following the insights of James more than anyone else, Duhigg suggests that to break your bad habits, you must identify the cues and rewards, then, you can change the routine. And following Peirce, for some for some of our habits, there's one other ingredient that's necessary, and that's belief. And though experience shows us that habits emerge within the brain and that we often do not have the ability to control them, when we become consciously aware of them, we are able create and cultivate new habits and forge our way for being in the world.

The Value of Relations for Thinking about the Development of Empathy

Certain experiences of relational empathy certainly may come more naturally to some than to others. But is there some innate or natural ability to be great at, say, empathic projection, empathic perspective-taking, or empathic care? Or is it the case that one achieves excellence at acting empathically by nurturing the skill of empathy as well as the habits, actions, and practices that help us to develop this or that type of empathy? This is the same basic structure of Meno's question: Is *arete* derived from some natural capacity or is it nurtured, learned, and developed? Historically, when theories have considered the possibility of empathic development, the abiding tendency has been to think of empathy as being derived from either nature or nurture. This dilemma, emerging out of an unnecessary and distorting dualism, in truth, does not provide for us two options for acting (even though it might be helpful for noting that certain empathic actions seem to be quite natural for some), for the only plan of action before us seems to lie in our attempts to try to develop empathy by creating the right habits to nurture the skills of our empathic powers.

Empathic contagion is an ability we have derived from nature, it is not right nor wrong in some abstract sense; rather, its moral truth or falsity is contingent upon whether we can draw certain relevant conclusions from empirical observations of how it is used in the context of one's life and what consequences experiences of it have or might produce. Empathic contagion, recall, arises whenever we unconsciously catch and co-experience the emotions, feelings, ideas, or perspectives of others. It is a common human experience of empathy and has its origins in the natural, biological, neurological traits and powers of the human body that give rise to this ability. Empathic mimicry, because of the interplay of the relations of feeling into and accurately feeling with, is evident very early in development, for example, when newborn infants cry in response to hearing and feeling another infant's distress. Infants, also, are able to imitate the head movements and tongue-protrusion of adults immediately after being born, and by the age of six weeks, infants can even imitate the actions and expressions of adults stored in their memories.[19] These mimetic powers at an early age can be said to have arisen from our natural and biological powers, but at early ages of childhood development, infants can't take another's perspective until they are at least aged 2.5 years old, but more commonly, not until ages 5–7.

Since our ability to experience empathic contagion, empathic mimicry, and empathic perspective taking occurs at different age levels, it follows from this that these three types of empathy are both limited by—but also enhanced by—biological stages of growth evident in early childhood development. However, it is not the case that all three of these experiences of empathy can equally be nurtured and developed. For instance, empathic contagion doesn't seem to be a type of empathy that can be learned or nurtured, though, I suppose, one could learn how to control this automatic and unconscious experience by other means. Empathic mimicry and empathic perspective-taking can likewise be experienced immediately, but often—as skills—they are not automatic natural processes or systems, but rather take an indefinite amount of time and thus can be developed.

Often, the question of empathic development is posed—not only by the way one defines what empathy is—but how the posing of something as problematic already predetermines the meaning of empathy by means of how the problem itself is perceived and defined. Take for example the experience of autism. Autism is spectrum "disorder," meaning that those who experience this way of being in the world fall on a spectrum between possessing and not possessing the ability both to grasp—feel into and feel with—the inner mentalities of others and communicate satisfactorily with them. As we have noted in the works of Husserl and Stein, the very idea that one could perceive the internal worlds of others by means of empathic perspective-taking and empathic inference is not an idea that is readily accepted by all theorists; nevertheless, certain experiences of autism in which one appears to be unable to *feel with* the mindsets of others are recognized as disorders brought on by nature and are the types of experiences in which one is unable, or at least finds it immensely challenging, to empathize with other people. Though, if one takes up the pluralistic perspective of relational empathy and chooses to think of empathy more broadly, we find that this common narrative is immediately challenged—and there are good reasons for doing this, for it will broaden our understanding by bringing about more inclusive interpretations of this phenomenon.

For instance, people who are classified as being autistic or having autistic traits often possess a remarkable artistic ability to reproduce and draw an object they see for only a few moments, a talent that requires them to both *feel into* and *feel with* objects with uncanny precision and in a manner that resembles the skill of *Einfühlung*, praised so highly by nineteenth-century aestheticians. Moreover, conceptualizing empathic experience according to the relational approach I have put forth here enables us to view empathic experience as feeling into, feeling with, or feeling for, or all three of these together, i.e., relational empathy; this may also help to dispel the falsehood that autistic children are unable to feel for others by expressing empathic concern toward others or providing empathic care to those they love—two ideas which stand as two terrible myths about autism today.

Or take the example of the so-called psychopath or sociopath, two names for persons who are believed to lack an appropriate amount of empathy to care for and act for the benefit of anyone other than themselves. There is a certain amount of vagueness to these two terms, and it is unclear to some if there is a recognizable—valid and observable—bodily pathological condition that is the cause of these ways of being in the world, much less if one's personhood can be described accurately as being either psychopathic or sociopathic.[20] Adding to the ambiguity, there are many narratives about empathy today that view a person's lack of empathy and care for others as a sign of either psychopathy, sociopathy, and/or narcissism. But as it is the case with other labels and forms of identity we affix to persons, the arrival of certain contextualized experiences can change the identity and/or change—or challenge—the meaning of the psychological condition.

A recent neuroscientific study has provided evidence for this claim. Specifically, when they scanned the brains of psychopathic criminals their initial findings discovered that criminals identified in this way were unable to produce a mirroring response when shown images of people in pain. However, when the same group of criminals were asked to focus diligently upon the victim's pain and try to imagine how it felt, their brains gained the capacity to mirror the suffering they witnessed.[21] This demonstrates, among other things, not only that one's definition of "empathy" can shape or reshape the meaning of the identities we affix to it, but also that the experiences of different modes of relational empathy can facilitate the functionality of other modes as was the case here when empathic perspective-taking facilitated empathic contagion.

These reflections upon the experiences of autism and the conditions we have classified as psychopathic or sociopathic do not serve to set a final meaning to these terms. Nor, by any stretch of the imagination should they be thought of as reproaches to those who use these categories out of necessity and for practical purposes. Rather, these reflections show how the acceptance of one definition of "empathy" rather than others, and the inclusion and naming of certain relations of experience as empathic while excluding others, change the very meaning of these experiences and conditions in such a way that previously ignored contexts of experience can provide for us more pluralistic—and accurate—accounts.

Consequently, the adoption of a narrow understanding of the experience of empathy can result in confusion, whereas the adoption of a pluralistic understanding of empathy provides a way for understanding the complexity of phenomena and classifications—these categories, labels, and forms of identity. What is also of note is that it seems the general question of whether empathy can or can't be developed is greatly enhanced when we think about the meaning of empathy contextually—in particular, how a specific notion of empathy has been understood historically, as well as the unique problem it is claimed could be resolved if only one were to adopt a given understanding of empathy and put it to work. The amount of time and practice it takes for any dimension of empathy to be developed is contingent upon certain natural tendencies as well as the arrival of certain developmental stages of childhood, but it is also contingent upon our ability to create and follow sound habits of mind and action that will allow us to put into practice that which is deemed necessary for positive transformation.

Taking up a pluralistic and pragmatic approach leaves one with a much richer perspective wherein one can speak of different dimensions of empathic experience rather than according to a sometimes arbitrary and exceptionally narrow approach. The question of the development of empathy as an experience is likewise seen from a fuller interpretative glance and what is seen as either problematic or beneficial with, e.g., different experiences of autism, is viewed under more appealing—or least differently revealing—lights. How one ought to define empathy and in what manner one ought to speak of empathic development are inextricability intertwined and if one is to think pragmatically, one ought to address these issues considering the uniqueness of different contexts of experiences and the conceivable consequences of thinking about them in one way rather than another.

Developing Relational Empathy

The nature versus nurture debate regarding empathy's possible development is a dead debate, for there is no other option than to try to nurture empathy by developing the habits of feeling into, feeling with, and feeling for that are necessary for personal or collective transformation. Empathy is a powerful skill that can be developed, and to act empathically consistently and in such a way that produces beneficial and satisfactory consequences is a form of excellence.

What "empathy" means is clearly important for determining how it can be developed, and my choice in adopting a pluralistic understanding of empathy means not only that the skill of being empathic is a plural reality, but also that there are multiple related, concomitant skills that will need to be honed to develop this relational type of empathic experience. Though the skill of empathy, whether one thinks of empathy as relational empathy or not, could be thought of as manner of flourishing and as an excellent representation of one's behavior, it can also be recognized in experiences that might be perceived by some as somewhat passive, banal, or ordinary, such as the art of listening empathically to another or even something as simple as holding the door open for someone.

Reflection upon the civilized behavior of holding the door open for another illustrates how relational empathy functions even in our most ordinary and everyday experiences. Imagine you are about to walk through a door at a local store. If you have developed the habit of holding the door open for people, even strangers, who immediately follow behind you as you enter a doorway, you have already practiced relational empathy. Let's say that you have instilled this habit of behavior and have made it a part of your character, the moment immediately before you about to enter through a doorway and reach for the door handle, you take a quick look behind you to see if anyone following you might be inclined to follow you through the passageway. Then, usually, there is a moment when you glean whether that person is intending to follow you through the door. And following this gesture, if you sense that the person aims to enter the passageway after you, then you extend the courtesy of holding the door open for the person.

Each part, the exercise of each relation, is crucial here, and if one step fails to see its completion or if the agent of this civilized act falters, it won't come to fruition. For example, if the agent turns around and doesn't see anyone, the act ends. If the agent fails to look behind (feel into) to see if a person is following him/her, the gesture never begins. If the person behind the agent decides not to follow her/him or the agent doesn't connect with (feel with) the person's intentions, the act falters. Or still yet, if the agent walking through the door looks back and notices that a person is following and wishes to enter the door, but decides to slam the door on the person (i.e., does not feel for), then all three movements of relational empathy did not take place and this act of civilizing behavior clearly did not come to pass.

Experiences of relational empathy, whether similar or dissimilar to the one above (in which all three relations of feeling into, feeling with, and feeling for cooperate in given activity) are myriad. Sometimes experiences like these occur rather naturally, other times they are the result of the habit formations of one's character, while others may arise because of strategic planning. Other understandings of empathy, whether narrowly or broadly conceived, might call for one to develop different types of habits, but for experiences of relational empathy to flower—and considering the history I have narrated—I sense that there are nine habits both to keep in mind and to practice for the purpose of developing the skill of relational empathy.

The first fundamental habit is mindfulness. Mindfulness is a skill that involves most notably, a skillful manner of experiencing the relation of feeling into. The relation—which we noted in the traditions of romanticism and aestheticism as well as in the works of theorists such as Novalis, Herder, Lotze, the Vischers, and Lipps, etc.—is a relation under which may be subsumed all exceptional skills of attentiveness; one of which is what is called *mindfulness*. Among contemporary parlance, mindfulness is often touted as a skill that we should all adopt, though quite often such a narrative, as it is expressed and summarized by the directive "Be mindful," lacks substantiation. Be mindful of what? The answer is not always clear because this maxim itself is devoid of meaning, absent of the object and purpose of one's mindfulness. Consequently, to be mindful means to be mindful of something, person, or situation and thus requires one to select an object(s) of one's attention at the expense of others. For our purposes, by "mindfulness" I mean possessing a lucid awareness of some object of one's conscious perception or reflection.[22] The literature on developing mindfulness as lucid awareness is abundant, especially concerning the skill of becoming lucidly aware of one's body and mind and one's breathing.[23] The practice of relational empathy requires that we are mindful of our present experience, i.e., that we are lucidly aware of some person, thing, and/or situation. The objects of which we are mindful requires us to both *feel into* acutely and *feel with* them correctly. One cannot experience empathy without first being mindful, i.e., that one *feels into* and *feels with* the presence of someone or something, and this involves the act of feeling for the object to such a degree that we desire to be mindful of it. For instance, if I am unable to be mindful of your presence, if I am unaware of your existence, and if I don't recognize your needs, desires, and circumstances as they stand in relation to my life, I cannot possibly have empathy for you because I do not sufficiently care about—feel for—your well-being to become lucidly aware of some aspect of it.

A helpful second habit is often referred to in the literature as *self-empathy*.[24] "Empathy" has most commonly been referred to as the ability to feel into, with, or for other people, but since, the object of empathic consciousness can refer to anything, several psychologists have considered the relational value of self-empathy. Self-empathy can also be seen more generally as a mode of empathic introspection. Relative to our broad understanding of empathy, introspection involves the act of feeling into oneself, while the self-knowledge or, more humbly, self-awareness is recognized when there is there is an apparent agreement or unity between the act of looking inward and understanding accurately or feeling with some trait, habit, or quality of one's character. Self-empathy also seems to entail that one feels for oneself, or put another way, that one has a healthy degree of self-love to make the turn inward for the purpose of becoming something different, someone relatively better that what one once was. The ancient Greeks proclaimed the value of certain type of looking inward, what was called the virtue of *sophrosyne*, which is a lost virtue that needs to be reexplored as a practice that likewise can be instrumental in developing empathy. *Sophrosyne*, which means "nothing in excess," "a balanced life," and "know thyself," as the practice and art of looking inward (feeling into) and grasping the subjective, existential truths that one finds by doing this, is instrumental not only for gaining a vision of what one must do in life but also for coming to terms with how one can act benevolently (feeling for) toward others.

Another habit we will call the *art of appreciation*. This third habit, whether as an activity by which one better understands a situation or as the act of assessing the good qualities and positive value of someone or something, puts to work the relations of feeling into and feeling with persons and things to produce some sense of empathic accuracy. Artistically minded people have mastered this art and exercise it during the process of creating their works. But so too has anyone who is able to appreciate aesthetic objects, for they have honed an ability to become lucidly aware of the objects observed, and subsequently, they are able to grasp with precision the qualities and properties of them. Practicing the art of appreciation also develops one's ability to feel for persons and things in that it cultivates one personal taste and as such assists one in knowing her/his interpretative approach in making judgments. This accomplishment often invites one to enter into dialogue with others concerning the manner in which they feel for persons and things. The art of appreciating the actions of another as well as the unique and admirable qualities of one's character can evoke a feeling of empathic connection with him or her, which can function as an act of feeling for and caring for that person's creative approaches in life. The habit of appreciating others, as the act of recognizing and accentuating the good and positive qualities of others, often serves to build unity between people, which is a foundational experience that establishes loyalty and trust. Opportunities to appreciate the good qualities of another, or the value of something, seem to come naturally for many people, but for those of us who don't appear to have this proclivity or penchant, the act of observing, and noting, how people act in different situations (e.g., "people watching") has the potential to stimulate the art of appreciating others, the circumstances in which they find themselves, as well as the unique quality of things. Observing and interpreting another's body language, whether by means of empathic mimicry or empathic contagion, can also stimulate a feeling of appreciation, which can be communicated to another person in a formative and constructive way. The act of connecting with others, in this or another way, has the potential to create common ground by which one can enter the world of another and simulate (perspective take) sentiments that are radically different from one's own.

A fourth habit, which may counter the illusory tendencies of feeling united or the "same" with other persons and things is the *habit of imagining—and recognizing—difference*. Often, when we have a feeling of being united with certain things rather than others, we tend to gloss over the biases that inform our tastes and loyalties, and we tend to project these biases as well as our falsely constructed presuppositions into the things with which we are feeling united or similar. Feeling united or connected with things as well as recognizing similarities between our experiences and those of others have their contextual places in the movements of positive transformation, but they can also be the source of our greatest folly, our most harmful expressions of ignorance. Our bodies have evolved to notice the similarities and differences of things and between things, and we learned this ability in order to survive. For without it, we wouldn't have survived as a species because we wouldn't have developed the capacity to note the difference between what keeps us alive and what kills us. Other times, noticing differences does not come that easy, especially in those instances when we magically make them the same as something we admire greatly or cherish fervently. The challenge of imagining difference, then, isn't only difficult because we sometimes think of things as the "same" as others—which are, in truth, quite different—but also because differences between things are always emerging through time and the transformations time engenders. One's practice of relational empathy ought to be sensitive to this truth.

Imagining—and accurately perceiving—differences can be enhanced by focusing upon the habit of maintaining openness to the worlds, wills, and experiences of others, whether that comes by means of traveling to a foreign culture or by reading a novel filled with characters whose experiences are radically different from one's own.[25] The contents of a novel as well as the places we visit are often understood accurately by means of *critical thinking skills*, a fifth habit that nurtures empathy. Critical thinking is rarely mentioned as a skill that can facilitate the development of empathy, and historically this has been the case because of the specious tendency to think of the experience of a reflective, cognitive process as being distinct from emotional, affective processes, whether this error in judgment is noted among the ancients or amid the discursive tendencies of contemporary psychologists and neuroscientists. Applying logic and exercising reasoning can help one to develop discernment as to how one should empathize, and for what purpose, and for whose benefit one should to this. Who might be excluded as a consequence of empathizing in one way rather than another, and how might one use reason along with empathic inference to guess what might be the conceivable consequences of one's actions? Both deductive and inductive forms of reasoning can aid one in sharpening one's observational skills (feeling into), and by using analogical reasoning one is better equipped to understand similarities and differences between oneself and others as one attempts to feel with people and things. Abductive reasoning, which is a type of reasoning that uses observation to construct hypotheses, is exceptionally good at assisting one in exercising empathic inference, and consequently, increasing one's empathic accuracy and perspective-taking abilities. Reasoning well can also sharpen one's understanding of cause and effect, enabling one to be able to spot and avoid logical fallacies, and each of these habits has the potential to help one be more accurate with how they empathize with others.

Sometimes the ability to feel with others and grasp what they are experiencing comes to us easily, as we instantly *feel with*, though not necessarily *agree with*, the perspective of another. Other times, we immediately "catch" another's emotion, also without even a modicum of difficulty—for instance, when what someone says resonates, seemingly automatically, within us. On the other side of the spectrum, the experiences, emotions, and perspectives of others are sometimes hidden from us, whether this occurs because we are willfully ignorant of them or simply uniformed. But even if we immediately feel with others, we could be misinformed, but empathically listening, specifically active listening—a sixth habit—can help us to be cautious when making judgments about our own thoughts in relation to the experiences of others. Active listening, though described variously, is generally a three-part movement in which (a) one listens mindfully to what another person is saying by feeling into the words and meaning of another with acuity, (b) by feeling with and grasping accurately what is being said, and (c) by repeating what the person said for the purpose of having the speaker know she/he is being heard, which is an act of feeling and caring for what another has said. All three of these parts of active listening should be conducted with the listener refraining from judgment. What exactly one means by "refraining from judgment" is subject to debate; however, the main idea here is meant to suggest that for one to hear clearly and grasp accurately what another person is feeling and thinking, one must refrain from criticizing the meaning of what one is hearing. Feeling into the words and meaning one is hearing during active listening is the good type of empathic projection and not the type of "projection" that psychologists dread, wherein one's interpretation of what one is hearing is deeply clouded, altered, and filtered, by one's own perspectives and ideals. At the foundation of active listening, as well as any form of empathic listening, lies the sincere act of feeling for another person to such a degree that their ideas, perspectives, and opinions are deemed important enough to hear and consider. Without care and concern, without feeling for the person to whom one is listening, the entire process of actively listening misses the mark.

The final useful skill for developing relational empathy, I will call pragmatic benevolence; it is a skill which, when practiced, involves the imparting of well-being to others through displays of empathic concern and empathic care. *Some* acts of benevolence, such as actions of kindness and helping behavior, have better results than others, and as acts of feeling for are *always* relative to certain relations of experience rather than others.[26] This last point is important to accentuate; since acts of benevolence are always relative to certain relations of experience rather than others, one's choice regarding to whom or to what one should extend benevolence always involves a selection of relations in experience and an exclusion of others. Why this is important should be relatively clear: one's choice to extend benevolence involves a tragic choice in which certain individuals or groups are included as recipients of such benevolence while others are excluded. Sometimes, the only act of the skill of pragmatic benevolence is simply to listen to someone without passing judgment, and sometimes this requires us to remain silent. Another successful way to extend benevolence, from a pragmatic perspective, has very little to do with one's interpersonal relationships but focuses on changing the cultural and social conditions that disallow people to flourish. Imagine two people: one person aims to extend benevolence to all her/his personal friends and acquaintances and another person who aims to extend benevolence by changing the cultural conditions and social structures that keep people from living flourishing lives. Which will have the greatest effects on each of these habits of action can only be worked out in experience; nevertheless, the performance of each approach can only enhance one's ability to empathize.

Technology and Empathic Development

Daily practice of these habits can assist one in nurturing relational empathy. But the future may hold something more for our attempts to develop empathy. In the last twenty years, advances in technology have drastically altered how we perceive the world and interact with one another. The noticeable and drastic effects technology has had upon our lives are interpreted in different ways and depending upon the context of our experience, the way we use technology is viewed as either good or bad, appropriate or inappropriate. If you are sending someone an emergency text, technology is viewed as good, but if someone walks into you accidentally while peering into the portal of an iPhone, technology is bad, a source uncivilized behavior.

Some folks think that we today are losing (or unable to develop) the basic skills of empathy required for the development of significant relationships because of the presence of technology in our lives.[27] In an age of a billion selfies, so the story goes, we are becoming more narcissistic, less courteous, and worst of all, less concerned for the plight of others.[28] A rival interpretation of our current interactions with technology paints a much rosier picture. Technological advances are allowing us to connect with others as never before in human history; and because of this, the world is becoming a smaller place and our opportunities to empathize with others are made available to us within seconds of major global events.[29] But technology doesn't allow us only to empathize with the pain and suffering of others, for it also allows us to make an immediate connection with the joy, exhilaration, and happiness of others.

So here we have two interpretations about technology's effect upon our ability to develop and experience empathy with others—each belief is true within a given context—but one thing is certain: there is no going back. The future will continue to become more computerized, technology will continue to experience exponential growth, and the connections we make with others will be directed, if not dictated, by such advances. Questions concerning what should be done about advances in technology resemble nature/nurture questions in that one side of each of these options confines us to resignation while the other side calls for us to act. On the side of resignation, we could simply continue to note how technological advances are problematic in relation to our ability to nurture relational empathy, while on the hand, we can think about how to use technology to nurture our ability to empathize with other people and things.

Over the last dozen years, forward-thinking people have already begun this task of controlling, or least guiding, technological advances for the purpose of nurturing relational empathy, and the majority of these people have focused on our experiences of how we *feel with* and/or *feel for* other persons and things.[30] Forms of extended reality (XR), specifically, which may include technological advances such as virtual reality, augmented reality, virtual humans, avatars, etc., have largely focused upon our ability to "see the world" through another's point of view by means of creating either embodied simulations that are intended to either test one's ability to perspective take or to widen a participant's view of some outstanding issue.

From a pragmatic perspective, the use of technology enhances our ability to empathize when it avoids the worlds of abstraction and idealism and focuses on real human problems that technology helps to solve—whether that be increasing mindfulness, teaching soft skills for making connections, and/or helping one feel for the well-being of others.[31]

Whatever technological advances may bring, we live in a rather unstable universe, and independent of how well-ordered and carefully structured our plans might be, they are susceptible to randomness and the overabundance of external conflict that works against the force of our wills. Habit formation is the power we have within us that mitigates the randomness when it has made an ally of our nervous system and assists us in establishing regularity and relative uniformity as a counter-measure to instability.[32] Relevant to this work, habit formation is the key to developing empathy, however defined. And although, as I have noted, certain dimensions of relational empathy seem to be much more readily developed than others within certain contexts of experience (e.g., the skill of empathic perspective-taking might be easier to develop than, say, empathic contagion for some people and/or in certain situations), the power of habit fueled by a strong will and an unyielding desire to evoke a recognizable, positive transformation of one's ability to empathize, stands as the great secret to invoke activities of flourishing and excellence.[33]

8

Empathic Democracy as a Way of Life

Quite early one morning, you awake well before your clock normally alarms you to rise and meet the day. The darkness of the night is withering, and the encroaching lights of the sun are dotting the clouded skies with hues of light blue and speckled gray. Now faced with the reality of having to welcome the day before you planned, you decide to go for a walk.

Only a few minutes into your walk, you see a path to your immediate right that you have never noticed before; it is a winding dirt path leading to a forested area. You take the path, but eventually, the differences between the original dirt path and several possible paths become indiscernible to you. Sufficiently awake for a little adventure, you decide to follow down a westward trail that is not well-trodden. After a long time of breaking branches, leaping over logs, and telling yourself over and over that you are quite the trailblazer, you finally reach a point of exhaustion and you sense that the only viable option is to return to the original dirt path.

As you slowly turn around and begin to head eastward back to the original path, your senses are immediately hypnotized by a gigantic and majestic spider web, adorned with thousands upon thousands of dewdrops. This sight alone would capture the perception of anyone who might come across it, but what you find even more interesting is that the light of the sun, now rising on the opposite side of this silky web, is penetrating each dewdrop, filling each with light and an array of different colors. This creates a mirroring effect, for unable to contain all the lights and colors entering it, each dewdrop—out of necessity—reflects its light and color toward other dewdrops. The entire web looks like a kaleidoscope, and you find it difficult to look away, as you stand mesmerized by this unexpected, yet wholly welcomed, sight.

This portrait of an enormous web resembles a popular image found in the traditions of both Hinduism and Buddhism called The Jeweled Net of Indra, a metaphor that is used to explain the interconnected and interrelated nature of all things.

Figure 8 The Guiding Light Appears, walking with John Stuhr.

Imagine a vast and wonderful net hung in the heavens and stretched out infinitely in all directions. Now visualize that at each place where the netting meets, at each node of the entire net where its silky threads meet, there hangs a single glittering jewel; and since the net itself is infinite, these nodes and the jewels placed upon them are likewise infinite in number. If we were to select any one of these jewels for inspection and look closely at it, we would discover that in its polished surface there are reflected all the other jewels in the net, infinite in number. Not only that, but each of the jewels reflected in this one jewel is also reflecting all the other jewels, so that the process of reflection is infinite. Every jewel, then, is intimately connected with all other jewels in the universe, and a change in the colors and lights within one jewel means a change, however slight, in every other jewel. *Whatever affects one jewel, affects them all.*

Though this quasi-religious, mystical description of the interconnected structure of the cosmos may seem to some to be somewhat ambiguous, it is useful as a metaphor for symbolizing the relational and interdependent structure of social reality as well the interconnectedness of communal experience. Extending this interpretation further, we may take the reflective and porous nature of the interrelated jewels upon the net to symbolize individuals within communities or even individual communities within a society.

The Relational Structure of Social Existence and Moral Luck

Relevant to the subject of this work, Indra's Net serves as a poetic image of the relational structure of social existence. Recall that a relation is a mode or manner by which two or more things are connected in experience; thus, the notion of a relational structure of social existence is meant to imply that social reality is *primordially* a relational phenomenon. Individuals and communities, then, are not fundamentally discrete. Their existence is—not unsimilar to the drops upon our silky web or the jewels of Indra's Net—porous, interconnected, and interdependent. Given this fact, relational empathy serves as a tool to improve our social-political relationships with others, contribute to the melioration of cultural conditions, and revive a notion of democracy often touted by American pragmatists: "democracy as a way of life." This notion of democracy as a way of life—fueled by the habits of relational empathy—I will call empathic democracy as a way of life.

The use of this metaphor to signify the relational structure of social existence may not fall gracefully upon the ears of some, considering that within several highly individualistic societies, e.g., in the United States of America, citizens are taught from a very young age that each of them, as an individual self and person, is not only unique and intrinsically special but also distinct from others and thus ultimately responsible for the direction and quality of his or her life. Accompanying this narrative, they are also taught of the importance of independence and self-reliance, two qualities of one's character that are certainly admirable. But within highly individualistic societies an obsessive focus upon these character traits often distorts one's perspective about his or her own social existence. We see evidence for this last claim in a certain type of *social amnesia*, which is recognized when individuals remember and recount the achievements of their lives, while forgetting to remember the roles others have contributed to their success. A central motif of this part of the narrative is often recognized as a belief in the "myth of rugged individualism," which exaggerates the role and power of the individual in society as it overemphasizes the power within the individual to shape his or her destiny.[1]

This mistake isn't simply an error in identifying the nature of the self but also in understanding social ontology, a mistake that was encouraged most notably by the rise of a biological myth of human development, i.e., Social Darwinism.[2]

What is rarely mentioned in this general narrative is that as soon as we enter this world, after making our departure from the dark and warm security of the womb, we are immediately and entirely *dependent* upon the care of others without whom, the cold naked world, with its seemingly unassuming indifference, would bring about a quick end to our existence. The care, concern, and assistance we receive from others during these important, yet impotent, stages of early life are reliant upon the guardians that watched over us, those who practiced the art of relational empathy for the benefit of our continued existence. This existential reliance upon the helpful behavior of others continued, until our budding bodies and blooming brains allow us to make certain choices relatively independently of the will of others.

Nevertheless, during infancy and early childhood, we learn the many different dimensions of empathic consciousness as we communicate our experiences with gestures, emotions; we learn to mimic others, and we eventually gain the capacity to imagine and adopt the roles and perspectives of others. We are socialized. We learn codes of conduct by which to live by, are taught ideas about right and wrong, and begin to formulate for ourselves, however embryonic, our own understanding of the difference between right and wrong behavior. As we grow older, we begin to reflect, question, and doubt things we are told. And spiraling from the early stages, life unfolds, and wholly separate from how we construct our character through the formation of unique habits and skills, we all find that unimaginable and unpredictable circumstances arise, not just in our own lives but in the lives of others.

Our instances of good fortune or triumph mingle with moments of difficulty, hardship, and even tragedy, and what those who observe carefully begin to realize is that the choices we make between the available options are not wholly dependent upon the strength of our wills and power of our actions. One doesn't choose many factors of his or her existence, such as one's ethnicity, the class into which one is born, or other significant factors that might shape one's experience of the world. We did not choose when and where we are born, and our entrance into this world is contingent upon the choices our parents or guardians made. Reflection upon these facts of our existence, one need not take too much time to realize that a host of factors predefine our identities and that, to varying degrees, shape our destinies; moreover, one quickly recognizes that these factors are wholly *independent* of the exercise of will and are wholly *dependent* upon the unfolding of fate. To think otherwise is not only a distortion of reality but also a habitual pattern of misinterpreting social reality by excluding the relations of experience that are empirically instrumental for shaping the *opportunity* that arises or fails to arise throughout our lives.

These opening reflections lay a foundation for establishing an important truism about social reality and democracy, namely that *we are fundamentally dependent beings subject to varying degrees of existential randomness that affect our capacity to self-actualize*. This truth stands as a starting point both for legitimizing democracy (as a form of government) and for embracing democracy as way of life, and what follows here is an attempt to convince you of democracy's inherent value as well as a few ideas as to how to practice empathic democracy as a way of life.

The legitimization of any government or political constitution has always and will always be the task of the political philosophers, who in the past have used various approaches to justify the rule of a government. Some attempts to legitimize the sovereign began with the attempt to establish what it was or what it might be like without the influence of the sovereign, e.g., the state of nature, to justify the sovereign's exercise of power.[3] Other attempts considered the legitimacy of the sovereign in perhaps a more roundabout way either by reflecting upon the nature of justice or by establishing the principles of justice.[4] Once the nature or principles of justice were agreed upon, only then could one reason about what legitimizes the sovereign's rule. I am taking a different path here by focusing on the fact that we are fundamentally dependent beings subject to varying degrees of existential randomness that affect our capacity to self-actualize, this social fact is what we will call *moral luck*. By "moral luck" I mean a force by which we become subject to varying degrees of existential randomness in which circumstances, conditions, and factors beyond our control affect our ability to flourish. Based on the most common way of thinking about the word moral, moral luck might appear as a strange term, and in consideration of this it is necessary to be clear about its meaning, its role in the history of political philosophy, and its importance for legitimizing democratic tendencies and realizing the benefits of practicing empathic democracy as a way of life.

Aristotle provides for us the best, i.e., most pragmatic, account of moral luck. There is no denying the fact that certain people are or will become disempowered in society because of what Aristotle called moral luck, and being disempowered by moral luck means that events and circumstances have affected a person's choices and thus his or her ability to flourish in any activity or in the whole of life.[5] Recall that the best of all possible ends according to Aristotle is to live a life of happiness or *eudaimonia*, which means good-spirited, doing well, and flourishing, and one who is exceedingly and exceptionally "happy" is also excellent. As our own experience shows us, there are many roadblocks that can get in the way of our doing well as well as prevent us from living a life of happiness and excellence. In the *Nicomachean Ethics*, Aristotle refers to two roadblocks on the path to excellence and exploring these will enlighten us as to the main differences between what philosophers call moral luck and what is generally known and understood in experience as simply ordinary luck.[6] Moral luck, whether good or bad, is that which happens to us in life over which we have no control whatsoever, while what I am calling ordinary luck is recognized as any experience in which what we will and over which we have at least a modicum of control is affected by chance circumstances. Moral luck then, has a hand in the shaping of our successes or failures and it is recognized in those moments when we are disempowered because certain circumstances or consequences of our actions lie well beyond our ability to control them.

Lack of control over oneself is another roadblock that can keep us from flourishing. Aristotle called this way of being in the world *akrasia*, i.e., "without power," which occurs when we lack self-restraint, exemplified, for instance, in those moments when we know what to do to flourish in life but voluntarily choose to do what will hurt our chances at flourishing. Perhaps the best translation of this word is being weak-willed. If you have a weak will, it is very unlikely that you will develop the habits necessary to build a strong character, which can empower you to do well in life. In most cases, being disempowered in this way has little, if anything, to do with luck in relation to one's ability to manifest a particular end. However, moral luck, which is our other roadblock on the path to doing well and living a flourishing life, hampers volition and seriously disempowers one's attempts at living happily. As it is the case with ordinary luck, moral luck comes in two forms: bad moral luck and good moral luck, whether the events and choices they have affected are judged good, bad, or simply indifferent.

There have been several contemporary philosophers who have explored moral luck, but most of them have done so for the purpose of calling into question Kant's claim that morality is immune from luck, as for Kant nothing is good except a good will.[7] And almost all writings on the subject, from Aristotle to the presents day, speak about moral luck in relation to moral responsibility, rational actions, the exercise of one's volition, the assignment of blame, and whether certain forms of punishment are just or unjust.[8] Here I want to do a bit more with the concept of moral luck—I want to locate how moral luck (as a force that lies outside of our ability to control its effects upon us) shapes the parameters of political opportunities and thus the ability of some to actualize their potential to flourish in a given activity and/or in life. Moreover, understanding the force of moral luck provides us with a fact of human existence that can be used to legitimize the practice of democracy and to elucidate the need for embracing empathic democracy as a way of life. With an understanding of the powerful effects of moral luck, the practice of relational empathy exercised as a mode of living democratically can function as something melioristic to lessen the potency of bad moral luck.

Three types of moral luck are especially relevant to our social lives and thus affect our chances at doing well in life; as such they help us think about some important questions concerning democracy's legitimacy: *circumstantial moral luck*, *constitutive moral luck*, and *consequential moral luck*.[9] Circumstantial moral luck is recognized in those instances when certain circumstances and conditions of one's life greatly affect that person's chance to flourish; constitutive moral luck is noted in those instances when a person's biological and/or psychological characteristics are a consequence of luck not choice; while consequential moral luck occurs when the future consequences of a person or a group's actions arise quite independently of one's intentions and are therefore not predictable. How precisely these types of moral luck unfold are, of course, a matter of degree and entirely relative to the context of the person or group's life and the way they are affected by the existential randomness of which I speak.

Even though context produces varied experiences of these three types of moral luck, a specific example (for illustrative purposes) is helpful. Imagine a couple in the United States who has just started a family. Each parent grew up in the town in which they now live, and their parents and grandparents were also born and raised locally. Quite unfortunately, moral luck greatly contributed the couple's lives of abject poverty. The parents and grandparents on the mother's side died early deaths after living lives of utter destitution and impoverishment, entirely devoid of opportunities for flourishing. The father's ancestors, on the other hand, lived long lives and tried their best to establish economic security and to live a flourishing life; despite their attempts, there were too many obstacles in the way, too many roadblocks of bad moral luck on their path to a happy and flourishing life. For instance, the father's great-grandparents were denied multiple business loans because of the institutional racism of the time. It was only by means of sheer determination and an uncanny work ethic that the great-grandparents were able to set up a will and leave some money and assets to their children. Unfortunately, the children, i.e., the grandparents of the couple were robbed of their inheritance because of certain loopholes in the laws that were established in their county's courts. Because of these unfortunate events, the couple's ability to flourish and do well in life were greatly affected by the arrival of unjust *circumstantial moral luck*. But that wasn't this couple's only brush with moral luck, for these events were brought into existence by *constitutive moral luck*, by which their physical appearance was deemed untrustworthy by those in power within a racist culture. This led to the couple developing certain psychological habits, such as paranoia and distrust of persons, which were likewise manifestations of this second type of moral luck. These forms of moral luck didn't have to arise in the lives of this couple if the intent of those who went before them were met with more empathic and caring responses regarding the well-being of others. Although the events, situations, and predicaments of circumstantial moral luck and constitutive moral luck cannot be altered by a person or group's will (for no amount of desire or effort can mitigate the full force of these), consequential moral luck can be affected, though not directed, and controlled, by reason and strategic planning. The best form of reasoning for this task is a form of abductive reasoning, an unheralded, though crucial, form of reasoning for social meliorism. Of course, all these types of moral luck do not always have to be roadblocks on the path to a flourishing life, for they can also benefit a person by increasing his/her chances to flourish in some arena of experience; abductive reasoning as the creation of moral hypotheses concerning social uplift, is a productive tool toward this end.[10]

Whatever one's thoughts on the subject, when it comes to issues of justice and fairness, moral luck has had its role to play in peoples' attempts to flourish in life, and as such it stands as a major phenomenon that must always be raised during debates about social justice. Though this is irrefutably true, moral luck ought not to function as an excuse for someone's inability to flourish, but instances of good or bad moral luck could shape a person's entire life and render their wills, however earnest or well-intended, entirely impotent. Good moral luck as a fortunate gift from the universe that one does not ask for, can enhance one's chance to flourish, while bad moral luck often has the opposite effect. And when the effects of moral luck are understood and taken seriously, egregious moral luck is discovered to be one of the fundamental forces of social inequality. We can all recognize this simply by looking at experience, though we might not all agree as to what ought to be done about it, that is, if anything should be done at all. Nevertheless, its presence *legitimizes* democratic ideals and when taken seriously, the fact of moral luck, I argue, can inspire one to practice empathic democracy as a way of life for the purposes of enlarging one's perspective about the human condition as well as for changing the cultural and historical conditions that have contributed to disadvantageous influences of bad moral luck.

The Many Faces and Criticisms of Democracy

It is difficult to appreciate empathic democracy as a way of life without addressing the relative vagueness of the term "democracy" as well as what many suggest are the shortcomings of the democratic process. Investigations into the latter show that the apparent failings of democracy are contingent upon the former, that is, ideas concerning the apparent failings of the process are often shaped by the ambiguity surrounding the term. What is democracy? Well, many things; "democracy" is a word with a long and varied history, democracy is a fluid and debatable concept, democracy is also an ideal, independent of whether a particular ideal becomes manifested in action; democracy also refers to a type of political constitution, a governmental body, a process for making decisions, and it can serve as an idea for establishing communal relationships and arrangements.[11]

There are a few immediate problems with "democracy" that one immediately notices with all meanings of democracy independent of their practical differences, namely, that the manner in which democratic government is run, the way its bureaucracies are structured and how its polices are implemented are often not democratic processes. Second, theorists defined democracy in accordance with what they deemed were the outstanding social problems, historical needs and events arising within the time and place in which they found themselves. Thus, their assessments of democratic governments as good or bad, productive, or problematic cannot be understood independent of their historical situatedness. Historical situations, then, often qualify the value of democratic practices; thus, there can be no final evaluation of democracy. Third, what is determined to be the value of democracy, whether as a democratic ideal, a systematic form of government, or a set of practices, arises out of the selective *interpretations* of value of the actual or conceivable consequences arising from different democratic processes.[12]

As an *ideal*, democracy is a social process in which the views, ideas, and contributions of all people concerned are considered and counted, to varying degrees, equally. We most often think of this process in terms of a governing body or political constitution, so democracy is also a *system* of applying, in the best practical manner, what is held to be ideal, and this can take a variety of forms as a systematic process, e.g., a direct democracy, representative democracy, or constitutional democracy. Democracy is also an assemblage of institutional or social *practices* including but not limited to the elections of officials, the act of voting, and possessing the liberty to express and exchange ideas. Whether as an ideal, a system, a collection of practices, or a combination of these, expressions of democracy are always drawn from historical frames, experiences, and contexts; they always function as temporal solutions to real, though equally, temporal problems and concerns; they are piecemeal and pragmatic answers to outstanding questions about justice, fairness, and inclusion. Democracy—in its best form—serves the needs and demands of changing social circumstances and provides avenues for people to flourish. Based on this, it seems that the most central commonality among conflicting definitions of democracy lies in how they, whether as ideals, systems, or sets of practices, contribute to satisfactory consequences—how they are interpreted to be either functional or dysfunctional within a given community, nation, or bureaucratic system for solving the problems of people. In this way, democracy is always a future-oriented political ideal that is instrumental for engendering positive social change.

But one need only to take a cursory glance at the history of political thought to discover that not everyone has believed democratic government has produced—or can produce—satisfactory consequences. We find this to be true, not only within contemporary theories, but also among the inventors of democracy itself. Plato's theory of the five regimes is exemplary of this; in this theory he describes his fear that democracy produces the disastrous consequence of tyrannical government. Plato's fear (and many similar fears evident through the history of philosophy) is grounded in a fundamental belief that people are not to be trusted with the affairs of the state because they are unable to make the correct political decisions that are necessary for creating a harmonious state.[13] They are also ruled by their irrational passions, so the story goes, and are generally ignorant concerning how political constitutions ought to be conducted. Hobbes contended something similar, namely that since human beings are generally ruled not only by their passions but also their fears, the artificial monster of the *Leviathan* must be formed for the purpose of avoiding a return to the state of nature, a perpetual state of war.

Others argue that the notion of equality is a problematic element of democracy; not so much as an ideal for shaping society by providing citizens with equal opportunity to flourish, but because the very idea of equality often functions to make all ideas equal, independent of their contextual and practical use. This engenders and supports a common narrative that one idea is no better than another, and that there is no ground, such as rationality or expertise, to justify one belief over another. One can argue that this democratization of ideas is one of the sources of what I have called traditional relativism. Some claim that this pattern in a democracy has produced disastrous social effects, in that it tends to produce a culture of uniformed and unenlightened citizens who have not developed the ability to discern between different truth claims; and in favoring the rule of the majority, as it does, the intrinsic dynamic of democracy is not contingent upon the knowledge and expertise of those that are part of the ruling majority.

Considering the fact that most people contend that greatness or expertise is crucial for bringing into existence the best possible results of any particular action, one may be genuinely bewildered at the fact that democracy seems to favor the will of the inexperienced and naïve in relation to the best political ends conceivable. The often-cited example that calls into question some people's loyalty to the democratic process, is an imagined situation in which one is ill and wishes to find and be assessed by the most competent person available. Imagine for a moment that someone has been diagnosed with a fatal illness and begins the process of seeking medical advice to cure her/his medical malady. Wouldn't this person seek out the very best expert in the medical field who might provide a cure? Wouldn't you seek out an expert in the field of medicine that would have the intelligence and means to help you rather than, say, put it to a vote, or some other democratic process in which nonexperts acted as the final arbiters. Analogously, if a society is not running smoothly, it would make sense to choose the politician or political group who were experts in running a government that would produce the best possible ends. And conversely, it doesn't seem to be best to leave the most important decisions a nation faces in the hands of those who have little information, or don't care, about politics. Neither does it seem to be best to allow a majority to make such decisions if they do care about politics but are so biased in their own view and have little empathy for the plight of their fellow citizens. Democratic government or any democratic process in which either nonexperts or biased experts have power to make decisions about the lives, livelihoods, and freedoms of others appears not to be ideal, in any sense of the word.

These common criticisms of democracy ought to be considered as serious threats to democracy's value, whether as an ideal, system, set of practices, or something else entirely, and failure to take them seriously would sound as another disharmonious note in the unreflective song of democratic triumphalism. The central problem with these criticisms is twofold. First, the supporters of these criticisms reject the whole of democracy by including into the calculus of their evaluation of it merely the consequences that they herald as significantly deleterious, while wholly ignoring those consequences of democracy that they have excluded from deliberation. No political constitution is perfect—in fact, nothing is perfect—and every political system that has ever existed has produced both good and bad consequences. Second, and very much related to this first point, those who promulgate these criticisms fail to consider the sociopolitical fact that democracy, rather than being some static entity, is a living and changing reality in which greater participation in its process often yields both a more nuanced understanding of both existing social problems as well as the needs of people. Accordingly, those who adopt these criticisms for the purpose of discounting democracy fail to note greater—more pragmatically beneficial—ends the democratic process may produce, e.g., the personal and social transformation generated from the inclusion of different voices, the personal growth one experiences by listening empathically and compassionately to viewpoints other than one's own, and the visible empowerment gained by the participants of the democratic process. If these criticisms—all of which have been voiced as concerns since democracy began—stand as the sole criteria by which democracy is judged and its progress measured—without a consideration of how democracy is a living entity and dynamic process and absent of a consideration of the other consequences that arise from the process—then clearly these criticisms fall short of providing a complete assessment of the value of democracy if they function as the sole criteria for judging it.

Empathic Democracy as a Way of Life

An attempt to defend all criticisms of democracy would be futile and fatuous, for there are myriad aspects, multiple dynamics of democracy as an ideal, a process, and a set of practices and addressing all of them is not beneficial for our purposes here. But what would be the value in thinking that the practice of democracy is something much larger than all the component parts that we commonly recognize as the fundamental and constituent parts of democracy? What if we were to think of democracy more broadly? What if democracy were understood as a *form of life* rather than simply an ideal, governmental system, bureaucratic process, and political practice? What would it mean to say that the practice of democracy is a *way of life*? And how might the practice of empathy I have outlined in this work facilitate the habits necessary for living democratically?[14]

These questions are not simply rhetorical; they are constructed for the purpose of putting into practice solutions to outstanding problems concerning government, questions about justice, and the challenges people face when trying to live a flourishing life. Meditation upon what pragmatists refer to as democracy as a way of life, I contend, sidesteps many criticisms of democracy by focusing upon the actions we might take to solve social problems as well as by accentuating the positive consequences that emerge out of the practice of democracy; moreover, practicing the habits of relational empathy can facilitate democratic action, specifically *democracy as a way of life*.

Often democracy is, as John Dewey pointed out, what people most commonly believe it to be, that is, a system of elections and conducting government. But it is far more than this, for originally democracy meant simply that "state and society is at one,"[15] which implies that whenever a society changes, the state *ideally* needs to follow the political transformations of society and serve the arising needs of all people within it. This involves the refashioning of the meaning of democracy itself, once there has been a serious consideration of both the effects wrought by social change as well as the significance of real human needs. Recognizing this, Dewey called for a more experimental ideal and practice of democracy that requires *our participation in the construction of its meaning*. He called this activity "creative democracy," a process in which we continually reconstruct the very idea of democracy for the purpose of reconstructing institutions so that they may meet the ongoing, emerging needs of people.

Understood this way, democracy is not some separate and distinct ideal and process unrelated to our lived experiences, but rather, as Dewey noted, "Democracy is a way of life controlled by a working faith in the possibilities of human nature ... put in force in the attitudes which human beings display to one another in all the incidents and relations of daily life."[16] Democracy as a way of life is the compilation of the habits of our lives (e.g., empathic habits), by which this working faith is put into action and is incarnated both in human relationships and in the social process of working together with others toward what are hoped to be socially beneficial ends. The habits of relational empathy are crucial for this creative activity, for they help us to reinvent, reconstruct, and refashion our hope for a better world in response to the problems that emerge from the changing circumstances of social life.

Life is superabundant; it proceeds; and as new sensations, perspectives, and thoughts arise, we become, in some way, something other than we once were. This process, this reality of change, in which life is always in transition, provides the opportunity to rethink and reconstruct our political visions and moral hypotheses. And by making these public, we allow the visions of our melioristic hopes for a better tomorrow to enter public and democratic deliberation. But because life is uncertain; and thus, the nature of "the good" (as well as the arrival of something good in our experiences that will shape a better tomorrow) is uncertain as well, all legitimate visions of democratic life—all acts of creative democracy—are fallible.

For we need not look very far before we discover that many acts of creative democracy end with disastrous results. For instance, we have seen creative constructions of the meaning of democracy in times of totalitarian governments, who used the concept of democracy to serve their own tyrannical campaigns. Sidney Hook, who along with Dewey also encouraged us to think of democracy as a way of life, noted this in the actions of Hitler, Stalin, and Mussolini and the strategies of their dictatorial regimes. Each of these demagogues, says Hook, insisted that their political movements, contrary to belief, were democracies "in the higher sense."[17] In contemporary times, the Democratic People's Republic of Korea, put a creative spin on the meaning of democracy when in its constitution defined the country as a "dictatorship of the people's democracy."[18] And although all these examples are clearly antidemocratic because the *citizens of these regimes are not empowered and have no real political capital*, the point here to be made should not be too difficult to conceive: Creative democracy is happening all the time and sometimes the consequences of creative constructions of democracy's meaning are oppressive. This fact should encourage anyone interested in using democracy as a force for liberation to become a part of its creative reconstruction.

One way we can participate in the construction of democracy's meaning that may help us to grasp the meaning of *democracy as a way of life* involves a rethinking of the Greek word Δημοκρατία ("dēmokratia"). Κρατία ("kratos"), among the ancients, meant both *rule or power*, but when used in reference to a political constitution or theory of government it generally means "rule," and when combined with δημο ("demo") most commonly means *rule by the people*. This, of course, signifies a meaning of democracy as a political constitution or government. But what if for the practical purpose of gaining a better understanding of democracy as a way of life, we interpret *kratos* to signify *power*? In this way when combined with *demo*, democracy as a way life can signify, among other things, *living life in a way that empowers people*. Taking this to another level of interpretation, what would be the instrumental value of thinking of democracy as a way of life, that is, as an approach to living in which one empathizes with the perspective of others, realizes that moral luck affects chances to flourish in life, and tries to empower others by changing the cultural conditions that perpetuate systematic bad moral luck? Could this approach—in addition to all the positive consequences it may produce—legitimize the very spirit of democracy?

Having faith in putting to work the habits of empathy, which serve as instruments for practicing democracy as a way of life, seems to require a certain disposition, character, and temperament, which might be described as a genuine openness to—and preparedness for—social change as well as a *persistent hope* that with collective effort combined with a democratic attunement of real-world problems that threaten human flourishing, our actions have the potential to bring about social meliorism. Throughout the history of philosophy, hope has signified many things, so to be clear about what I mean here, the most common understanding of hope, which I will call expectant hope, is vastly different from the pragmatic hope I endorse here that is relative to both relational empathy and a lived practice of democracy—I will call this pragmatic hope simply *hope in action*.

Expectant hope signifies an internalized, sometimes verbalized, desire for certain outcomes to arise in the future, while hope in action signifies this internalized desire as well as the actions one enacts for the purpose of engendering an individual or group's desires.[19] Hope in action is fundamentally social; it is a socially recognizable act arising from internalized desires in relation to and in consideration of the desires and expectations of others, and in this way it is a version of what pragmatists call *social hope*. Though it is unclear to say that our experiences of hope serve either the individual's personal goals or a community's collective goals, expectant hope often lies dormant within the internalized psychology of an individual. And although this expression of hope sometimes contributes to one's motivation or confidence to act, hope in action is the hope for and the act of engaging and communicating with others, listening to their desires, and working together with them to engender collectively satisfactory outcomes. This requires a willingness to change our desires, reshape of our perceptions, and recognize our biases for the purpose of planning and working together with others democratically.

Throughout the history of philosophy, hope has been defined primarily as expectant hope.[20] In the writings of Dewey and Rorty, we find two well-articulated understandings of social hope. For Dewey, social hope is meliorism—an optimistic stance toward the world, which suggests that we may be able to contribute to human progress, but there is no guarantee that our actions and efforts will result in the ends we desire. The object of meliorism is democracy, which Dewey defines as the simple idea "that political and ethical progress hinges on nothing more than persons, their values, and their actions."[21] Rorty operationalizes social hope by its relevance to liberalism and the need for ongoing conversation. In the act of engaging others in political conversation, hope, says Rorty, operates as a "hope for agreement, or at least, exciting and fruitful disagreement," as well as "an attempt to create solidarity out of shared experiences and interests."²² I take my cue from each of these thinker's articulations of social hope by suggesting that hope in action refers to a social action perpetuated by the spirit of meliorism and reconstructed through the process of conversation, movements of inclusivity, and actions aimed to change unjust cultural conditions. Conceived in this way, hope in action as a mode of social hope is also a continual pragmatic fashioning of reality, which the American Pragmatist John Stuhr notes, "is always an ongoing refashioning and always a hope for a better understanding, a different understanding."²³

The mood to furnish this character and temperament of hope in action, by which one is open to and prepared for social change, is what James called the *strenuous mood*. An adoption of the strenuous mood provokes one to recognize the existence of conflicting ideals and hopes as well as the fact that while some hopes are fulfilled, others are dashed; thus, pragmatic pluralism as well as all melioristic social projects, says James, "has to fall back on a certain ultimate hardihood, a certain willingness to live *without assurances or guarantees*."²⁴ By adopting the strenuous mood, the question of the legitimization of one's social hope is displaced by an honest recognition of the smallness, fragility, and shortsightedness of every melioristic hope for a better future. Certain idealists, rationalists, and other absolutists were for James *dispellers of uncertainty*—they feared uncertainty and wished to banish it by successfully completing what Dewey called "the quest for certainty."²⁵ The faith in absolutes, exemplified by those dispellers of uncertainty who were quite often rationalists, was for James similar to taking a permanent moral holiday from our feelings of moral uncertainty and incompleteness.²⁶ Instead of taking a moral holiday, an adoption of the strenuous mood calls us to turn and return to experience and fall back "on a certain ultimate hardihood, a certain willingness to live without assurances or guarantees."²⁷ James contrasts this strenuous mood with the *easygoing mood*, in which shrinking from present ill is our ruling consideration. The difference between these two moods, says James, is the deepest practical difference in the moral life of people. An adoption of the strenuous mood provokes one to recognize the existence of conflicting democratic ideals and melioristic hopes as well as the fact that while some hopes are fulfilled, others are dashed. These truths of experience, rather than being interpreted as problematic, ought to be recognized as opportunities to practice relational empathy, to strive toward a greater ideal—inclusivity.

An ethical philosophy based on empathy and inclusivity as well as all other ethical philosophies, as James notes, do not engender a "final truth" *until the last person has had her or his experience and her or his say*.²⁸ This is a gentle way of stating that since life is always in transition, there can never be a final truth in ethics because there will never be a time when everyone has had their say. We are always on the way to doing well in life and life itself is always in transition, and it follows from this that the exercise of relational empathy, as a vehicle for democratic engagement with others toward inclusive ends, may be perceived accurately as a perpetual act that never reaches a final terminus. Adopting the terminology of James and being playful with his perspective, relational empathy, when combined with living democratically, can function as a habit of hope in action that aims to satisfy—at all times—as many demands as it can, while awakening the least sum of dissatisfactions for the purpose of producing the best whole, that is, the *most inclusive whole*.[29]

Relational empathy as a tool for satisfying demands and engendering the most inclusive whole, following James's philosophical spirit, requires the cooperation of many independent persons, which arises because of the precursive faith in one another of those immediately concerned.[30] Without faith in and cooperation with others, acts of satisfying demands will never give rise to or allow us to question the meaning and attainment of the most inclusive whole. Recognizing the uncertainty of our social hope for a better tomorrow may not seem very inviting to those who believe that their visions for a better tomorrow are infallible; the deep-seated emotional connection to our melioristic visions is difficult to challenge or abandon, even when we recognize their impracticality. But it is the reality of this uncertainty that one must embrace if one is concerned with solving the greater problems that arise *when social hopes clash* or *when moral goods conflict* with one another.

The claim that relational empathy can serve as a vehicle for manifesting social hope—as hope in action—is a moral hypothesis (as is every goal of bringing about a better world), and its success hinges on the uncertainties of limited perspectives. If one is disinclined to embrace this truth, this patent uncertainty, one can always find a secure sanctuary for one's mind by following the patterns of Western philosophy—for instance, by believing in eternal Forms, an overarching *logos*, an Unmoved Mover, the One, the unfolding of Geist, Monads, the categorical imperative, the transcendental ego, the thing-in-itself. Or perhaps, some other mythological construction from a non-European culture will suffice for banishing the unwanted feelings that uncertainty brings? Or maybe, we should begin another "quest for certainty" and finality in order to feel the soft, warming—sometimes delusional—glow that feelings of certainty about the future bring.[31] One can always find sanctuary in the history of philosophy and its declarations of soothing absolutes and final truths about experience, but those who adopt the strenuous mood resist this temptation, however seductive it might be.

The ideality of hope in action guided by the strenuous mood is tamed by the realization that we are deeply biased, and we are so, not intentionally, but rather because of the limits of our experiences and the relative selectiveness of our interpretations. Often when we think about biases, we tend to think of them in terms of something that are generally bad and ought to be banished from our lives. I suggest that just the opposite ought to be the ideal—namely, we ought to admit and make public the way we are biased for the purpose of entering into a quite humbling democratic deliberation with others. Practicing the habits of relational empathy has the potential to encourage us to recognize and challenge our presuppositions, which provides the conceptual spaces to reflect upon and admit the shortsightedness of our humanistic visions and our moral hypotheses, as well as the biases that sustain these. Recognizing that our biases are part and parcel of our interpretations of the world is not usually considered an important goal to be attained in any circumstance, much less when one thinks about one's social hopes. Admitting our biases seems contrary to our intuitions, perhaps, for it seems that biases are those aspects of ourselves we often ignore (or hide from the view of others). Experiencing the habits of relational empathy, however, can provoke us to challenge our presuppositions, to admit our biases, and even to reprogram our minds and to change our habits of behavior by considering the needs of others. For by projecting thoughts and feelings out of ourselves—not unlike a movement of ecstasy—we put ourselves in a position to reevaluate our ideas and beliefs as we encounter the experiences of others. This, in turn, affords us the opportunity to feel with and feel for others who have radically different senses than ours. This movement resembles dialogue or open and direct conversation, but without challenging the presuppositions that fuel our social activities and participation in each democratic process, we are simply regurgitating our presuppositions and biases. There are no guarantees that practicing the habits of relational empathy will, independent of our intent, affect the world in some morally satisfactory way. Life is uncertain; and thus, satisfactory moral ends—as well as hope for a better tomorrow—is uncertain as well.

Nevertheless, I think one could admit, without causing much of a stir, that adopting the habits of empathy can help us to widen the windows of our perception and expand the limits we place upon our own interpretations, each of which in turn can help us to admit our biases as we practice democracy as a way of life. The habit of empathic projection, for instance, in which we feel our way into things, propels us out of ourselves and encourages us to move beyond the limits of what we currently believe is obvious or uncontestably true in life. When exercised as a daily activity, empathic projection also impels us to encounter how others are both similar and different from ourselves, and these types of encounters can encourage us to feel for and act for the benefit and well-being of others. One consequence of this habit can be open and beneficial dialogue within a community, whether this stimulates what Rorty called a conversation of agreement or exciting and fruitful disagreement or, in Stuhr's words, a hope for a better and different understanding. Practicing the habit of feeling for, in which we show public concern and care for other persons or things, likewise assists us in widening the windows of our perception. For by expressing our concerns and cares socially, we display our interests and acts of care publicly; and consequently, we put ourselves in a position to engage with others, listen attentively to their viewpoints, and take seriously the actions they take to exhibit their ideas and perspectives socially.

Relational empathy combined with the practice of democracy as a way of life can also propel one beyond what she/he currently conceives to be political and social justice issues, and this in turn has the potential to expand one's sociopolitical imagination. Often what we believe is socially problematic is wholly confined to and defined by the ingrained and limited perspectives we have learned as well as the political allegiances we hold. Polarization in political life solidifies biases and confines our thoughts, but empathy is the vehicle by which we can visit, grasp, and access the positions of those wholly opposed to one's political loyalties.

This might sound nice in the abstract, but you only need to turn to your own experiences to recognize that, if you are politically loyal to certain ideas over others, then it might not be best to forsake you own political beliefs if indeed what you believe in is consistently producing socially beneficial ends, for example, more opportunities for people to flourish in life. Practicing empathy when considering political views that oppose one's own will probably not lead to one abandoning the political ideals, allegiances, and actions that one favors—this rarely, if ever, happens and probably shouldn't be the goal. Nevertheless, becoming mindful, perceiving acutely, and grasping accurately the political positions others hold can assist one in feeling for others and how circumstances in life have contributed to one's own position as well as the positions of others.

Too often throughout its history, empathy has been conceived as a capacity, an intellectual and sentimental tool, by which we only attain agreement with others—whether that be by being empathically accurate with other's perspective or whether we recognize that our experiences and perspectives are like others.

The aforementioned ideas concerning the benefits of applying the habits of empathy as one practices democracy as a way of life resists this, and for good reason. How often do we believe that our thoughts or actions agree with those of others, only to find out upon another moment of reflection that our assessment of similarity between our ideas and actions and those of others has been made in haste or that we have assumed far too much in the act of such a comparison?

Historically, the study of empathy as *feeling with* has fixed its attentive gaze upon the apparent agreement between observers and object(s) observed. The agreement is recognized in many different manifestations of this relation, such as the arrival of agreement between two people who once had different perspectives; an agreement between an observer and a work of art; an emotional agreement between two or more persons who, say, might equally find a certain subject to be humorous; or even a kinesthetic agreement between the movements of two dogs who are functionally in unison while pulling a sled. But what if empathic acts of feeling into and feeling with other people or things do not yield neither a sense of agreement nor a recognition of similarity? Recognition of the similarity between things as well as the act of designating "sameness" between two things that are distinctly different phenomenologically are functionally and practically useful actions, but it is also clear that these two actions also function to satisfy, even mollycoddle, our senses when we are assigned the difficult task of recognizing important differences between ourselves and others. And sometimes, despite one's intentions, the recognition of *similarity* and/or the designation of *sameness* can lead to a certain type of ignorance in which empathy as an expression of goodwill does more harm than good or even when it reinforces violence.[32]

Contesting the feeling of similarity—and identity—between our perspectives and those of other persons need not lead us to think that having a feeling of empathic connection with them is misguided. Nor should our skepticism concerning these relations between our beliefs and the opposing beliefs of others lead to a rejection of our experiences of *empathic connection* with them. For the experience of empathic connection, as a type of resonance—but not agreement—with beliefs and lifestyles different from our own, provides the opportunity for having solidarity with others, even if we don't wholly understand or agree with their perspectives. The social solidarity I have in mind here resembles what Cynthia Willett has coined a *solidaric mode of empathy*, an experience of empathy as the relation of *feeling with* that Willett notes "can travel across conflicting social groups."[33] So, although feeling with others is often assumptive, by falsely imagining that one's own positions, perspectives, and beliefs are the same as others, *feeling with others as a solidaric mode of feeling*, a connection or resonance with the experience of others, seems both more realistic and practical while avoiding the—all too common—tendency to assume identity between ones experiences and those of another when none exists.

One way we can both widen our perspectives and challenge our presuppositions and biases is by reflecting upon the problem of moral luck, as well as the indefatigable truth that moral luck extends into every person's life and affects every person's capacity to invite well-being into their lives. Let's call the realization of the problem of moral luck in one's life as well as in the lives of others, *a recognition of the mirrored circumstance of moral luck*. Recognizing the mirrored circumstance of moral luck is available to anyone at any moment if they only are inclined to indulge in it. This type of reflection begins by feeling into the situations, circumstances, as well as good or ill fortune that has affected one's own life choices, one's will—and even destiny—in life, and becoming mindful of how moral luck has influenced one's opportunities in life. This is followed by feeling with and grasping the influence of those moments and events of empathic connection that one can quite easily recognize as being either beneficial or detrimental to one's ability to self-actualize and flourish in life. Feeling for, caring about, and showing concern for the forces of moral luck as it influences the lives of others is an act of awareness, occurring whenever one *feels into* and *feels with* the conditions, situations of one's experiences, and how these disallow one to flourish. Recognition of one's own brushes with the power of moral luck, then, serves as an impetus for one to recognize—or imagine—this reality in the lives of others.

We are alive for a short time; we—all of us—are momentary and moving beings of flesh and bone who arise out of the earth, will return to the earth, and—within one sliver of the truth—are the eyes and sensations of the earth. And among and throughout this flash of existence we call life, we can develop certain habits—as skills—to the extent fate allows. One of these skills is empathy, which is a power that we can harness; it is a strength with which we can produce good, bad, or indifferent consequences. It is a gift, here for us to open at any moment by the power of our will, and we can use this gift to increase our power to understand and love and to empower others to so the same. The enemy of these movements is discovered in another fact of our existence, namely that we are all trapped in our interpretative circles which, laced with biases and presuppositions, keep us hypnotized by the thundering sounds of our limited perspectives. Acts of transcending our perspective and leaving behind our situatedness are not options; though, by the exercise of relational empathy we are always invited to widen our perspective and wonder about the state of our situatedness in relation to the experiences of others.

The theory I have put forth here of relational empathy, drawn from historical conceptualizations of what were deemed to be empathic experiences, should not be considered as an attempt to stipulate the final word about empathy. There can never be a final word about empathy, any more than there can be a final word about experience. Ultimately, the value of the type of empathy I have narrated here will be recognized in the consequences the practice of it produces in life; though, I do suspect that what I have called "relational empathy" here will someday just be referred to as "empathy proper," once—and if—it runs through the classic stages of a theory's career:

> First, you know, a new theory is attacked as absurd; then it is admitted to be true, but obvious and insignificant; finally it is seen to be so important that its adversaries claim that they themselves discovered it.[34]

Notes

Preface

1 Edith Stein, *On the Problem of Empathy*, trans. Waltraut Stein (The Hague: Martinus Nijhoff, [1917] 1964), 63.
2 Jean Decety, *Empathy: From Bench to Bedside* (Cambridge, MA: MIT Press, 2012), vii.
3 Simon Baron-Cohen, *The Science of Evil: On Empathy and the Origins of Cruelty* (New York: Basic Books, 2012), 16.
4 Frederique de Vignemont and Tania Singer, "The Empathic Brain: How, When, and Why?," *Trends in Cognitive Sciences* 10, no. 10 (2006): 435–441.
5 William Ickes, *Empathic Accuracy* (New York: Guilford Press, 1997); and Nicolas Danziger, Kenneth M. Prkachin, and Jean-Claude Willer, "The Perception of Others' Pain in Patients with Congenital Insensitivity to Pain," *Brain* 129, no. 9 (2006): 2494–2507.
6 Edward B. Titchener, *Lectures on the Experimental Psychology of the Thought-Processes* (New York: MacMillan, 1909).
7 Carl Rogers, "The Necessary and Sufficient Conditions of Personality Change," *Journal of Consulting Psychology* 21, no. 2 (1957): 95–103.
8 Baron-Cohen, *Science of Evil*; and Simon Baron-Cohen, "The Male Condition," *New York Times*, August 8, 2005, A15.
9 Peter Goldie, *The Emotions: A Philosophical Explanation* (Oxford: Oxford University Press, 2002), 195.
10 C. Daniel Batson and Kathryn C. Oleson, "Current Status of the Empathy-Altruism Hypothesis," in *Prosocial Behavior*, ed. Margaret S. Clark (Newbury Park, CA: SAGE, 1991), 63; Nancy Eisenberg and Richard A. Fabes, "Prosocial Development," in *Handbook of Child Psychology: Social, Emotional, and Personality Development*, ed. William Damon and Nancy Eisenberg (Hoboken, NJ: John Wiley & Sons, 1998), 702; and Martin Hoffman, *Empathy and Moral Development: Implications for Caring and Justice* (Cambridge: Cambridge University Press, 2000), 4.
11 Margaret Graver, *Cicero and the Emotions: Tusculan Disputations 3 and 4* (Chicago: University of Chicago Press, 2002), 79; Dana LaCourse Munteanu, *Tragic Pathos: Pity and Fear in Greek Philosophy and Tragedy* (Cambridge: Cambridge University Press, 2012), 50; and Aquilino Cayuela, "Vulnerable: To Be between Life and Death," in *Human Dignity of the Vulnerable in the Age of Rights: Interdisciplinary Perspectives*,

ed. Aniceto Mansferrer and Emilio Garcia-Sanchez (New York: Springer International, 2016), 63–79.

12 William James, "A World of Pure Experience," in *Essays in Radical Empiricism*, ed. William James (New York: Longmans, Green, and Co., [1912] 1996), 39–91.

Chapter 1

1 Adam Smith's notion of "sympathy" is *close* to what people today mean by empathic perspective-taking. See, Adam Smith, *Theory of Moral Sentiments*, ed. David Daiches Raphael and Alec Lawrence Macfie (Indianapolis, IN: Liberty Fund, [1779] 1984), 9–13. For a few contemporary definitions of empathy as empathic perspective-taking, see Goldie, *Emotions*, 195; Jean Decety and Andrew N. Meltzoff, "Empathy, Imitation, and the Social Brain," in *Empathy: Philosophical and Psychological Perspectives*, ed. Amy Coplan and Peter Goldie (Oxford: Oxford University Press, 2011), 76; Heidi L. Maibom, "Introduction: Almost Everything You Ever Wanted to Know about Empathy," in *Empathy and Morality*, ed. Heidi L. Maibom (New York: Oxford University Press, 2014), 12; and Derek Matravers, *Empathy* (Malden, MA: Polity Press, 2017), 1–2.

2 See C. Daniel Batson, "Two Forms of Perspective Taking: Imagining How Another Feels and Imagining How You Would Feel," in *Handbook of Imagination and Mental Simulation*, ed. Keith S. Markman, William M. P. Klein, and Julie A. Juhr (New York: Psychology Press, 2009), 267–279. See also Batson's earlier collaborative work on this distinction: C. D. Batson, Shannon Early, and Giovanni Salvarani, "Perspective Taking: Imagining How Another Feels versus Imagining How You Would Feel," *Personality & Social Personality Bulletin* 23, no. 7 (1997): 751–758.

3 The social psychologist William Ickes has conducted several studies of empathic inference and its relation to empathic accuracy (i.e., "mindreading"), defining the latter as the measure of ones' ability to infer accurately the specific content of other people's thoughts and feelings; see William Ickes, *Empathic Accuracy* (New York: Guilford Press, 1997), 2–6. For an earlier account, see Rogers, "Necessary and Sufficient Conditions"; and Norman Malcolm, *Knowledge and Certainty: Essays and Lectures* (Englewood Cliffs, NJ: Prentice-Hall, 1963), 130–140. For contemporary descriptions of the mode of empathy, see Alvin I. Goldman, *Simulating Minds: The Philosophy, Psychology and Neuroscience of Mindreading* (New York: Oxford University Press, 2006); and Karsten Stueber, *Rediscovering Empathy: Agency, Folk Psychology, and the Human Sciences* (Cambridge, MA: MIT Press, 2010), 5–19, 202. For another definition of "empathy" as empathic inference, see Danziger, Prkachin, and Willer, "Is Pain the Price of Empathy?," 2494.

4 Empathic contagion is recognized as a part of David Hume's early account of sympathy, which he describes as a bodily psychological mechanism with which we

"catch" the sentiments/passions of others via the conversion of an idea into a felt impression. See David Hume, *Treatise of Human Nature*, ed. L. A. Selby-Bigge (New York: Oxford University Press, [1738] 1978), 319–320. See also David Hume, *Enquiries Concerning Human Understanding and Concerning the Principles of Morals*, ed. L. A. Selby-Bigge (New York: Oxford University Press, [1748] 1975), 75–79, 250–251. For contemporary accounts of this mode of empathy, see Michael Slote, *Moral Sentimentalism* (New York: Oxford University Press, 2010), 15; and Jesse Prinz, "Is Empathy Necessary for Morality?," in Coplan and Goldie, *Empathy*, 212.

5   See Frans de Waal, *The Age of Empathy* (New York: Harmony Books, 2009), 52, and his entire discussion on synchrony as exemplary of empathic connection (pp. 46–53). For other elaborations on the notion of synchrony as a fundamental part of empathic connection, see Robert W. Levenson and Anna M. Ruef, "Physiological Aspects of Emotional Knowledge and Rapport," in Ickes, *Empathic Accuracy*, 44–69. On empathic connection as a type of empathy, see Ervin Staub, "Commentary on Part I," in *Empathy and Its Development*, ed. Nancy Eisenberg and Janet Strayer (New York: Cambridge University Press, 1990), 110–111, 114; and Roman Krznaric, *Empathy: Why It Matters, and How to Get It* (New York: Random House, 2014), 43, 55. On empathic connection and mirror neurons, see Marco Iacoboni, *Mirroring People: The New Science of How We Connect with Others* (New York: Farrar, Straus and Giroux, 2008); and Marco Iacoboni and Mirella Dapretto, "The Mirror Neuron System and the Consequences of Its Dysfunction," *Nature Reviews Neuroscience* 7, no. 12 (2006): 942–951.

6   See Sheldon J. Korchin, *Modern Clinical Psychology: Principles of Intervention in the Clinic and Community* (New York: Joanna Cotler Books, International Edition, 1978), 148–149; Janet Beavin Bavelas et al., "Motor Mimicry as Primitive Empathy," in Eisenberg and Strayer, *Empathy and Its Development*, 317–338; Tiffany M. Field et al., "Discrimination and Imitation of Facial Expression by Neonates," *Science* 218, no. 4568 (1982): 179–181; see also De Waal, *Age of Empathy*, 53–65.

7   See C. Daniel Batson and Laura L. Shaw, "Evidence for Altruism: Toward a Pluralism of Prosocial Motives," *Psychological Inquiry* 2, no. 2 (1991): 107–122; Marco Dondi, Francesca Simion, and Giovanna Caltran, "Can Newborns Discriminate between Their Own Cry and the Cry of Another Newborn Infant?," *Developmental Psychology* 35, no. 2 (1999): 418–426; and Jean Decety and Claus Lamm, "Empathy versus Personal Distress: Recent Evidence from Social Neuroscience," in *The Social Neuroscience of Empathy*, ed. Jean Decety and William Ickes (Cambridge, MA: MIT Press, 2009), 199–213.

8   See Yoni K. Ashar et al., "Empathic Care and Distress: Predictive Brain Markers and Dissociable Brain Systems," *Neuron* 94, no. 6 (2017): 1263–1273; and Decety, *Empathy*, vii.

9. Anna Aragno, "The Language of Empathy: An Analysis of Its Constitution, Development, and Role in Psychoanalytic Listening," *Journal of American Psychoanalytic Association* 56, no. 3 (2008): 714.
10. See Gregory Currie, "Empathy for Objects," in Coplan and Goldie, *Empathy*, 82–98; and Graham McFee, "Empathy: Interpersonal vs. Artistic?," in Coplan and Goldie, *Empathy*, 185–210.
11. Novalis bemoaned the rigid views of his contemporaries, whose representations of nature failed to be substantially moved by the beauty and wonder of nature. Mystical experiences, which seem to be the core of all religious experiences, are often described as having feelings of being at one with all things.
12. Johann Gottlieb Herder, "Vom Erkennen und Empfinden der menschlichen Seele," in *Herders Werke*, Vol. 3 (Berlin: Aufbau Verlag, [1774] 1964), 3:7–8.
13. Johann Gottlieb Herder, *Sämmtliche Werke*, ed. Bernhard Suphan (Berlin: Weidmann, 1877–1937), 5:502–503, 506.
14. See Amy Coplan, "Will the Real Empathy Please Stand Up? A Case for a Narrow Conceptualization," *The Southern Journal of Philosophy* 49, supp. 1 (2011): 40–65.
15. Coplan, "Will the Real Empathy Please Stand Up?," 44.
16. Coplan notes, "I consider these processes to be distinctive enough to warrant distinctive labels. In addition, the terms 'emotional empathy' and 'cognitive empathy' are not used uniformly. Thus, some researchers use emotional empathy to refer to emotional contagion, while others use emotional empathy to refer to any empathic process involving an emotion, and still others use the term to refer to cases of empathizing with someone who is experiencing emotion (as opposed to someone who is thinking or reasoning)" (Coplan, "Will the Real Empathy Please Stand Up?," 51, n. 17).
17. See, for instance, Elaine Hatfield, John T. Cacioppo, and Richard L. Rapson, *Emotional Contagion* (Cambridge: Cambridge University Press, 1994); Stephen Darwall, "Empathy, Sympathy, Care," *Philosophical Studies* 89, no. 2–3 (1998): 261–282; Hoffman, *Empathy and Moral Development*; and De Waal, *Age of Empathy*.
18. This is well known. Jean Decety and Kalina J. Michalska argue that the "construct of empathy needs to be 'broken down' into a model that includes bottom-up processing of affective communication and top-down reappraisal processing in which the perceiver's motivations, intention, and attitudes influence the extent of empathic experience" (Decety, *Empathy*, 167).
19. Slote, *Moral Sentimentalism*, 15; see also Michael Slote, *The Ethics of Care and Empathy* (New York: Routledge, 2007).
20. Slote, *Moral Sentimentalism*, 33.
21. Jesse Prinz, "Against Empathy," *The Southern Journal of Philosophy* 49, supp. 1 (2011): 212.
22. See Xiaojing Xu et al., "Do You Feel My Pain? Racial Group Membership Modulates Empathic Neural Responses," *Journal of Neuroscience* 29, no. 26 (2009): 8525–8529;

and Jennifer N. Gutsell and Michael Inzlicht, "Empathy Constrained: Prejudice Predicts Reduced Mental Simulation of Actions during Observations of Outgroups," *Journal of Experimental Social Psychology* 46, no. 5 (2010): 841–845.

23. C. Daniel Batson et al., "Immorality from Empathy-Induced Altruism: When Compassion and Justice Conflict," *Journal of Personality and Social Psychology* 68, no. 6 (1995): 1042–1054.

24. Prinz, "Against Empathy," 213, 214–233.

25. This is his most recent and succinct definition of empathic concern. See C. Daniel Batson, *A Scientific Search for Altruism: Do We Only Care about Ourselves?* (New York: Oxford University Press, 2019), 29.

26. C. Daniel Batson, "These Things Called Empathy: Eight Related but Distinct Phenomena," in Decety and Ickes, *Social Neuroscience of Empathy*, 3–15.

27. Decety and Ickes, *Social Neuroscience of Empathy*, 3–15; and Prinz, "Against Empathy."

28. Stephanie D. Preston and Frans de Waal, "Empathy: Its Ultimate and Proximate Bases," *Behavioral and Brain Sciences* 25, no. 1 (2002): 4, emphasis mine.

29. Amy Coplan, "Understanding Empathy: Its Features and Effects," in Coplan and Goldie, *Empathy*, 5, n. 19.

30. Historically, several philosophical voices have had their say about what many call today "empathy." For instance, the Counter-Enlightenment romanticists of the late eighteenth century, the moral sentimentalists of the Scottish Enlightenment, and early twentieth-century phenomenologists (e.g., Scheler and Stein) have all had their say. More recently, psychologists, neuroscientists, and analytic philosophers have seemed to dominate the academic perspective on this debatable and attractive phenomenon. Very little, however, has been offered explicitly from the tradition of pluralistic pragmatism (with the exception of George Herbert Mead), but it is this tradition, primarily as it was envisioned though the perceptive eyes of William James, that I will follow for the purpose of creating a more encompassing vision for understanding and practicing empathy.

31. William James, *A Pluralistic Universe: Hibbert Lectures at Manchester College on the Present Situation of Philosophy* (Lincoln: University of Nebraska Press, [1909] 1996), 97.

32. Decety and Ickes, *Social Neuroscience of Empathy*, vii.

33. Baron-Cohen, *Science of Evil*, 16.

34. de Vignemont and Singer, "Empathic Brain," 435.

35. Danziger, Prkachin, and Willer, "Is Pain the Price of Empathy?," 2494.

36. Baron-Cohen, "Male Condition," A15.

37. Goldie, *Emotions*, 195.

38. Matravers, *Empathy*, 1–2.

39. See, for example, Batson and Oleson, "Current Status," 63; Eisenberg and Fabes, "Prosocial Development," 702; and Hoffman, *Empathy and Moral Development*, 4.

40 Throughout the history of philosophy, we find an obsessive focus upon philosophical problems that are never resolved, the so-called perennial problems of philosophy: the mind-body problem, the problem of evil, even something called the "problem of other people's minds." If we understand these as the "eternal" problems of philosophy, we are excluded from thinking about them according to different relations, e.g., the historical and cultural relations that have contributed to their rise, the relations of their practical use, etc. By focusing on these often-ignored relations, however, we can recast these so-called perennial problems and inject some color into them by historicizing, contextualizing, and pluralizing them, which helps us to consider their value in relation to lived experience.

41 James, *Essays in Radical Empiricism*. Pure experience, as James describes it in *Essays in Radical Empiricism*, is the one primal stuff or material in the world, the immediate flux of life, and the undifferentiated flow of experiential relations, which "furnishes the material to our later reflection with its conceptual categories ... full both of oneness and manyness, but in respects that don't appear; changing throughout, yet so confusedly that its phases interpenetrate, and no points, either of distinction or of identity, can be caught" (pp. 93–95).

42 See Marcus Tullius Cicero and Margaret R. Graver, *Cicero on the Emotions: Tusculan Disputations 3 and 4* (Chicago: University of Chicago Press, 2002), 79; Munteanu, *Tragic Pathos*, 50; Cayuela, "Vulnerable." See also the O.E.D. definition of pathos (2a): "To have experience of; to meet with; to feel or undergo"; Margaret Graver describes this general and neutral sense of *pathos* as "a broad and colorless term, roughly equivalent to 'experience' in English"; in Plato's *Gorgias*, we find one such example of *pathos* as a general experience: "Well, Callicles, if human beings didn't share common experiences [*pathos*], some sharing one, others sharing another, but one of us had some unique experience [*pathos*] not shared by others, it wouldn't be easy for him to communicate what he experienced [*pathema*] to the other" (Plato, *Complete Works*, trans. John M. Cooper (Indianapolis, IN: Hackett, 1997), 481c, 826).

43 For more on philosophical genealogy, see Mark Bevir, "What Is Genealogy?," *Journal of the Philosophy of History* 2, no. 3 (2008): 263–275; Brian Lightbody, *Philosophical Genealogy: An Epistemological Reconstruction of Nietzsche and Foucault's Genealogical Method*, Vol. 1 (New York: Peter Lang, 2010); see also Brian Lightbody, *Philosophical Genealogy: An Epistemological Reconstruction of Nietzsche and Foucault's Genealogical Method*, Vol. 2 (New York: Peter Lang, 2010).

Chapter 2

1 See Chapter 1, n. 42, of this work.

2   Aristotle, *Rhetoric*, trans. W. Rhys Roberts (Fairhope, AL: Mockingbird Classics, 2015), 1378a20–23. The Aristotelian portrait of *pathé* is often distorted by translating this Greek word into the English word "emotion." Besides the fact that the word "emotion" and its numerous historical formations and transformations were not available to the ancient Greeks because the word "emotion" hadn't been invented yet, there are a number of other serious problems with this translation, which I will address throughout this work.
3   Aristotle, *Rhetoric*, 1378a21.
4   Aristotle, *Rhetoric*, 1356a4.
5   Aristotle, however, holds the view that certain *pathé*, such as envy or spite, are always bad.
6   Aristotle, *Nicomachean Ethics*, trans. W. D. Ross (Lawrence, KS: Digireads, 2016), 1106b10–12, emphasis added.
7   For more on this and Epicurus's understanding of *pathos*, see book ten of Diogenes Laertius, *Lives of Eminent Philosophers*, Vol. 2, trans. Robert Drew Hicks (Cambridge, MA: Harvard University Press, 2005). Also see David Konstan, "Epicurean 'Passions' and the Good Life," in *The Virtuous Life in Greek Ethics*, ed. Burkhard Reis (New York: Cambridge University Press, 2006), 194–205.
8   Epicurus, *Letter to Menoeceus*, trans. Cyril Bailey (Oxford: Clarendon Press, 1926), 129. Limited by our access to only mere fragments, Epicurus understanding of *pathos* has been disputed. See Martha Nussbaum, *The Therapy of Desire* (Princeton, NJ: Princeton University Press, 1994). Nussbaum notes that Epicurus sometimes used the term "pathos" to mean an experience of "suffering," i.e., in the fragment: "Empty is that philosopher's argument by which no human suffering [*pathos*] is therapeutically treated. For just as there is no use in a medical art that does not cast out the sicknesses of bodies, so too there is no use in philosophy, if it does not throw out the suffering [*pathos*] of the soul" (Nussbaum, *Therapy of Desire*, 13). But Nussbaum is also sensitive to the plurality of meaning of *pathos* and notes that *pathos*, in general, signifies "feeling" (Nussbaum, *Therapy of Desire*, 102, n. 1). My understanding of Epicurus is derived from this general sense of feeling, which is similar to the interpretations of David Konstan who defines Epicurus's notion of *pathos* as both the "elementary forms of awareness, operating at the level of the non-rational psyche" and the "non-rational sensations of pleasure and pain." See Konstan, "Epicurean Passions," 201, 203.
9   According to Diogenes, Epicurus contended that we "choose the virtues ... on account of pleasure and not for their own sake, as we take medicine for the sake of health ... Epicurus describes virtue as the *sine qua non* of pleasure, i.e., the one thing without which pleasure cannot be; everything else, food, for instance, being separable, i.e., not indispensable to pleasure" (Diogenes, *Lives of Eminent Philosophers*, 663).

10 According to Nussbaum, it appears that Democritus developed this analogy "at length in a clearly philosophical context. 'Medicine,' he wrote, 'heals the sicknesses of bodies; but wisdom (*sophié*) rids the soul of its sufferings [pathé]' ... elsewhere he draws attention to analogies between bodily diseases and diseases of thought and desire; he stresses the causal efficacy of his art in balancing the soul and restoring it to health" (Nussbaum, *Therapy of Desire*, 51).

11 What is the Stoic meaning of soul/psyche? Though we can recognize different parts of the body and their functions, what are the parts of the soul? Also, what are the relations between the parts of the soul, what are the relations between the body and the soul; that is, how do the body and the soul affect one another? From the perspective of ancient philosophers, this first question is relatively simple to answer. Although some philosophers entertained or claimed that our souls existed before our births and/or that they might survive after our physical deaths, the soul (*psuché*/psyche), as it relates to psychological or bodily health, was generally believed to consist of certain faculties, vital functions, or animations of living bodies arising from the internal movements, operations, and processes within, and interactions between, different parts of the physical body. Disagreements between the theorists of antiquity concerning the parts of the soul were widespread. For instance, Aristotle contended that there weren't any parts of the soul, for the soul is a single substance with different powers; Chrysippus and a number of other Stoics believed that there was only one part of the soul; others contended that there were two parts, one rational and one irrational (Epicurus, Lucretius); still others, that there were three parts—the rational, spirted, and appetitive (Plato, Hippocrates, Galen), etc. These different narratives of the relations between the body and psyche/soul were supported by the belief that each part of the psyche was "housed" within a specific part of the body. Hippocrates, Plato, and Galen believed that the three distinct parts of the psyche are located within different bodily organs, namely reason is located in the brain, spirit is within our heart, and appetite dwells in the liver. As a consequence of this, the pathos and sickness of the psyche/soul was often seen as a sign of the *noséma* of the body and vice versa, leaving the diseases of the body and the sickness of the soul ambiguously demarcated. Take, for instance, black bile, one of the four so-called humors of the body, an unnatural and dysfunctional excess of black bile within the body was often asserted to give rise to two types of pathos: fear (*phobos*) and depression (*dysthymia*). Chronic feelings of fear and/or depression, on the other hand, were regularly seen as symptoms of an excess of black bile within the body. When these or other types of imbalances were observed as chronic conditions of the body-soul, they were interpreted to be diseases. For instance, melancholy is a *pathos* of the soul meaning "pensive sadness," but also, it means, literally "black bile disease," which was also conceived to be an ancient variety of madness.

12 Anthony Arthur Long and David N. Sedley, *The Hellenistic Philosophers, Volume 1* (Cambridge: Cambridge University Press, 1987), 417.
13 Long and Sedley, *Hellenistic Philosophers*, 417–418, emphasis added.
14 See Galen, *The Doctrines of Hippocrates and Plato* (Berlin: Akademie-Verlag, 1984), 27; cf. Margaret Graver, *Stoicism and Emotion* (Chicago: University of Chicago Press, 2007), 39.
15 He was reported as saying, "And as there are said to be certain infirmities (*arróstmata*) in the body, as for instance gout and arthritic disorders, so too there is in the soul: love of fame, love of pleasure, and the like. By infirmity is meant disease accompanied by weakness, and by disease (*noséma*) is meant a fond imagining of something that seems desirable [a type of pathos]. And as in the body there are tendencies to certain maladies such as colds and diarrhea, so it is with the soul, there are tendencies like enviousness, pitifulness, quarrelsomeness, and the like" (Diogenes, *Lives of Eminent Philosophers*, 7.115).
16 Long and Sedley, *Hellenistic Philosophers*, 383; and Diogenes, *Lives of Eminent Philosophers*, 197.
17 According to Cicero, the meaning of virtue, mentioned here, differed from Zeno's predecessors, who "claimed that not every virtue belonged to reason" and that some virtues were "brought to perfection through natural dispositions and habit." See Marcus Tullius Cicero, *On Academic Scepticism* (Indianapolis, IN: Hackett, 2006), 102. Zeno, however, considered all virtues to be rational; thus, reason and virtue are inseparable. Moreover, and also in opposition to philosophers who came before him, the disposition of virtue, rather that the mere exercise of a particular virtue, is alone intrinsically virtuous or excellent. Consequently, no one can possess virtue without exercising it continually.
18 For instance, the Stoic Cleanthes described it as "living in agreement with nature," and according to Chrysippus this disposition is our ability to live "in accordance with experience of the actual course of nature" (Diogenes, *Lives of Eminent Philosophers*, 7.87).
19 *Logos* is also synonymous with God/Zeus, which is both the origin of the cosmos as well as the rational order and providence indwelling within it. As the source of universe, then, the *Logos* is not a supernatural being existing outside of the material world; rather, it is nature itself, or more precisely, it is Reason (God) that begins, governs over, and permeates all matter.
20 In the words of Chrysippus, "our natures are part of the nature of the universe. Therefore, the goal becomes 'to live following nature,' that is, according to one's own nature and that of the universe" (Diogenes, *Lives of Eminent Philosophers*, 663, 7.88; cf. 7.135–141).
21 For instance, *pathé*, are, according to Zeno, "irrational and unnatural" movements of our souls.

22 *Pathos* as "excessive impulse" is an impulse or *hormē* (hormone) that "went too far," and the name for this principle of "going too far" was *pleonasmos*.

23 Chrysippus uses an analogy to elucidate this position: "When someone walks in accordance with his impulse, the movement of his legs is not excessive but commensurate with the impulse, so that he can stop or change whenever he wants to. But when people run in accordance with their impulse, this sort of thing no longer happens. The movement of their legs exceeds their impulse, so that they are carried away and unable to change obediently, as soon as they have started to do so. . . . The excess of running is called "contrary to the impulse," but the excess in the impulse is called "contrary to reason." For the proportion of a natural impulse is what accords with reason and goes only so far as reason itself thinks right" (Galen, *Doctrines of Hippocrates*, 4.2, 10–18; and Long and Sedley, *Hellenistic Philosophers*, 65J, 414).

24 Joy, according to the Stoics, is the opposite of pleasure, consisting in well-reasoned swelling [elation]; and watchfulness is the opposite of fear, consisting in well-reasoned shrinking. For the wise man will not be afraid at all, but he will be watchful. They say that wishing is the opposite of appetite, consisting in well-reasoned stretching [desire]. Just as certain *pathē* fall under the primary ones, so too with the primary good feelings. Under wishing: kindness, generosity, warmth, affection. Under watchfulness: respect, cleanliness. Under joy: delight, sociability, cheerfulness (Diogenes, *Lives of Eminent Philosophers*, 7.116, SVF 3.431).

25 Cicero, *De Finibus Bonorum et Malorum* (Cambridge, MA: Harvard University Press, 1931), 255, my translation.

26 Cicero, *De Finibus Bonorum*, 4.10.

27 Cicero, *De Finibus Bonorum*, 4.27, 28.

28 *Passio* among Christian thinkers was used *commonly*—but not only—to signify the movements of one's will toward the lower appetites and desires of the body; *passio* and *affectus* were used both positively and pejoratively, though the latter more often signified a movement of the will toward God.

29 In Aristotelian philosophy, the word "sin" (*harmatia*) meant literally "to miss the mark" of *arete* (excellence) in an activity; it is the failure to act virtuously. But Christian philosophers, following the theology of St. Paul, expanded this notion of failure by interpreting sin not only as missing the mark of virtue but also as a cosmic failure to act in accord with the will and goodness of God. When an individual commits a sin, he/she is guilty by following the passions (*pathē*) of the body rather than the goodness, lawfulness, and spirit of God. But, independent of any particular guilt-inducing act of sin, all human beings, as the story goes, are born into sin, they are guilty (*sontis*) from birth, as a consequence of the Fall. Humans, merely by their births, are guilty of rebellion against God; they are separated from God because of the stain of "original sin."

30 In contrast to the Stoics, Christian thinkers invented a much more complex psychology in which the body and soul are sick and/or imperfect at the moment of birth; they are each in need of a divine cure because of "original sin." Indulgence in the lower passions and appetites of the physical body is induced by the desires of one's soul toward worldly objects of sense and away from the spirit, reason, goodness, and will of God. This further sickens the soul, which, devoid of a cure, results not only in a life without virtue and happiness but also in separation from God. The desires and appetites of the corporeal corrupts both the physical body and the soul whenever one's lower passions (e.g., lust, greed, pride) leads to sin; however, whenever one aspires toward and is inspired by the spiritual effects of the intellect and will (e.g., love, joy, and even, a hatred of sin), the soul moves toward God and motivates one to act virtuously. This latter movement toward the goodness of God, which is simultaneously a movement away from and rejection of evil, operates as part of the Christian cure for the sick, fallen, and sinful nature of humanity.
31 In whatever manner Augustine used these terms contextually, they are always understood as desires or movements of the body-soul within the Great Chain of Being—a hierarchical and systematic order of Being that, according to the Christian and spiritual version of it, places God at the top of the chain and the Devil at the bottom of it. Upon this cosmic grid of the order of things, God represents the perfection of eternal Being and goodness, while the Devil represents the absence of God, nonbeing, and evil.
32 See Augustine, "The City of God, Vol. 1," in *The Works of Aurelius Augustine*, ed. Marcus Dods (Edinburgh: T. & T. Clark, 1913), 331, 355–358.
33 Augustine, "The City of God," section 14.9.
34 Augustine, "The City of God," section 14.6.
35 Augustine's distinction between the *Civitas Dei* (The City of God) and *Civitas Terrena* (The City of Man) expresses the tension between these two inner movements of the will, which further represents the differences between the Christian and non-Christian life. The former movement of the will encourages the love of God and the love of neighbor, while the latter encourages the love of self. Augustine suggested that a number of philosophers, for example Plato (Augustine, "The City of God," 9.16, 10.12), could have been members of the City of God due to their emphasis on friendship and their idea of and love for a transcendent Good.
36 St. Thomas Aquinas, *Summa Theologiae*, trans. Fathers of the English Dominican Province (Westminster: Christian Classics, 1981); 1:77.1, 78.1.
37 Drawing from Aristotle's *De Anima*, Aquinas describes each of these faculties as appetitive, but makes some important distinctions between them. Though the objects of each of these faculties is good, what "good" means for each is not the same. The objects of the sensitive appetite power of the soul are particular goods within

the world of sense, whereas the objects of the rational appetite or will are universal objects of good, such as truth, goodness, and virtue.
38 Aquinas, *Summa Theologiae*, IIaIIae 141.2, 24.1.co.
39 Aquinas, *Summa Theologiae*, Ia.II.ae. 22.2.
40 Aquinas, *Summa Theologiae*, I–II 30.1 ad I, ST I–II 22.3 ad I.
41 *Pathé* are passions of the soul, i.e., perceptions, sensations, or emotions of the soul or psyche, which are caused, maintained, or fortified by some movement of the "animal spirits."
42 René Descartes, *The Philosophical Writings of Descartes*, Vols. 1 and 2, ed. and trans. John Cottingham, Robert Stoothoff, and Dugald Murdoch (Cambridge: Cambridge University Press, 1985), 1:339.
43 Nevertheless, this view rejects the Christian metaphorical understanding of the body and soul and replaces it with a literal ontological dualism in which the body and soul are conceived as two distinct substances: an extended physical substance (body) and a thinking substance (soul). See René Descartes, *Meditations on First Philosophy*, 3rd ed., trans. Donald A. Cress (Indianapolis, IN: Hackett, [1641] 1993).
44 Descartes, *Philosophical Writings*, 1:347.
45 Descartes, *Philosophical Writings*, 1:343, 381.
46 René Descartes, *The Philosophical Writings of Descartes*, Vol. 3: *The Correspondence*, ed. and trans. John Cottingham, Robert Stoothoff, Dugald Murdoch, and Anthony Kenny (Cambridge: Cambridge University Press, 1991), 306.
47 Within both the Cartesian mechanistic system as well as the Christina theological worldview, we find that a higher ontological status was granted to the operations of the soul. Within the Cartesian vision, this was believed to be necessary for both creating a foundation for scientific inquiry as well as for living a virtuous, happy life. With the Christian tradition, the higher status assigned to the movements of the soul was necessary for living a virtuous, happy life, but also for moving one closer to the will of a loving God.
48 Descartes's introduction of and hopes for the philosophical usefulness of the word "*émotion*" certainly did not become realized in his lifetime. There are at least two reasons this came to pass. First, the modern philosophers that followed him either wrote in Latin (Spinoza) or wrote in both Latin and English (Hobbes). *Pathos*, then, continued to be represented by the Latin word *passio* and the English word *passion* rather than Descartes's new French philosophical word, *émotion*. Second, although Descartes claimed that certain *pathé* have their origins in bodily changes, his soul/body dualism, which conceived of the soul/psyche as a nonspatial thinking substance, disallowed any serious scientific inquiry to emerge. As a consequence of this, a serious scientific study of the emotions in both human and nonhuman animals didn't arise until the mid-nineteenth century.

49 Thomas Hobbes, *Leviathan*, ed. John Charles Addison Gaskin (Oxford: Oxford University Press, [1651] 1996), 10.
50 Hobbes, *Leviathan*, 66.
51 For instance, Hobbes notes that sense as a motion is an "internal motion" within the body "caused ... by the pressure, that is, by the motion of external things upon our eyes, ears, and other organs" (Hobbes, *Leviathan*, 10). See also page 117 in Thomas Hobbes, "Concerning Body," in *The Metaphysical System of Hobbes*, ed. Mary Whiton Calkins (Chicago, IL: Open Court, [1656] 1963), where Hobbes defines sense as "a phantasm, made by the reaction and endeavor outwards in the organ of sense, caused by an endeavor inward from the object, remaining for some time more or less." Though most of my representation of Hobbes's view of the passions is drawn from the *Leviathan*, my account of Hobbes's view is drawn from both *Elements of Law* (1640) and "Concerning Body" (1656). For relevant passages of the former concerning the passions side by side with relevant passages from the *Leviathan*, see Deborah Baumgold, *Three-Text Edition of Thomas Hobbes's Political Theory* (Cambridge: Cambridge University Press, 2017).
52 Hobbes links a number of passions with their motions in *Elements of Law*, where he compares life to a race in which the only goal is to be foremost. "And in it [the race]: To endeavour is appetite. To be remiss is sensuality. To consider them behind is glory. To consider them before is humility. To lose ground with looking back vain glory. To be holden, hatred. To turn back, repentance. To be in breath, hope. To be weary, despair. To endeavour to overtake the next, emulation. To supplant or overthrow, envy. To resolve to break through a stop foreseen, courage. To break through a sudden stop, anger. To break through with ease, magnanimity. To lose ground by little hindrances, pusillanimity. To fall on the sudden is disposition to weep. To see another fall, disposition to laugh. To see one out-gone whom we would not is pity. To see one out-go we would not, is indignation. To hold fast by another is to love. To carry him on that so holdeth, is charity. To hurt one's-self for haste is shame. Continually to be out-gone is misery. Continually to out-go the next before is felicity. And to forsake the course is to die." See the end of chapter nine in part one of Thomas Hobbes, *Elements of Law: Natural and Politic*, ed. Ferdinand Tönnies (New York: Routledge, [1640] 1889).
53 Baruch Spinoza, *Ethics: Proved in Geometric Order*, trans. Michael Silverthorne and Matthew J. Kisner (Cambridge: Cambridge University Press, 2018), Part I (D6).
54 The concepts of adequacy and inadequacy alone do not form the dualism I mention here. The dualism arises when these words are combined with others to create different terms in Spinoza's *Ethics*. For instance, adequate ideas/inadequate ideas and adequate causes/inadequate causes. These terms are not merely useful distinctions to describe experience; they are dualisms because Spinoza employs them to describe the ontology and metaphysical nature of both ideas and causes.

55 Spinoza, *Ethics*, Part III (D1).
56 See, for instance, Book II, Part III, Sections 4–10 of Hume, *Treatise of Human Nature*; and Part VII, Section III, Chapter 2 of Smith, *Theory of Moral Sentiments*.
57 For instance, in the opening lines of *The Theory of Moral Sentiments*, Smith includes the following description of the powers of sympathy, which is clearly a description of what Hume calls sympathy: "When we see someone poised to smash a stick down on the leg or arm of another person, we naturally shrink and pull back our own leg or arm; and when the stick connects, we feel it in some measure, and are hurt by it along with the sufferer. When a crowd are gazing at a dancer on a slack rope, they naturally writhe and twist and balance their own bodies, as they see him do, and as they feel they would have to do if they were up on the rope where he is. . . . Men notice that when they look at sore eyes they often feel soreness in their own eyes."
58 Smith talks about entering into gratitude, surprise, admiration, resentments, pusillanimity, weakness, sentiments, pain, pleasure, passion, disgusting appetites, anxiety, anguish, eagerness, satisfaction, hopes, and another's mind-set, etc. Here is one example of how Smith describes our experience of the relation of *feeling into*: "We see or think about a man being tortured on the rack; we think of ourselves enduring all the same torments, *entering into his* body (so to speak) and becoming in a way the same person as he is. In this manner we form some idea of his sensations, and even feel something that somewhat resembles them, though it is less intense" (Smith, *Theory of Moral Sentiments*, Part I, Section 1, Chapter 1, 1, emphasis added). In addition to this relation, Smith includes the relation of *feeling for* as either a part of the sympathetic process or as in need of sympathy as *feeling with* to be realized, as Smith notes: "So my thesis is that our *fellow feeling for* the misery of others comes from our imaginatively changing places with the sufferer, thereby coming to conceive what he feels or even to feel what he feels" (Smith, *Theory of Moral Sentiments*, Part I, Section 1, Chapter 1, 1). The relation of *feeling into* is likewise identified as, at least, a necessary of our feeling for others: "But if we don't entirely enter into and go along with a person's joy, we have no sort of regard or *fellow feeling for* it" (Smith, *Theory of Moral Sentiments*, Part I, Section 3, Chapter 1).
59 For instance, Thomas Dixon has written a brilliant and concise article on the troubled history of the multiple meanings assigned to the word "emotion." See Thomas Dixon, "'Emotion': The History of a Key Word in Crisis," *Emotion Review* 4, no. 4 (2012): 338–344.
60 William James, "What Is an Emotion," *Mind* 9, no. 34 (1884): 189–190.
61 James, "What Is an Emotion," 189.
62 For example, the works of Antonio Damasio and Jesse Prinz. See Antonio Damasio, *The Feeling of What Happens: Body and Emotion in the Making of Consciousness* (New York: Harcourt, Brace, 2000); and Jesse Prinz, *Gut Reactions: A Perceptual Theory of Emotion* (Oxford: Oxford University Press, 2004).

63 Antonio Damasio, *Emotion, Reason, and the Human Brain* (New York: HarperCollins, 1994).
64 During his ongoing pen-pal relationship with Elisabeth, Descartes diagnoses a "low grade fever" from which Elisabeth has been suffering as caused by sadness or melancholy and recommends the familiarly Stoic-sounding remedy of reading Seneca, while reflecting on her mind and its ability to master bodily based passions.
65 William James, "The Sentiment of Rationality," in *The Will to Believe, and Other Essays in Popular Philosophy*, ed. William James (New York: Longmans, Green, and Co., [1882] 1905), 63–110.
66 James, "Sentiment of Rationality," 64.

Chapter 3

1 For the best work on this subject, see Lidewij Niezink and Katherine Train, *The Self in Empathy: Self-Empathy* (South Africa: Lidewij Niezink and Katherine Train, 2021).
2 By "modern" here, I mean modern in a philosophical sense: modern philosophy—the period of time, roughly, between Francis Bacon (1561–1626) and G. W. F. Hegel (1770–1831). Adam Smith is most widely recognized for *The Wealth of Nations* and thus for being the so-called father of capitalism. What many people fail to recognize today is that this work cannot be adequately understood without consulting his *Theory of Moral Sentiments*.
3 Smith, *Theory of Moral Sentiments*, Chapter 2, n. 48.
4 When compared with other theories of empathy and/or sympathy, Smith's account of moral sentiment most closely resembles my theory of relational empathy.
5 Roger Hausheer, "Fichte and Shelling," in *German Philosophy since Kant*, ed. Anthony O'Hear (Cambridge: Cambridge University Press, 1999), 3.
6 Herder, *Sämmtliche Werke*, 5:502–503, 506.
7 See Stueber, *Rediscovering Empathy*, for an exhaustive and insightful work on this point.
8 See Johann Gottlieb Herder, *Herder on Social and Political Culture*, ed. Frederick M. Barnard (Cambridge: Cambridge University Press, 1969), 186.
9 Herder, *Herder on Social*, Chapter 1, n. 14.
10 Novalis, *Schriften*, Vol. 2, ed. Paul Kluckhorn and Richard H. Samuel (Stuttgart, Germany: Kohlhammer 1928] 1965), 289.
11 Hermann Lotze, *Microcosmus: An Essay Concerning Man and His Relation to the World*, Vol. 1, 4th ed. (Edinburgh: T. & T. Clark, 1856), 584, emphasis added.
12 Though this break locates a distinct historical difference in the meaning of empathy between late-eighteenth-century Counter-Enlightenment/romanticists thinkers and mid-late nineteenth-century aestheticians and psychologists, Herder was definitely a

forerunner of this change. See, for example, Joe K. Fugate, "The Relationship between Aesthetics and Psychology," in *The Psychological Basis of Herder's Aesthetics*, ed. Joe K. Fugate (The Hague: Mouton, 1966), 16–70.

13 Robert Vischer, *Empathy, Form and Space: Problems in German Aesthetics, 1873–1893*, ed. Harry Francis Mallgrave and Eleftherios Ikonomou (Santa Monica, CA: Getty Center for the History of Art and the Humanities, [1873] 1994), 92, emphasis added.

14 See Karl Groos, *The Play of Man* (New York: D. Appleton, 1901), 323.

15 Groos, *Play of Man*.

16 See Herbert Sidney Langfeld, *The Aesthetic Attitude* (New York: Harcourt, Brace, 1920), 114.

17 Langfeld, *Aesthetic Attitude*, 115, emphasis added.

18 For more on this, see Theodor Lipps, "Einfühlung und Ästhetischer Genuß," *Die Zukunft* 54, no. 16 (1906): 100–114.

19 Theodor Lipps, *Ästhetik: Psychologie des Schoenen und der Kunst* (Leipzig, Germany: L. Voss, 1914).

20 Lipps, *Ästhetik*, 121–126.

21 See Robin Curtis and Richard George Elliott, "An Introduction to Einfühlung," *Art in Translation* 6, no. 4 (2015): 366.

22 Samuel Taylor Coleridge, "Letter to W. Sotheby," in *Letters of Samuel Taylor Coleridge*, ed. Ernest Hartley Coleridge (London: William Heinemann, 1895), 1:372.

23 These lines were written in Whitman's notebooks immediately before he wrote the first lines of *Leaves of Grass*. See "Foreword to Section 21," *Song of Myself* (New York: Dodd, Mead, [1964] 1971).

24 See Gustav Jahoda, "Theodor Lipps and the Shift from 'Sympathy' to 'Empathy,'" *Journal of the History of the Behavioral Sciences* 41, no. 2 (2005): 153–154.

25 This would continue in the unilinear theories of human development and cultural evolution exemplified in the writings of Auguste Comte (1798–1857), Herbert Spencer (1820–1903), Edward Burnett Tylor (1832–1917), James George Frazier (1854–1941), and Lucien Lévy-Brühl (1857–1939).

26 William James, "On a Certain Blindness in Human Beings," in *On Some of Life's Ideals*, ed. William James (New York: Henry Holt, 1899), 8.

Chapter 4

1 We find a similar meaning of sympathy in *Politics*, in which Aristotle states that the power of music produces similar emotional and psychological states between individuals, i.e., when two or more people listen to the same piece of music, a corresponding feeling arises within them and they *feel with* one another, experiencing the same general emotional sensation provoked by the music (1340a).

Both of these usages of sympathy signify experiences of feeling with others, in which our sensations of what another is feeling is provoked by something outside of ourselves, and thus our feeling and sensations are not consequences of our conscious deliberations.

2. This isn't as strange as it may seem. Today, we describe nervous systems as sympathetic and parasympathetic. In Plato's *Charmides*, Socrates speaks of Critias as experiencing sympathy as a type of suffering and contagion with others, like yawning. Critias believed that he had arrived at the same intellectual impasse (*aporia*) as Socrates did concerning the nature of moderation. But while Socrates difficulties arrived after the long process of reasoning and doubting, Critias merely "caught" the beliefs and feelings of Socrates. This usage of "sympathy" signifies experiences of feeling with others in which our sensations of what another is feeling is provoked by something outside of ourselves, and thus is not a consequence of our conscious deliberations.

3. In Plato's *Republic*, the concept of sympathy, i.e., as a unity between the parts of the city-state, is an operating concept of Plato's notion of the tripartite soul in which one part of the soul (reason) was believed to control and keep in check the two other parts of the soul (the appetitive and the spirited), creating balance, unity, and agreement (i.e., "sym") between all of its parts. This, in turn, becomes the starting point for Plato in this dialogue to investigate the corresponding parts of the *polis*: the guardians, the auxiliaries, and the producers, which when functioning together in unity might allow for the harmony and order of a future city-state, the so-called "ideal" city.

4. See René Brouwer, "Stoic Sympathy," in *Sympathy: A History*, ed. Eric Schliesser (Oxford: Oxford University Press, 2013), 15–35. The collection of writings in this work edited by Schliesser are some of the best sources I have encountered for understanding the historical and semantic variations of the word "sympathy."

5. To say that the cosmos is at sympathy with itself implies a few things. First, that all parts of the cosmos are united together—connected by *pneuma*—and that the cosmos itself is well-ordered and coherent, and the *Logos* permeates throughout it. Second, the tensional force of *pneuma* causes affinities, sympathetic relations, between certain parts of the cosmos. Consequently, third, the cosmos operates and unfolds as a causal chain of relational events within which a part could affect, influence, excite, or change another part, even independent of the apparent distance of time or space between them. Regarding this last point about spatial distance, think of the human body. The toes and the head are spatially distant from one another, but if one stubs her/his toe, this affects the head instilling the sensation of pain, for each of these parts are connected by the nervous system. Similarly, the cosmos is connected by the fiery breath of *Logos* (*pneuma*) and the seemingly independent parts of it affect each other: the moon affects the tides, causing the

waters to flow and ebb, and along with this, sea creatures are affected by these movements of the waters. Likewise, as some Stoics insisted, the movements of stars or planets could affect the lives and destinies of human beings, and in the same manner, a person's action(s) could affect another part of the cosmos either intentionally or even independently of the motive, intent, or aim of her/his action.

6 For more on this, see Menahem Luz, *Cosmic Sympathy: The Teachings of Posidonius* (Albany, CA: Berkeley Hills Books, 2007).

7 Long and Sedley, *Hellenistic Philosophers*, SVF 2.1189, 261.

8 See Cicero, *On Divination*, trans. William Armistead Falconer (Cambridge, MA: Harvard University Press, 1923), section 2.34. The roman Stoic Seneca viewed sympathy as "fellow-feeling" and crucial to the philosopher's aims, noting that the "first thing which philosophy undertakes to give is fellow-feeling with all men; in other words, sympathy and sociability." See Letter V., section IV in Seneca, *Letters from a Stoic*, trans. Robin Campbell (London: Penguin Classics, 1969).

9 Take, for example, the following English words: "embroider" (to ornament something; to inlay, i.e., put into or embed some object with a different material); "embalm" (to put spices into a corpse); "embitter" (to infuse with bitterness; to put bitterness into something); "emblaze" (to set in a blaze); "embellish" (to put beauty into something); "employ" (to make use of; to apply or place into a purpose, effort or work into something); "empower" (to make powerful, to inject potency into a person).

10 Think: "symmetry" (similar parts or the unity, agreement, and/or harmony of parts with each other and the whole); "symbol" (something similar to something else that stands for, represents, or denotes it); "symbiosis" (living together harmoniously); "symphony" (harmony of sound or agreement between sounds); "symposium" (a drinking party; to drink with others). These different significations of "sym," have each been used to operationalize particular meanings of sympathy for different purposes.

11 See Lauren Wispé, *The Psychology of Sympathy* (New York: Plenum Press, 1991), 70. See also Phillip Mercer, *Sympathy and Ethics: A Study of the Relationship between Sympathy and Morality with Special Reference to Hume's Treatise* (Oxford: Clarendon Press, 1972).

12 Of all the theorists we have explored thus far, Smith's account of sympathy most closely resembles what I have called relational empathy as Smith was one of the few thinkers to include the relation of *feeling into*. For example, Smith notes: "When we have read a book or poem so often that we can no longer enjoy reading it by ourselves, we can still take pleasure in reading it to a companion . . . we *enter into* the surprise and admiration that it naturally arouses in him but can no longer arouse in us . . . and we enjoy by *sympathy* his enjoyment that thus enlivens our own" (Smith, *Theory of Moral Sentiments*, Book I, Part I, Section 17–18).

13 Dermot Moran, "The Problem of Empathy: Lipps, Scheler, Husserl, and Stein," in *Amor Amicitiae: On the Love That Is Friendship; Essays in Medieval Thought and beyond in Honor of the Rev. Professor James McEvoy*, ed. Thomas A. F. Kelly and Philipp W. Rosemann (Leuven, Belgium: Peeters, 2004), 269–312.
14 Theodor Lipps, "Das wissen von fremden ichen," *Psychologischen Untersuchungen* 1, no. 4 (1907): 694–722.
15 Lipps, "Das wissen," 713–714.
16 How can I be certain that my acts of projection and mimicry are more a sign of my selfhood than knowledge of what is expressed in the other? How can I internally reproduce another's ego (consciousness) in such a way that I "know" that my reproduced and inward account matches, or is even similar to the others? To use C. Daniel Batson's terminology described earlier, how do I know that my perspective of another's expression is grasped by means of an imagine-other perspective rather than an imagine-self perspective?
17 Lipps could not provide an answer to this question because, in Husserl's mind, Lipps never provided a thorough in-depth phenomenological account of the self as a "living body" and "spiritual subject." Lipps, says Husserl, is "blind to the fact that the perception of another mainly requires an understanding of the living body as a living body, and above all understanding of the relationship between body and subject in the sense of the spiritual subject."
18 Stein, *On the Problem of Empathy*, 14. Stein uses the experience of joy to illuminate what she means in this section about empathy as a nonprimordial/primordial experience. I can experience joy about having just passed an exam, and my friend can relate to me her joy that she experienced when she passed an exam. If I were to try to empathize with the joy she felt when she passed her exam, I would be experiencing primordially my joy about the joy she felt, but I wouldn't be co-experiencing her original primordial experience of joy.
19 Max Scheler, *The Nature of Sympathy* (London: Transaction, [1923] 2009), 12.
20 Scheler, *Nature of Sympathy*, 18.
21 Moran, "Problem of Empathy," 287–288.
22 For more on empathy, hermeneutics, and the social sciences, see Hans Herbert Kögler and Karsten Stueber, *Empathy & Agency: The Problem of Understanding in the Human Sciences* (New York: Routledge, 1999); also see Stueber, *Rediscovering Empathy*.
23 Sigmund Freud, "Jokes and the Relation to the Unconscious," in *The Standard Edition of Freud's Works*, Vol. 8, trans. James Strachey (London: Hogarth Press, 1955–1964), 9.
24 Sigmund Freud, "Das Interesse an der Psychoanalyse," *Scientia* 14, no. 31–32 (1913): 240–250, 369–384.
25 Sigmund Freud, "Further Recommendations in the Technique of Psychoanalysis: On Beginning the Treatment," in *Therapy and Technique*, trans. Joan Riviere (New York: Crowell-Collier, [1913] 1964), 121–144.

26 Sigmund Freud, "Remembering, Repeating and Working-Through," in *The Standard Edition of Freud's Works*, Vol. 12, trans. James Strachey (London: Hogarth Press, 1914), 145–156.
27 See Sigmund Freud, "Recommendations to Physicians Practicing Psycho-Analysis," *The Standard Edition of Freud's Works*, Vol. 12, trans. James Strachey (London: Hogarth Press, 1912), 109–120, esp. 115.
28 Titchener, *Lectures on the Experimental Psychology*, 22.
29 Titchener, *Lectures on the Experimental Psychology*, 205, footnote b.
30 See, for example, Carl Rogers, "Empathy: An Unappreciated Way of Being," *The Counseling Psychologist* 5, no. 2 (1975): 2–10; see also Heinz Kohut, "On Empathy," *International Journal of Psychoanalytic Self Psychology* 5, no. 2 (1981): 122–131.
31 This focus on empathy as an interpersonal phenomenon led many theorists to reject the idea of empathy as any type of projection, favoring instead definitions of empathy chiefly as interpersonal connection. By the middle of the twentieth century, this narrative that empathy means *feeling with* others not *feeling into* others even led to support by some to replace the German word *Einfühlung* with a "more accurate" word, namely *Empathie*.
32 See George Herbert Mead, *Mind, Self, and Society: From the Standpoint of Social Behaviorist*, ed. Charles W. Morris (Chicago: University of Chicago Press, 1934), 154–156.
33 De Waal, *Age of Empathy*, 59–61.
34 Danziger, Prkachin, and Willer, "Is Pain the Price of Empathy?," 2494.
35 Ickes, *Empathic Accuracy*, 3; also see William Ickes et al., "Naturalistic Social Cognition: Empathic Accuracy in Mixed-Sex Dyads," *Journal of Personality and Social Psychology* 59, no. 4 (1990): 730–742.
36 See Claus Lamm, C. Daniel Batson, and Jean Decety, "The Neural Substrate of Human Empathy: Effects of Perspective-Taking and Cognitive Appraisal," *Journal of Cognitive Neuroscience* 19, no. 1 (2007): 42–58.
37 See Jean Decety and Phillip L. Jackson, "The Functional Architecture of Human Empathy," *Behavioral and Cognitive Neuroscience Reviews* 3, no. 2 (2004): 71–100. See also Rick B. van Baaren et al., "Being Imitated: Consequences of Nonconsciously Showing Empathy," in Decety and Ickes, *Social Neuroscience of Empathy*, 31–42.
38 See Giuseppe di Pellegrino et al., "Understanding Motor Events: A Neurophysiological Study," *Experimental Brain Research* 91, no. 1 (1992): 176–180; Vittorio Gallese et al., "Action Recognition in the Premotor Cortex," *Brain* 119, no. 2 (1996): 593–609; and Giacomo Rizzolatti et al., "Premotor Cortex and the Recognition of Motor Actions," *Cognitive Brain Research* 3, no. 2 (1996): 131–141.
39 For a good start for investigating the ongoing discourse surrounding the concepts of mirror neurons and/or mirroring processes, see Iacoboni, *Mirroring People*; Iacoboni and Dapretto, "The Mirror Neuron System"; and Christian Keysers, *The Empathic*

Brain: How the Discovery of Mirror Neurons Changes Our Understanding of Human Nature (Lexington, KY: Social Brain Press, 2011).

40 See Gregory Hickok, *The Myth of Mirror Neurons: The Real Neuroscience of Communication and Cognition* (New York: W. W. Norton, 2014).

41 De Waal, *Age of Empathy*, 61.

42 Empathy has been described similarly. Take, for example, the following definition by Evelyne Schwaber: "Empathy . . . is that mode of attunement which attempts to maximize a singular focus on the patient's subjective reality, seeking all possible cues to ascertain it. . . . As a scientific modality, empathy employs our cognitive, perceptual, as well as affective capacities" (Evelyne Schwaber, "Empathy: A Mode of Analytic Listening," *Psychoanalytic Inquiry* 1, no. 3 (1981): 357–392.

43 The word "affect" in this sense ought not be conceived dualistically, i.e., opposed to our experiences of reasoning, etc., but rather as the experience of being moved in any manner, including the experience of being moved intellectually.

44 I draw this notion of the "art of affect attunement" from Cynthia Willett's extremely well-conceived and pluralistic understanding of empathy as described in her forwarding work on interspecies ethics. See Cynthia Willett, *Interspecies Ethics* (New York: Columbia University Press, 2014), 15, 80–99.

Chapter 5

1 See Colin Turnbull, *The Forest People* (New York: Simon & Schuster, 1961).

2 See Douglas Cohen and Janet Strayer, "Empathy in Conduct-Discorded and Comparison Youth," *Developmental Psychology* 32, no. 6 (1996): 988–998; also see Nancy Eisenberg and Richard A. Fabes, "Empathy: Conceptualization, Measurement, and Relation to Prosocial Behavior," *Motivation and Emotion* 14, no. 2 (1990): 131–149.

3 See Nancy Eisenberg et al., "Personality and Socialization Correlates of Vicarious Emotional Responding," *Journal of Personality and Social Psychology* 61, no. 3 (1991): 459–470. Also see Norma D. Feshbach and Seymour Feshbach, "Empathy Training and the Regulation of Aggression: Potentialities and Limitations," *Academic Psychology Bulletin* 4, no. 3 (1982): 399–413.

4 See De Waal, *Age of Empathy*, 67–68, 214–218. These recognizable advantages should be interpreted judiciously and cautiously, as De Waal points out, "Men and women differ on average, but quite a few men are more empathic than the average woman, and quite a few women are less empathic than the average man. With age, the empathy levels of men and women seem to converge" (De Waal, *Age of Empathy*, 68).

5 Carl Rogers, "A Theory of Therapy, Personality and Interpersonal Relationships as Developed in the Client-Centered Framework," in *Psychology: A Study of Science:*

Formulations of the Person and the Social Context, ed. Sigmund Koch (New York: McGraw Hill, 1959), 210–211.
6. Rogers, "Empathic," 7, emphasis mine.
7. C. Daniel Batson, *Altruism in Humans* (New York: Oxford University Press, 2011), 11.
8. For an early work on this distinction in which Batson et al. use the term "empathic emotion" rather than "empathic concern," see C. Daniel Batson et al., "Is Empathic Emotion a Source of Altruistic Motivation?," *Journal of Personality and Social Psychology* 40, no. 2 (1981): 290–302. For more developed and in-depth accounts of Batson's empathy-altruism hypothesis, see C. Daniel Batson, *The Altruism Question: Toward a Social-Psychological Answer* (New York: Psychology Press, 1991); Batson, *Altruism in Humans*; and for his most recent explanation and defense of the empathy-altruism hypothesis, see Batson, *Scientific Search for Altruism*.
9. See Batson et al., "Immorality from Empathy-Induced Altruism," 1042–1054.
10. Batson, "These Things Called Empathy."
11. Hoffman, *Empathy and Moral Development*, 3–4.
12. Eisenberg and Fabes, "Prosocial Development," 702.
13. See also Nancy Eisenberg and Natalie D. Eggum, "Empathic Responding: Sympathy and Personal Distress," in Decety and Ickes, *Social Neuroscience of Empathy*, 71–83.
14. Baron-Cohen, *Science of Evil*.
15. These theories were used to create social conditions that favored the so-called stronger races by putting them in positions of power and subjugated what were believed to be inferior races who, as the story goes, have experienced some type of arrested development at some point in their phylogenic history. This notion was also promulgated in the mid-nineteenth century by Robert Knox, who believed that the development of all species was contingent upon the past through a sequence of what Knox called mysterious metamorphosis and that embryogenesis is best understood by adhering to three transcendental laws: the tendency to variety, the tendency to heredity, and the tendency to return to the type of the race, or to perish altogether. See Robert Knox, *The Races of Men: A Philosophical Enquiry into the Influence of Race over the Destinies of Nations* (Cambridge, MA: Harvard University Press, [1850] 2008).
16. See Ben-Ami Bartal, Jean Decety, and Peggy Mason, "Empathy and Pro-Social Behavior in Rats," *Science* 334, no. 6061 (2011): 1427–1430.
17. See Preston and De Waal, "Empathy," 4.
18. Their definition is similar to mine in that it also encapsulates the meanings of numerous definitions of empathy. My reason for adopting a similarly broad approach is to provide a historically inclusive and pragmatic understanding of empathy grounded upon on three general relations of empathic experience rather than on those things and activities we call empathic.

19 Preston and De Waal, "Empathy," 2.
20 De Waal, *Age of Empathy*, 208–209.
21 Preston and De Waal, "Empathy," 17. On this page, however, he also notes, "The more similar or familiar the subject and object, the more their representations will be similar, which in turn produces more state matching, better accuracy, and less projection.... The degree to which it is empathy rather than projection depends purely on the extent to which the subject's representations are similar to those of the object, or include information about the object, which in turn determine accuracy." I interpret this to mean that although projection is always part and parcel of the process of empathizing as some form of "attended perception," with greater empathic accuracy, there is only projection similar to what I have called direct perception and thus an experience of instantaneous feeling with another person or thing similar to when one views a sunset and instantaneously feels with its beauty without the need for acute, detailed, and prolonged observation or perception of it.
22 De Waal, *Age of Empathy*, 65.
23 See Russell D. Clark and Larry E. Wood, "Where Is the Apathetic Bystander? Situational Characteristics of the Emergency," *Journal of Personality and Social Psychology* 29, no. 3 (1974): 279–287.
24 See Shaun Nichols, "Mindreading and the Cognitive Architecture Underlying Altruistic Motivation," *Mind & Language* 16, no. 4 (2001): 425–455.
25 Danziger, Prkachin, and Willer, "Is Pain the Price of Empathy?," 2494.
26 Jean Decety, "The Neurodevelopment of Empathy in Humans," *Developmental Neuroscience* 32, no. 4 (2010): 258.
27 Decety, *Empathy*, vii.
28 See Tania Singer and Claus Lamm, "The Social Neuroscience of Empathy," *Annals of the New York Academy of Science* 1156, no. 1 (2009): 81–96.
29 Jean Knox, "'Feeling for' and 'Feeling with': Developmental and Neuroscientific Perspectives on Intersubjectivity and Empathy," *Analytical Psychology* 59, no. 4 (2013): 495.
30 Knox, "'Feeling for' and 'Feeling with,'" 498.
31 Steven Pinker, *The Better Angels of Our Nature* (New York: Viking, 2011), 576. For a recent example of this usage, see Lee A. McBride III, *Ethics and Insurrection: A Pragmatism for the Oppressed* (London: Bloomsbury Press, 2020), 81.
32 McBride, *Ethics and Insurrection*, 573–578.
33 McBride, *Ethics and Insurrection*.
34 See Marian D. Sigman et al., "Responses to the Negative Emotions of Others by Autistic, Mentally Retarded, and Normal Children," *Child Development* 63, no. 4 (1992): 797–807.
35 Goethe, *Faust*, Part 1.

36 See, for example, Jean Jacques Rousseau, *The Social Contract and Discourses* (London: J. M. Dent and Sons, [1761] 1923); and Hume, *Treatise of Human Nature*, 581–582.

37 On enhanced empathy in relation to in-groups, see Divya Mathur et al., "A Transient Niche Regulates the Specification of Drosophila Intestinal Stem Cells," *Science* 327, no. 5962 (2010): 210–213.

38 On self-other merging and empathy, see Robert B. Cialdini et al., "Reinterpreting the Empathy-Altruism Relationship: When One into One Equals Oneness," *Journal of Personality and Social Psychology* 73, no. 3 (1979): 481–494. On the in-group/out-group distinction in relation to empathy for the pain of others, see Benoît Montalan et al., "Behavioural Investigation of the Influence of Social Categorization on Empathy for Pain: A Minimal Group Paradigm Study," *Frontiers in Psychology* 3, no. 389 (2012): 2–5.

39 See Vani A. Mathur et al., "Neural Basis of Extraordinary Empathy and Altruistic Motivation," *NeuroImage* 51, no. 4 (2010): 1468–1475; and Grit Hein et al., "Neural Responses to Ingroup and Outgroup Members' Suffering Predict Individual Differences in Costly Helping," *Neuron* 68, no. 1 (2010): 149–160.

40 See Brian B. Drwecki et al., "Reducing Racial Disparities in Pain Treatment: The Role of Empathy and Perspective-Taking," *Pain* 152, no. 5 (2011): 1001–1006; see also Vani A. Mathur, Tokiko Harada, and Joan Y. Chiao, "Racial Identification Modulates Default Network Activity for Same and Other Races," *Human Brain Mapping* 33, no. 8 (2012): 1883–1893; and Mathur et al., "Neural Basis of Extraordinary Empathy."

41 For example, when one acts out of consideration and is courteous for another person by walking through a public doorway, she experiences relational empathy instantly. For as she opens the door to enter it, she immediately feels into her surroundings, especially the spaces behind her. She then, let's say, notices a man who appears as though he intends also to enter the door. In this moment, she must feel into and try to feel with the man's intentions, perhaps by feeling into his body language or by noticing the direction of his eyes. If she feels with the intention of the man accurately, which is to walk through the door after her, she will feel for, care for, and show compassion toward the man by holding the door for him to pass through it. Or think about another, perhaps less banal, example: friendship. Friendships oftentimes begin by each person feeling into the character, personality, habits, and general temperament of another. Though what each person notices in the other may not be the same, the friends find attractive, useful, and/or admirable qualities in each other that produces a mutual affinity—a reciprocal sense of connection or feeling with—between these persons. Experiences of these two relations alone (e.g., feeling into the character of the other and having mutual feelings of affection for each other) could not alone be called a friendship with experiences of the relation of feeling for and caring for the other.

42 See Mark Fagiano, "Relational Empathy as an Instrument of Democratic Hope in Action," *Journal of Speculative Philosophy* 33, no. 2 (2019): 200–219.

Chapter 6

1 "Words strain, crack and sometimes break, under the burden, under the tension, slip, slide, perish, decay with imprecision, will not stay in place, will not stay still" (T. S. Eliot, "Burnt Norton," in *Four Quartets*, ed. T. S. Eliot (New York: Mariner Books, 1943)).
2 William James, *Pragmatism* (New York: Longmans, Green, and Co.), 43.
3 James, *Pragmatism*.
4 This sentiment comes from Donald Davidson, "A Nice Derangement of Epitaphs," in *Truth and Interpretation*, ed. Ernest Lepore (Oxford: Blackwell, 1989). Davidson further states that "we should realize that we have abandoned not only the ordinary notion of a language, but we have erased the boundary between knowing a language and knowing our way around the world generally. For there are no rules for arriving at passing theories that work.... There is no more chance of regularizing, or teaching, this process than there is of regularizing or teaching the process of creating new theories to cope with new data—for that is what this process involves.... We must give up the idea of a clearly defined shared structure that language users master and then apply to cases ... We should give up the attempt to illuminate how we communicate by appeal to conventions" (Davidson, "A Nice Derangement of Epitaphs," 446).
5 James, *Pragmatism*, 53.
6 James, *Pragmatism*.
7 As adjectives, "moral" and "ethical" serve to qualify the value of actions and behaviors as good and right, but as nouns, "ethics," and "morality"—most generally—denote the study of the moral principles that guide and govern our behavior and conduct.
8 Here I am following C. Daniel Batson's stipulation of the meaning of "principlism," see C. Daniel Batson, *What's Wrong with Morality: A Social-Psychological Perspective* (New York: Oxford University Press, 2016). Within the last few decades, "principlism" has taken on a different meaning than how I am defining it here, and my employment of this term bears little or no resemblance to this usage. "Principlism" in this other, recent, sense has been defined as a practical approach of *medical ethics*, in which ethical principles (i.e., respect for autonomy, beneficence, nonmaleficence, and justice) are used to examine real ethical dilemmas and are applied to facilitate decision-making. Much like the narrow versus the broad debate about the word "empathy," I find that the isolation of this word "principlism," in which it only refers to medical ethics, limits the greater and more accurate meaning, namely an

understanding of how ethical theories throughout history have fallen under the common impression and oft-repeated belief that merely holding the "correct" moral principles will govern and guide moral behavior. This has been shown to be a dubious claim over the last few decades by the conclusions of unique and ingenious social scientific studies. A "principle," accordingly is: "A fundamental truth or proposition on which others depend; a general statement or tenet forming the (or a basis of a system of belief, etc." O.E.D. 3a).

9 On the Axial Age, see Karl Jaspers, "The Axial Period," in *The Origin and Goal of History*, trans. Michael Bullock (London: Routledge & Kegan Paul, 1953), 1–22, 51–57; and Robert Bellah and Hans Joas, eds., *The Axial Age and Its Consequences* (Cambridge, MA: Belknap Press, 2012).

10 William James, "The Moral Philosopher and the Moral Life," *International Journal of Ethics* 1, no. 3 (1891): 330, emphasis added.

11 James, "Moral Philosopher," 337.

12 Rogers, "Theory of Therapy"; Kohut, *On Empathy*; and Aragno, "Language of Empathy."

13 John Lawson, Simon Baron-Cohen, and Sally Wheelwright, "Empathizing and Systemizing in Adults with and without Asperger Syndrome," *Journal of Autism and Developmental Disorders* 34, no. 3 (2004): 301–310.

14 Michalinos Zembylas, "The Politics of Trauma: Empathy, Reconciliation, and Education," *Journal of Peace Education* 4, no. 2 (2007): 207–224.

15 Pinker, *Better Angels*, 573–592.

16 David Nash, "Ethics, Empathy, and the Education of Dentists," *Journal of Dental Education* 74, no. 6 (2010): 575.

17 James Zaki, *The War for Kindness* (London: Penguin, 2019).

18 Batson, *Altruism Question*, 1991.

19 Baron-Cohen, *Science of Evil*, 194.

20 Baron-Cohen, *Science of Evil*, 183.

21 Slote, *Moral Sentimentalism*, 15.

22 For example, you could feel my pain if I were to step upon a four-inch nail without shoes, but if I were to attempt to rob you under the covering darkness of a moonless night as the nail entered the bottom of my foot, you probably wouldn't feel for (sympathize with) me. Similarly, I could sympathize with you, caring deeply for your well-being, without feeling your pain. For example, one could feel for or sympathize with someone who is depressed or humiliated without vicariously experiencing such a person's depression or humiliation.

23 Slote, *Moral Sentimentalism*, 13, 27.

24 Slote, *Moral Sentimentalism*, 33.

25 See Frans de Waal, *Primates and Philosophers: How Morality Evolved*, ed. Stephen Macedo and Josiah Ober (Princeton, NJ: Princeton University Press, 2006).

26 De Waal, *Age of Empathy*, 225.
27 Hoffman, *Empathy and Moral Development*, 134.
28 Hoffman, *Empathy and Moral Development*, 282.
29 Krznaric, *Empathy*, 194.
30 Jeremy Rifkin, *The Empathic Civilization: The Race to Global Consciousness in a World in Crisis* (New York: Jeremy P. Tarcher, 2009).
31 V. S. Ramachandran, "Mirror Neurons and Imitation Learning as the Driving Force Behind 'the Great Leap Forward' in Human Evolution," *Edge.org*, May 29, 2000.
32 Nils Bubandt and Rane Willerslev, "The Dark Side of Empathy: Mimesis, Deception and the Magic of Alterity," *Comparative Studies in Society and History* 57, no. 1 (2015): 5.
33 Bubandt and Willerslev, "Dark Side of Empathy," 7.
34 Prinz, "Is Empathy Necessary for Morality?," 212.
35 Batson et al., "Immorality from Empathy-Induced Altruism," 1042–1054.
36 See, for instance, Xu et al., "Do You Feel My Pain?," 8525–8529; Gutsell and Inzlicht, "Empathy Constrained," 841–845. See also Stefan Stürmer, Mark Snyder, and Allen M. Omoto, "Prosocial Emotions and Helping: The Moderating Role of Group Membership," *Journal of Personality and Social Psychology* 88, no. 3 (2005): 532–546; and Lisa M. Brown, Margaret M. Bradley, and Peter J. Lang, "Affective Reactions to Pictures of In-Group and Out-Group Members," *Biological Psychology* 71, no. 3 (2006): 303–311.
37 Paul Bloom, *Against Empathy: The Case for Rational Compassion* (New York: HarperCollins, 2016), 3, 16. As an alternative to empathy, Bloom emphasizes and extols the practical benefits of intelligence and self-control, which when coupled with compassion and kindness, helps us to focus on long-term consequences and produce greater moral outcomes than empathy does.
38 Bloom, *Against Empathy*, 38.
39 Bloom, *Against Empathy*, 130; cf. 3.
40 Bloom, *Against Empathy*, 2–3.
41 Bloom, *Against Empathy*, 36.
42 Richard Rorty, "Pragmatism, Relativism, and Irrationalism," in *The New Social Theory Reader: Contemporary Debates*, ed. Steven Seidman and Jeffrey C. Alexander (New York: Routledge, [1980] 2001), 151, emphasis added.
43 See, for example, Gottlieb Frege, *Grundgesetze der Arithmetik: Begriffsschriftlich Abgeleitet*, Vol. 1 (Jena, Germany: Pohle, 1883); and Edmund Husserl, *Logische Untersuchungen: Erster Band Prolegomena zur reinen Logik*, ed. Elmar Holenstein (The Hague: Nijhoff, [1900] 1975).
44 In Karl Popper's words: "One of the more disturbing aspects of the intellectual life of our time is the way in which irrationalism is so widely advocated ... one of the

components of modern irrationalism is relativism" (Karl Popper, *The Myth of the Framework: In Defense of Science and Rationality* (London: Routledge, 1994), 33).

45 Indeed, pour through the pages of history, read about ruthless wars, racial injustice, totalitarian regimes, and human cruelty, and you will find a horde of absolutists had a hand in the rise of these atrocities, not relativists, however defined.

46 William James, *The Meaning of Truth* (New York: Dover, [1909] 2002), 165.

47 James, *Meaning of Truth*, 163.

Chapter 7

1 See Plato, *Meno*, trans. Georges Maximilien Antoine Grube (Indianapolis, IN: Hackett, 1976).

2 Homer, for instance, recognized virtue, i.e., *arete*, in the activities of wrestling and war; the Olympic champions were recognized as excelling at different activities of physical virtue, and even things, such as a well-built house or a well-crafted piece of pottery, were described as possessing virtue because of virtuous actions. Isocrates noticed virtue in the greatness of the orator; in this sense of word, a person could be a virtuous, i.e., excellent, speaker. In addition to these various meanings, a person who had seemed to have mastered all the moral and intellectual virtues necessary for the best, flourishing life was described as possessing a virtuous character. *Arete* is cognate with "aristos," which means "the best" (recognized in the word "aristocracy," which means ruled by the best people). Related to this, a member of an aristocracy could have been considered as possessing *arete* as a politician or statesman.

3 While this approach sometimes serves some practical and desired ends, it is fundamentally an antipluralistic and ahistorical approach in that it disregards the practical import of recognizing the incompleteness of things and views the variations between things of the same class as insignificant for obtaining knowledge of them—their essences. Knowledge of anything, accordingly, is produced by means of excluding all the "nonessential" or "accidental" qualities and properties of a particular thing as well as the nonessential relations and qualities of things that are classified as and belong to the same class.

4 Noting the pragmatic shortcomings of this familiar philosophical approach, William James noted that it is exemplary of, what he called, "viscous intellectualism" and "vicious abstractionism" (two synonymous terms for the same general idea), a form of reflection that often makes experiences and our understanding of *reality itself less intelligible*. James defines "vicious intellectualism" in *Essays in Radical Empiricism* as "the treating of a name as excluding from the fact named what the name's definition fails positively to include" (James, *Essays in Radical Empiricism*, 60). This process of abstraction is necessary and natural. However, such processes become vicious

whenever one makes the claim that the abstraction and representations of a particular thing, for instance, the internal relations of a thing, are abstracted out of the flow of pure experiences and are thought to be more ontologically real than the excluded relations of that thing. James recognizes that this trend of vicious intellectualism has been with us since the dawn of philosophy stating, "ever since Socrates we have been taught that reality consists of essences, not of appearances, and that the essences of things are known whenever we know their definitions" (James, *Essays in Radical Empiricism*, 218).

5 William James, "The Thing and Its Relations," in James, *Essays in Radical Empiricism*, 97.
6 James, "Thing and Its Relations," 141.
7 See John Stuhr, "Introduction: Classical Philosophy," in *Pragmatism and Classical American Philosophy: Essential Readings & Interpretive Essays*, 2nd ed., ed. John Stuhr (New York: Oxford University Press, 2000), 1–12.
8 Fallibilism, as an important dimension of pragmatic pluralism, claims that propositions concerning empirical knowledge cannot be proved with certainty; therefore, we could be wrong, even about those propositions that appear to be irrefutably true.
9 See Zaki, *War for Kindness*, 28–32.
10 Charles Sanders Peirce, "How to Make Our Ideas Clear," in *The Essential Peirce*, Vol. 1, ed. Nathan Houser and Christian Kloesel (Bloomington: Indiana University Press, 1878 [1992]), 132.
11 David Hume, "An Abstract of a Treatise of Human Nature," in *An Enquiry Concerning Human Understanding*, ed. Charles W. Hendel (New York: Bobbs-Merrill, 1955), 187.
12 Peirce, "How to Make Our Ideas Clear," 129.
13 Peirce, "How to Make Our Ideas Clear," 130.
14 See William James, "Does Consciousness Exist?," in *The Writings of William James: A Comprehensive Edition*, ed. John J. McDermott (Chicago: University of Chicago Press, 1996), 170.
15 Quoted in William James, "Habit," in *The Heart of William James*, ed. Robert Richardson (Cambridge, MA: Harvard University Press, [1892] 2010), 102.
16 James, "Habit," 105.
17 James, "Habit," 110, 111.
18 James, "Habit."
19 Andrew Meltzoff and Keith Moore, "Imitation in Newborn Infants: Exploring the Range of Gestures Imitated and the Underlying Mechanisms," *Developmental Psychology* 25, no. 6 (1989): 954–962. For other studies of this phenomenon, see Andrew Meltzoff and Keith Moore, "Imitation of Facial and Manual Gestures by Human Neonates," *Science* 198, no. 4312 (1977): 75–78; Andrew Meltzoff and Keith

Moore, "Newborn Infants Imitate Adult Facial Gestures," *Child Development* 54, no. 3 (1983): 702–709; and Andrew Meltzoff and Keith Moore, "Imitation, Memory, and the Representation of Persons," *Infant Behavior and Development* 17, no. 1 (1994): 83–99.

20 For more on the apparent vagueness of these terms, their similar usages, and the lack of consensus regarding their meaning in the scientific community, see Bloom, *Against Empathy*, 197–202.

21 Zaki, *War for Kindness*, 46.

22 For another interesting, two-component model, definition of mindfulness, see Scott R. Bishop et al., "Mindfulness: A Proposed Operational Definition," *Clinical Psychology: Science and Practice* 11, no. 1 (2004): 230–241.

23 For works on how to integrate the habit of mindfulness into one's life, see Thich Nhat Hanh, *The Miracle of Mindfulness*, trans. Mobi Ho (Boston, MA: Beacon Press, 1975); John Kabat Zinn, *Mindfulness for Beginners: Reclaiming the Present Moment and Your Life* (Boulder, CO: Sounds True, 2016). Zinn's work is not always philosophically carefully, as he often uses ambiguous terminology such as "universal," "wholeness," and "the present moment"; but his guidance for developing mindfulness is very seminal and exceedingly helpful to many practitioners. On mindfulness and higher education, see Narelle Lemon and Sharon McDonough, eds., *Mindfulness in the Academy: Practices and Perspectives from Scholars* (New York: Springer, 2018).

24 Lemon and McDonough, *Mindfulness in the Academy*, Chapter 3, n. 2.

25 See Suzanne Keen, *Empathy and the Novel* (New York: Oxford University Press, 2007).

26 By "kindness" here, I do not mean being kind in the sense that someone is simply nice to everyone without considering the value and conceivable consequences of such an act. Sometimes, we can be nice without being truthful, and to be nice when you ought to be truthful may not produce well-being at all; in fact, depending upon the circumstances, it could produce just the opposite. Also, we can extend kindness to someone and that could encourage that person to continue to act in such a way that perpetuates their tendencies to be unwell.

27 For instance, our daily experiences and interactions with technology, such as the bombardment of text messages, emails, and voicemails from our cellphones—our satellite leashes—are overwhelming us to the point that our senses are being distorted and along with it, our empathy for others.

28 If you are old enough, you might remember that many folks in the 1950s had a similar response to technological advance with the advent of television. Between 1945 and 1950, the number of television sets in American homes jumped from ten thousand to six million, and people noticed that social interactions were being influenced by the hypnotizing glow of televisions.

29 Think of some recent tragic or joyous events. Moments after the brunt of Hurricane Katrina wreaked havoc on the citizens of New Orleans, images of stranded people waiting to be rescued from the roofs of their homes beamed into our living rooms, and we were able to empathize with their plight; within only a few moments after the Haitian earthquake, tweets, posts, and cellphone pictures appeared instantly across the internet, and we experienced their sorrow as if it were our own. And for some of us, these flashes of instantaneous empathy convinced us to reach out and care for those in need of our help.

30 I believe this new theory of empathy will find an important application in healthcare. One of the biggest problems in healthcare is that patients don't feel cared for. Unless we are already inclined to note what exactly is at stake here, this may seem unimportant for many of us who do not grasp the consequences of this problem. Gone are the days when successful medical outcomes were the only criteria used to measure effective treatment in healthcare. Today, patient perception of care matters—patient satisfaction matters, both financially and medically. Using virtual reality, or some other form of extended reality, to teach healthcare professionals the habits of relational empathy will only help them to feel for their patients and coworkers. To solve these and other problems, I do think that the new language of relational empathy can help bring clarity to scientific investigations and thus feel that this work fulfills what Press Ganey's Chief Medical Officer, Thomas Lee, has noted to be necessary, namely, to drive sustained improvement in healthcare throughout the United States, "we need measures, we need data, and we need wisdom about how to use them" (p. 85); moreover, Lee states that in order to increase empathic care throughout the healthcare industry, "we also need a new language" (p. 7) (Thomas Lee, *An Epidemic of Empathy in Healthcare: How to Deliver Compassionate, Connected Patient Care That Creates a Competitive Advantage* (New York: McGraw Hill Education, 2016).

31 Over the last ten years, there have been many remarkable studies into the value and function of using technology for creating embodied experiences of learning. For a few recent resources in this arena of research, see Christine M. Bachen, Pedro F. Hernández-Ramos, and Chad Raphael, "Simulating REAL LIVES Promoting Global Empathy and Interest in Learning through Simulation Games," *Simulation & Gaming* 43, no. 4 (2012): 437–460; Tabitha C. Peck et al., "Putting Yourself in the Skin of a Black Avatar Reduces Implicit Racial Bias," *Consciousness and Cognition* 22, no. 3 (2013): 779–787; Belinda Gutierrez et al., "'Fair Play': A Videogame Designed to Address Implicit Race Bias through Active Perspective Taking," *Games for Health Journal* 3 no. 6 (2014): 371–378; Konstantina Kilteni, Raphaela Groten, and Mel Slater, "The Sense of Embodiment in Virtual Reality," *Presence* 21, no. 4 (2012): 373–387; Fernanda Herrera et al., "Building Long-Term Empathy: A Large-Scale Comparison of Traditional and Virtual Reality Perspective-Taking," *PLoS ONE* 13,

no. 10 (2018); and Philippe Bertrand et al., "Learning Empathy through Virtual Reality: Multiple Strategies for Training Empathy-Related Abilities Using Body Ownership Illusions in Embodied Virtual Reality," in *The Impact of Virtual and Augmented Reality on Individuals and Society*, ed. Mel Slater, María V. Sanchez-Vives, Albert Rizzo, and Massimo Bergamasco (Lausanne, Switzerland: Frontiers Media), 169–186.

32 This idea comes from James: "The great thing, then, in all education, is to make our nervous system our ally instead of our enemy. It is to fund and capitalize our acquisitions, and live at ease upon the interest of the fund.... There is no more miserable human being than one in whom nothing is habitual but indecision, and for whom the lighting of every cigar, the drinking of every cup, the time of rising and going to bed every day, and the beginning of every bit of work, are subjects of express volitional deliberation" (William James, *The Principles of Psychology* (Cambridge, MA: Harvard University Press, [1890] 1981), 130).

33 What this implies and what I have implicitly claimed throughout is that virtue is a skill. For more on this truth, see Matt Stitcher, *The Skillfulness of Virtue* (Cambridge: Cambridge University Press, 2018).

Chapter 8

1 See Charles A. Beard, *The Myth of Rugged Individualism* (New York: Strafford Press, 1931).

2 For the best work on this subject and its unfolding in the United States, see Richard Hofstadter, *Social Darwinism in American Thought* (Boston, MA: Beacon Press, 1944).

3 For a comparative investigation into this, see John D. Carlson, *The State of Nature in Comparative Political Thought: Western and Non-western Perspectives* (Lanham, MD: Lexington Books, 2013); also see Wojciech Sadurski, *Legitimacy: The State and Beyond* (Oxford: Oxford University Press, 2019).

4 See Plato, *Republic*, trans. Georges Maximilien Antoine Grube (Indianapolis, IN: Hackett, 1992).

5 Contemporary accounts seem preoccupied with moral luck in relation to responsibility and blame and have not sufficiently considered the relationship between those forces that affect human flourishing. Therefore, a turn to Aristotle is best for my purposes here.

6 For an interesting work on this point and an all-round excellent book on the concept of moral luck, see Nafsika Athanassoulis, *Morality, Moral Luck, and Responsibility* (New York: Palgrave MacMillan, 2005), 4–25.

7 For instance, Kant remarks, "A good will is not good because of what it effects or accomplishes, because of its fitness to attain some proposed end, but only because of

its volition, that is, it is good in itself ... Even if, by a special disfavor of fortune ... this will should wholly lack the capacity to carry out its purpose—if with its greatest efforts it should yet achieve nothing and only the good will were left (not, of course, as a mere wish but as the summoning of all means insofar as they are in our control)—then, like a jewel, it would still shine by itself, as something that has its full worth in itself. Usefulness or fruitlessness can neither add anything to this worth nor take anything away from it" (Immanuel Kant, *Groundwork of the Metaphysics of Morals*, ed. Mary Gregor (Cambridge: Cambridge University Press, [1784] 1998), 4:394.

8 Two famous examples are writings about moral luck by Thomas Nagel and Bernard Williams. See, Thomas Nagel, *Mortal Questions* (New York: Cambridge University Press, 1979); and Bernard Williams, *Moral Luck* (Cambridge: Cambridge University Press, 1981).

9 I am embracing some liberty here in speaking of these three ways of thinking about moral luck that deviates from the most common ways of describing and using the term drawn from Nagel's distinctions.

10 Imagine a child is born from parents who are exceedingly wealthy. From a very young age this child became interested in questions of justice and the problems of abject poverty around the world. And ever since she could remember she wanted to become a philanthropist and bring about positive social change. At the age of eighteen, her parents gave her access to a $500 million bank account so she could pursue her noble desire to relieve a lot of unnecessary human suffering. Her ability to flourish in the activity was clearly greatly enhanced by the good moral luck bestowed upon her by her parents.

11 For more on the nature, function, and value of democracy, see Alexis de Tocqueville, *Democracy in America*, trans. Henry Reeve, Vols. 1 and 2 (New York: The Century Co., 1898); Anthony H. Birch, *The Concepts and Theories of Modern Democracy* (New York: Routledge, 2001); Takashi Inoguchi, *The Changing Nature of Democracy* (Tokyo: United Nations University Press, 1998); and David A. Moss, *Democracy: A Case Study* (Cambridge, MA: The Belknap Press of Harvard University, 2017). On pluralism and democracy, see Arend Lijphart, *Democracy in Plural Societies* (New Haven, CT: Yale University Press, 1977); and Robert Dahl, *Dilemmas of Pluralist Democracy: Autonomy vs. Control* (New Haven, CT: Yale University Press, 1982).

12 For instance, though the ancient Greeks invented democratic thought and practice, not everyone believed it was a praiseworthy form of government. Nevertheless, those who praised it as well as those who warned against it agreed in that their definitions of democracy arose from their selective interpretations of the historical events in which democratic governments produced either constructive or disastrous consequences.

13 See Plato, *Republic*, 380.

14 For works on democracy and empathy, see Michael E. Morrell, "Empathy and Democratic Education," *Public Affairs Quarterly* 21, no. 4 (2007): 381–403; and Michael E. Morrell, *Empathy and Democracy: Feeling, Thinking, and Deliberation* (University Park, PA: Penn State University Press, 2010).
15 "It will do no harm to recall that ... democracy originally meant and was state and society at one, the citizen body governing itself directly, though active participation in politics, a duty which fell upon every citizen at one time or another" (Anthony Arblaster, *Democracy*, 2nd ed. (Minneapolis: University of Minnesota Press, 1994), 24).
16 John Dewey, *The Middle Works: 1899–1924: Human Nature and Conduct*, Vol. 14 (Carbondale: Southern Illinois University Press, 1924), 226, emphasis added.
17 Sidney Hook, "The Democratic Way of Life," in *Reason, Social Myths, and Democracy*, ed. Sidney Hook (New York: Humanities Press, 1940), 283–297. See also John Stuhr's brilliant essay on democracy as a way of life: John Stuhr, "Democracy as a Way of Life," in *Philosophy and the Reconstruction of Culture*, ed. John Stuhr (Albany, NY: State University of New York Press, 1993), 37–58.
18 See Chapter 1, Article 10 of the *Socialist Constitution of the Democratic People's Republic of Korea*.
19 Expectant hope may be thought as a type of "action" as well; after all, it is a movement of one's will manifested in the desire and expectation for something to arise in the future, but this is not what I mean by saying hope in action is an action.
20 For the Greeks, expectant hope was largely perceived as either negative or positive experience according to the way it contributed to one's personal character. For example, viewed through his doctrine of the mean, Aristotle finds hope to be negative when it leads us to miss the mark of courage, and positive when it provides us with the confidence necessary for courageous behavior. According to the Stoic worldview, expectant hope isn't desirable. For example, Seneca viewed expectant hope as a psychological experience very similar to the experience of fear, and fear and hope certainly weren't the experiences that contributed to the goal of *apatheia* or a disposition of *ataraxia*, for these experiences were not believed to be in concord with the rationality of the divine *Logos*. Among premodern religious philosophers, expectant hope was understood by most as a relation to other psychological states such as belief, confidence, and courage, but also in connection to the possibility of the afterlife. When they weren't rethinking the philosophical positions of the ancients or reworking the theories of premodern philosophers, modern philosophers generally deemed that an understanding of experiences of expectant hope was crucial for grasping our moral psychology as well as for determining what motivates us to act both rationally and irrationally. This focus on the rationality of hope lead to Immanuel Kant's famous question: For what may I hope? Kant's answer to this question was multifaceted and answered in many ways depending upon

whether the question was directed at moral progress, the hope for the afterlife, the hope for divine assistance, or the hope for happiness. According to Kant, hope for a better future in which one expects something desired lies within the *Grenze* or border of reason and is rational when directed at our moral progress and the benefit of the common good. And although Kant considered the relation between expectant hope in relation to larger communal or global concerns, he largely ignored the social problems that arise when hopes conflict and when desires for different moral goods clash. In the twentieth century, there arose the American philosophy of pragmatic pluralism, and it is this philosophical tradition that stands most prominently against Kant's articulation, and, in general, the Enlightenment conceptualization of expectant hope.

21 John Dewey, "Democracy and Education," in Dewey, *Middle Works*, 107.
22 Richard Rorty, *Philosophy and the Mirror of Nature* (Princeton, NJ: Princeton University Press, 1979), 318; and Richard Rorty, *Philosophy and Social Hope* (Middlesex: Penguin Books, 1999), 87.
23 John Stuhr, *Pragmatic Fashions: Pluralism, Democracy, Relativism, and the Absurd* (Bloomington: Indiana University Press, 2016), 149, emphasis added.
24 William James, "Pragmatism and Humanism," in McDermott, *Writings of William James*, 455–466, emphasis added.
25 John Dewey, "The Quest for Certainty," in *The Later Works*, Vol. 4, ed. Jo Ann Boydston (Carbondale: Southern Illinois University Press, [1929] 1988).
26 William James, "The Absolute and the Strenuous Life," in James, *Meaning of Truth*, 226.
27 James, "Absolute," 229.
28 James, "Moral Philosopher," 610–611.
29 James, *Will to Believe*, 205.
30 James, *Will to Believe*, 24.
31 The inspiration for this sentiment comes from John Dewey. See Dewey, "Quest for Certainty."
32 For an example of how empathy as "feeling with" and "feeling for" can lead to ignorance, see Janine Jones, "The Impairment of Empathy in Goodwill Whites for African Americans," in *What White Looks Like: African American Philosophers on the Whiteness Question*, ed. George Yancy (London: Routledge, 2004); for an example of how empathy can function violently, see Saidiya V. Hartman, *Scenes of Subjection: Terror, Slavery, and Self-Making in Nineteenth-Century America* (New York: Oxford University Press, 1997).
33 Cynthia Willett, *Uproarious: How Feminists and Other Subversive Comics Speak Truth* (Minneapolis: University of Minneapolis Press, 2019), 124.
34 William James, "Pragmatism's Conception of Truth," in *Pragmatism: A New Name for Some Old Ways of Thinking*, ed. William James (New York: Longmans, Green, and Co., 1907), 76.

Bibliography

Aquinas, St. Thomas. *Summa Theologiae*, translated by Fathers of the English Dominican Province. Westminster: Christian Classics, 1981.

Aragno, Anna. "The Language of Empathy: An Analysis of Its Constitution, Development, and Role in Psychoanalytic Listening." *Journal of American Psychoanalytic Association* 56, no. 3 (2008): 714.

Arblaster, Anthony. *Democracy*. 2nd ed. Minneapolis: University of Minnesota Press, 1994.

Aristotle. *Nicomachean Ethics*, translated by W. D. Ross. Lawrence, KS: Digireads, 2016.

Aristotle. *Politics*, translated by R. Rackham. Cambridge, MA: Harvard University Press, 1932.

Aristotle. *Rhetoric*, translated by W. Rhys Roberts. Fairhope, AL: Mockingbird Classics, 2015.

Ashar, Yoni K., Jessica R. Andrews-Hanna, Sona Dimidjian, and Tor D. Wager. "Empathic Care and Distress: Predictive Brain Markers and Dissociable Brain Systems." *Neuron* 94, no. 6 (2017): 1263–1273.

Athanassoulis, Nafsika. *Morality, Moral Luck, and Responsibility*. New York: Palgrave MacMillan, 2005.

Augustine. "The City of God, Vol. 1." In *The Works of Aurelius Augustine*, edited by Marcus Dods. Edinburgh: T. & T. Clark, 1913.

Bachen, Christine M., Pedro F. Hernández-Ramos, and Chad Raphael. "Simulating REAL LIVES Promoting Global Empathy and Interest in Learning through Simulation Games." *Simulation & Gaming* 43, no. 4 (2012): 437–460.

Baron-Cohen, Simon. "The Male Condition." *New York Times*, August 8, 2005, A15.

Baron-Cohen, Simon. *The Science of Evil: On Empathy and the Origins of Cruelty*. New York: Basic Books, 2012.

Bartal, Ben-Ami, Jean Decety, and Peggy Mason. "Empathy and Pro-Social Behavior in Rats." *Science* 334, no. 6061 (2011): 1427–1430.

Batson, C. Daniel. *Altruism in Humans*. New York: Oxford University Press, 2011.

Batson, C. Daniel. *The Altruism Question: Toward a Social-Psychological Answer*. New York: Psychology Press, 1991.

Batson, C. Daniel. *A Scientific Search for Altruism: Do We Only Care about Ourselves?* New York: Oxford University Press, 2019.

Batson, C. Daniel. "These Things Called Empathy: Eight Related but Distinct Phenomena." In *The Social Neuroscience of Empathy*, edited by Jean Decety and William Ickes. Cambridge, MA: MIT Press, 2011.

Batson, C. Daniel. "Two Forms of Perspective Taking: Imagining How Another Feels and Imagining How You Would Feel." In *Handbook of Imagination and Mental Simulation*, edited by Keith S. Markman, William M. P. Klein, and Julie A. Suhr. New York: Psychology Press, 2009.

Batson, C. Daniel. *What's Wrong with Morality? A Social-Psychological Perspective*. New York: Oxford University Press, 2016.

Batson, C. Daniel, Bruce D. Duncan, Paula Ackerman, Terese Buckley, and Kimberly Birch. "Is Empathic Emotion a Source of Altruistic Motivation?" *Journal of Personality and Social Psychology* 40, no. 2 (1981): 290–302.

Batson, C. Daniel, Shannon Early, and Giovanni Salvarani. "Perspective Taking: Imagining How Another Feels Versus Imagining How You Would Feel." *Personality & Social Personality Bulletin* 23, no. 7 (1997): 751–758.

Batson, C. Daniel, Trica R. Klein, Lori Highberger, and Laura L. Shaw. "Immorality from Empathy-Induced Altruism: When Compassion and Justice Conflict." *Journal of Personality and Social Psychology* 68, no. 6 (1995): 1042–1054.

Batson, C. Daniel, and Kathryn C. Oleson. "Current Status of the Empathy-Altruism Hypothesis." In *Prosocial Behavior*, edited by Margaret S. Clark. Newbury Park, CA: SAGE, 1991.

Batson, C. Daniel, and Laura L. Shaw. "Evidence for Altruism: Toward a Pluralism of Prosocial Motives." *Psychological Inquiry* 2, no. 2 (1991): 107–122.

Baumgold, Deborah. *Three-Text Edition of Thomas Hobbes's Political Theory*. Cambridge: Cambridge University Press, 2017.

Bavelas, Janet Beavin, Alex Black, Charles R. Lewmery, and Jennifer Mullett. "Motor Mimicry as Primitive Empathy." In *Empathy and Its Development*, edited by Nancy Eisenberg and Janet Strayer, 317–338. New York: Cambridge University Press, 1987.

Beard, Charles A. *The Myth of Rugged Individualism*. New York: Strafford Press, 1931.

Bellah, Robert, and Hans Joas, eds. *The Axial Age and Its Consequences*. Cambridge, MA: Belknap Press, 2012.

Bertrand, Philippe Jérôme Guegan, Léonore Robieux, Cade Andrew McCall, Franck Zenasni. "Learning Empathy through Virtual Reality: Multiple Strategies for Training Empathy-Related Abilities Using Body Ownership Illusions in Embodied Virtual Reality." In *The Impact of Virtual and Augmented Reality on Individuals and Society*, edited by Mel Slater, María V. Sanchez-Vives, Albert Rizzo, and Massimo Bergamasco, 169–186. Lausanne, Switzerland: Frontiers Media, 2019.

Bevir, Mark. "What Is Genealogy?" *Journal of the Philosophy of History* 2, no. 3 (2008): 263–275.

Birch, Anthony H. *The Concepts and Theories of Modern Democracy*. New York: Routledge, 2001.

Bishop, Scott R., Mark Lau, Shauna Shapiro, Linda Carlson, Nicole D. Anderson, James Carmody, et al. "Mindfulness: A Proposed Operational Definition." *Clinical Psychology: Science and Practice* 11, no. 3 (2004): 230–241.

Bloom, Paul. *Against Empathy: The Case for Rational Compassion*. New York: HarperCollins, 2016.
Brouwer, René. "Stoic Sympathy." In *Sympathy: A History*, edited by Eric Schliesser, 15–35. Oxford: Oxford University Press, 2013.
Brown, Lisa M., Margaret M. Bradley, and Peter J. Lang. "Affective Reactions to Pictures of In-Group and Out-Group Members." *Biological Psychology* 71, no. 3 (2006): 303–311.
Bubandt, Nils, and Rane Willerslev. "The Dark Side of Empathy: Mimesis, Deception and the Magic of Alterity." *Comparative Studies in Society and History* 57, no. 1 (2015): 5–34.
Carlson, John D. *The State of Nature in Comparative Political Thought: Western and Non-western Perspectives*. Lanham, MD: Lexington Books, 2013.
Cayuela, Aquilino. "Vulnerable: To Be between Life and Death." In *Human Dignity of the Vulnerable in the Age of Rights: Interdisciplinary Perspectives*, edited by Aniceto Mansferrer and Emilio Garcia-Sanchez, 63–79. New York: Springer International, 2016.
Cialdini, Robert B., Stephanie L. Brown, Brian P. Lewis, Carol Luce, Steven L. Neuberg. "Reinterpreting the Empathy–Altruism Relationship: When One into One Equals Oneness." *Journal of Personality and Social Psychology* 73, no. 3 (1979): 481–494.
Cicero, Marcus Tullius. *De Finibus Bonorum et Malorum*. Cambridge, MA: Harvard University Press, 1931.
Cicero, Marcus Tullius. *On Academic Scepticism*. Indianapolis, IN: Hackett, 2006.
Cicero, Marcus Tullius. *On Divination*, translated by William Armistead Falconer. Cambridge, MA: Harvard University Press, 1923.
Cicero, Marcus Tullius, and Margaret R. Graver. *Cicero on the Emotions: Tusculan Disputations 3 and 4*. Chicago: University of Chicago Press, 2002.
Clark, Russell D., and Larry E. Wood. "Where Is the Apathetic Bystander? Situational Characteristics of the Emergency." *Journal of Personality and Social Psychology* 29, no. 3 (1974): 279–287.
Cohen, Douglas, and Janet Strayer. "Empathy in Conduct-Discorded and Comparison Youth." *Developmental Psychology* 32, no. 6 (1996): 988–998.
Coleridge, Samuel Taylor. "Letter to W. Sotheby." In *Letters of Samuel Taylor Coleridge*, Vol. 1, edited by Ernest Hartley Coleridge. London: William Heinemann, 1895.
Cooper, John M. *Plato Complete Works*. Indianapolis, IN: Hackett, 1997.
Coplan, Amy. "Understanding Empathy: Its Features and Effects." In *Empathy: Philosophical and Psychological Perspectives*, edited by Amy Coplan and Peter Goldie, 3–18. Oxford: Oxford University Press, 2011.
Coplan, Amy. "Will the Real Empathy Please Stand Up? A Case for a Narrow Conceptualization." *The Southern Journal of Philosophy* 49, supp. 1 (2011): 40–65.
Currie, Gregory. "Empathy for Objects." In *Empathy: Philosophical and Psychological Perspectives*, edited by Amy Coplan and Peter Goldie, 82–98. Oxford: Oxford University Press, 2011.

Curtis, Robin, and Richard George Elliott. "An Introduction to Einfühlung." In *Art in Translation* 6, no. 4 (2015): 353–376.

Dahl, Robert. *Dilemmas of Pluralist Democracy: Autonomy vs. Control*. New Haven, CT: Yale University Press, 1982.

Damasio, Antonio. *Emotion, Reason, and the Human Brain*. New York: HarperCollins, 1994.

Damasio, Antonio. *The Feeling of What Happens: Body and Emotion in the Making of Consciousness*. New York: Harcourt Brace, 2000.

Danziger, Nicolas, Kenneth M. Prkachin, and Jean-Claude Willer. "Is Pain the Price of Empathy? The Perception of Others' Pain in Patients with Congenital Insensitivity to Pain." *Brain* 129, no. 9 (2006): 2494–2507.

Darwall, Stephen. "Empathy, Sympathy, Care." *Philosophical Studies* 89, no. 2–3 (1998): 261–282.

Davidson, Donald. "A Nice Derangement of Epitaphs." In *Truth and Interpretation*, edited by Ernest Lepore, 433–446. Oxford: Blackwell, 1989.

Decety, Jean. *Empathy: From Bench to Bedside*. Cambridge, MA: MIT Press, 2012.

Decety, Jean. "The Neurodevelopment of Empathy in Humans." *Developmental Neuroscience* 32, no. 4 (2010): 257–267.

Decety, Jean. *The Social Neuroscience of Empathy*, edited by Jean Decety and William Ickes. Cambridge, MA: MIT Press, 2009.

Decety, Jean, and Phillip L. Jackson. "The Functional Architecture of Human Empathy." *Behavioral and Cognitive Neuroscience Reviews* 3, no. 2 (2004): 71–100.

Decety, Jean, and Claus Lamm. "Empathy versus Personal Distress: Recent Evidence from Social Neuroscience." In *The Social Neuroscience of Empathy*, edited by Jean Decety and William Ickes, 199–213. Cambridge, MA: MIT Press, 2009.

Decety, Jean, and Andrew N. Meltzoff. "Empathy, Imitation, and the Social Brain." In *Empathy: Philosophical and Psychological Perspectives*, edited by Amy Coplan and Peter Goldie, 58–81. Oxford: Oxford University Press, 2011.

Descartes, René. *Meditations on First Philosophy*, 3rd ed., translated by Donald A Cress. Indianapolis, IN: Hackett, [1641] 1993.

Descartes, René. *The Philosophical Writings of Descartes*, Vols. 1 and 2, edited and translated by John Cottingham, Robert Stoothoff, and Dugald Murdoch. Cambridge: Cambridge University Press, 1985.

Descartes, René. *The Philosophical Writings of Descartes*, Vol. 3: *The Correspondence*, edited and translated by John Cottingham, Robert Stoothoff, Dugald Murdoch, and Anthony Kenny. Cambridge: Cambridge University Press, 1991.

de Tocqueville, Alexis. *Democracy in America*, translated by Henry Reeve, Vols. 1 and 2. New York: The Century Co., 1898.

de Vignemont, Frederique, and Tania Singer. "The Empathic Brain: How, When, and Why?" *Trends in Cognitive Sciences* 10, no. 10 (2006): 435–441.

de Waal, Frans. *The Age of Empathy*. New York: Harmony Books, 2009.

de Waal, Frans. *Primates and Philosophers: How Morality Evolved*, edited by Stephen Macedo and Josiah Ober. Princeton, NJ: Princeton University Press, 2006.

Dewey, John. "Democracy and Education." In *The Middle Works, 1899–1924*, Vol. 7, edited by Jo Ann Boydston. Carbondale: Southern Illinois University Press, [1916] 1980.

Dewey, John. *The Middle Works: 1899–1924: Human Nature and Conduct*, Vol. 14. Carbondale: Southern Illinois University Press, 1924.

Dewey, John. "The Quest for Certainty." In *The Later Works*, Vol. 4, edited by Jo Ann Boydston. Carbondale: Southern Illinois University Press, [1929] 1988.

Diogenes Laertius. *Lives of Eminent Philosophers*, Vol. 2, translated by Robert Drew Hicks. Cambridge, MA: Harvard University Press, 2005.

di Pellegrino, Giuseppe, Luciano Fadiga, Leonardo Fogassi, Vittorio Gallese, and Giacomo Rizzolatti. "Understanding Motor Events: A Neurophysiological Study." *Experimental Brain Research* 91, no. 1 (1992): 176–180.

Dixon, Thomas. "'Emotion': The History of a Key Word in Crisis." *Emotion Review* 4, no. 4 (2012): 338–344.

Dondi, Marco, Francesca Simion, and Giovanna Caltran. "Can Newborns Discriminate between Their Own Cry and the Cry of Another Newborn Infant?" *Developmental Psychology* 35, no. 2 (1999): 418–426.

Drwecki, Brain B., Colleen F. Moore, Sandra E. Ward, and Kenneth M. Prkachin. "Reducing Racial Disparities in Pain Treatment: The Role of Empathy and Perspective Taking." *Pain* 152, no. 5 (2011): 1001–1006.

Eisenberg, Nancy, and Richard A. Fabes. "Prosocial Development." In *Handbook of Child Psychology: Social, Emotional, and Personality Development*, edited by William Damon and Nancy Eisenberg, 646–719. Hoboken, NJ: John Wiley & Sons, 1998.

Eisenberg, Nancy, and Natalie D. Eggum. "Empathic Responding: Sympathy and Personal Distress." In *The Social Neuroscience of Empathy*, edited by Jean Decety and William Ickes, 71–83. Cambridge, MA: MIT Press, 2009.

Eisenberg, Nancy, and Richard A. Fabes. "Empathy: Conceptualization, Measurement, and Relation to Prosocial Behavior." *Motivation and Emotion* 14, no. 2 (1990): 131–149.

Eisenberg, Nancy, Richard A. Fabes, Mark Schaller, Paul Miller, Gustavo Carlo, Rick Poulin, Cindy Shea, and Rita Shell. "Personality and Socialization Correlates of Vicarious Emotional Responding." *Journal of Personality and Social Psychology* 61, no. 3 (1991): 459–470.

Eliot, T. S. "Burnt Norton." In *Four Quartets*, edited by T. S. Eliot. New York: Mariner Books, 1943.

Epicurus. *Letter to Menoeceus*, translated by Cyril Bailey. Oxford: Clarendon Press, 1926.

Fagiano, Mark. "Relational Empathy as an Instrument of Democratic Hope in Action." *Journal of Speculative Philosophy* 33, no. 2 (2019): 200–219.

Feshbach, Norma D., and Seymour Feshbach. "Empathy Training and the Regulation of Aggression: Potentialities and Limitations." *Academic Psychology Bulletin* 4, no. 3 (1982): 399–413.

Field, Tiffany M., Robert Woodson, Reena Greenberg, and Debra Cohen. "Discrimination and Imitation of Facial Expression by Neonates." *Science* 218, no. 4568 (1982): 179–181.

Frege, Gottlieb. *Grundgesetze der Arithmetik: Begriffsschriftlich Abgeleitet*, Vol. 1. Jena, Germany: Pohle, 1883.
Freud, Sigmund. "Das Interesse an der Psychoanalyse." *Scientia* 14, no. 31–32 (1913): 240–250, 369–384.
Freud, Sigmund. "Further Recommendations in the Technique of Psychoanalysis: On Beginning the Treatment." In *Therapy and Technique*, translated by Joan Riviere, 121–144. New York: Crowell-Collier, [1913] 1964.
Freud, Sigmund. "Jokes and the Relation to the Unconscious." In *The Standard Edition of Freud's Works*, Vol. 8, translated under the supervision of James Strachey. London: Hogarth Press, 1955–1964.
Freud, Sigmund. "Recommendations to Physicians Practicing Psycho-Analysis." In *The Standard Edition of Freud's Works*, Vol. 12, translated under the supervision of James Strachey, 109–120. London: Hogarth Press, 1912.
Freud, Sigmund. "Remembering, Repeating and Working-Through." In *The Standard Edition of Freud's Works*, Vol. 12, translated under the supervision of James Strachey, 145–156. London: Hogarth Press, 1914.
Fugate, Joe K. "The Relationship between Aesthetics and Psychology." In *The Psychological Basis of Herder's Aesthetics*, edited by Joe K. Fugate. The Hague: Mouton, 1966.
Galen. *The Doctrines of Hippocrates and Plato*. Berlin: Akademie-Verlag, 1984.
Gallese, Vittorio, Luciano Fadiga, Leonardo Fogassi, and Giacomo Rizzolatti. "Action Recognition in the Premotor Cortex." *Brain* 119, no. 2 (1996): 593–609.
Goldie, Peter. *The Emotions: A Philosophical Exploration*. Oxford: Oxford University Press, 2002.
Goldman, Alvin I. *Simulating Minds: The Philosophy, Psychology and Neuroscience of Mindreading*. New York: Oxford University Press, 2006.
Graver, Margaret. *Cicero and the Emotions: Tusculan Disputations 3 and 4*. Chicago: University of Chicago Press, 2002.
Graver, Margaret. *Stoicism and Emotion*. Chicago: University of Chicago Press, 2007.
Groos, Karl. *The Play of Man*. New York: D. Appleton, 1901.
Gutierrez, Belinda, Anna Kaatz, Sarah Chu, Dennis Ramirez, Clem Samson-Samuel, and Molly Carnes. "'Fair Play': A Videogame Designed to Address Implicit Race Bias through Active Perspective Taking." *Games for Health Journal* 3, no. 6 (2014): 371–378.
Gutsell, Jennifer N., and Michael Inzlicht. "Empathy Constrained: Prejudice Predicts Reduced Mental Simulation of Actions during Observations of Outgroups." *Journal of Experimental Social Psychology* 46, no. 5 (2010): 841–845.
Hanh, Thich Nhat. *The Miracle of Mindfulness*, translated by Mobi Ho. Boston, MA: Beacon Press, 1975.
Hartman, Saidiya V. *Scenes of Subjection: Terror, Slavery, and Self-Making in Nineteenth-Century America*. New York: Oxford University Press, 1997.

Hatfield, Elaine, John T. Cacioppo, and Richard L. Rapson. *Emotional Contagion*. Cambridge: Cambridge University Press, 1994.

Hausheer, Roger. "Fichte and Shelling." In *German Philosophy since Kant*, edited by Anthony O'Hear. Cambridge: Cambridge University Press, 1999.

Hein, Grit, Giorgia Silani, Kerstin Preuschoff, C. Daniel Batson, and Tania Singer. "Neural Responses to Ingroup and Outgroup Members' Suffering Predict Individual Differences in Costly Helping." *Neuron* 68, no. 1 (2010): 149–160.

Herder, Johann Gottlieb. *Herder on Social and Political Culture*, edited by Frederick M. Barnard. Cambridge: Cambridge University Press, 1969.

Herder, Johann Gottlieb. *Sämmtliche Werke*, Vol. 5, edited by Bernhard Suphan. Berlin: Weidmann, 1877–1937.

Herder, Johann Gottlieb. "Vom Erkennen und Empfinden der menschlichen Seele." In *Herders Werke*, Vol. 3, edited by Johann Gottlieb Herder. Berlin: Aufbau Verlag, [1774] 1964.

Herrera, Fernanda, Jeremy Balienson, Erik Weisz, Elise Ogle, and Jamil Zaki. "Building Long-Term Empathy: A Large-Scale Comparison of Traditional and Virtual Reality Perspective-Taking." *PLoS ONE* 13, no. 10 (2018): e0204494.

Hickok, Gregory. *The Myth of Mirror Neurons: The Real Neuroscience of Communication and Cognition*. New York: W. W. Norton, 2014.

Hobbes, Thomas. "Concerning Body." In *The Metaphysical System of Hobbes*, edited by Mary Whiton Calkins. Chicago, IL: Open Court, [1656] 1963.

Hobbes, Thomas. *Elements of Law: Natural and Politic*, edited by Ferdinand Tönnies. New York: Routledge, [1640] 1889.

Hobbes, Thomas. *Leviathan*, edited by John Charles Addison Gaskin. Oxford: Oxford University Press, [1651] 1996.

Hoffman, Martin. *Empathy and Moral Development: Implications for Caring and Justice*. Cambridge: Cambridge University Press, 2000.

Hofstadter, Richard. *Social Darwinism in American Thought*. Boston, MA: Beacon Press, 1944.

Hook, Sidney. "The Democratic Way of Life." In *Reason, Social Myths, and Democracy*, edited by Sidney Hook, 283–297. New York: Humanities Press, 1940.

Hume, David. "An Abstract of a Treatise of Human Nature." In *An Enquiry Concerning Human Understanding*, edited by Charles W. Hendel. New York: Bobbs-Merrill, 1955.

Hume, David. *Enquiries Concerning Human Understanding and Concerning the Principles of Morals*, edited by L. A. Selby-Bigge. New York: Oxford University Press, [1748] 1975.

Hume, David. *Treatise of Human Nature*, edited by L. A. Selby-Bigge. New York: Oxford University Press, [1738] 1978.

Husserl, Edmund. *Logische Untersuchungen: Erster Band Prolegomena zur reinen Logik*, edited by Elmar Holenstein. The Hague: Nijhoff, [1900] 1975.

Iacoboni, Marco. *Mirroring People: The New Science of How We Connect with Others*. New York: Farrar, Straus and Giroux, 2008.

Iacoboni, Marco, and Mirella Dapretto. "The Mirror Neuron System and the Consequences of Its Dysfunction." *Nature Reviews Neuroscience* 7, no. 12 (2006): 942–951.

Ickes, William. *Empathic Accuracy*. New York: Guilford Press, 1997.

Ickes, William, Linda Stinson, Victor Bissonnette, and Stella Garcia. "Naturalistic Social Cognition: Empathic Accuracy in Mixed-Sex Dyads." *Journal of Personality and Social Psychology* 59, no. 4 (1990): 730–742.

Inoguchi, Takashi. *The Changing Nature of Democracy*. Tokyo: United Nations University Press, 1998.

Jahoda, Gustav. "Theodor Lipps and the Shift from 'Sympathy' to 'Empathy.'" *Journal of the History of the Behavioral Sciences* 41, no. 2 (2005): 151–163.

James, William. "The Absolute and the Strenuous Life." In *The Meaning of Truth*, edited by William James, 226–229. New York: Longmans, Green, and Co., 1911.

James, William. "Does Consciousness Exist?" In *The Writings of William James: A Comprehensive Edition*, edited by John J. McDermott, 169–183. Chicago: University of Chicago Press, [1904] 1996.

James, William. *Essays in Radical Empiricism*. New York: Longmans, Green, and Co., 1912.

James, William. "Habit." In *The Heart of William James*, edited by Robert Richardson, 101–115. Cambridge, MA: Harvard University Press, [1892] 2010.

James, William. *The Meaning of Truth*. New York: Dover, [1909] 2002.

James, William. "The Moral Philosopher and the Moral Life." *International Journal of Ethics* 1, no. 3 (1891): 340–354.

James, William. "On a Certain Blindness in Human Beings." In *On Some of Life's Ideals*, edited by William James, 229–264. New York: Henry Holt, 1899.

James, William. *A Pluralistic Universe: Hibbert Lectures at Manchester College on the Present Situation of Philosophy*. Lincoln: University of Nebraska Press, [1909] 1996.

James, William. *Pragmatism*. New York: Longmans, Green, and Co., 1909.

James, William. "Pragmatism and Humanism." In *The Writings of William James: A Comprehensive Edition*, edited by John J. McDermott, 455–466. Chicago: University of Chicago Press, [1907] 1996.

James, William. "Pragmatism's Conception of Truth." In *Pragmatism: A New Name for Some Old Ways of Thinking*, edited by William James, 76–91. New York: Longmans, Green, and Co., 1907.

James, William. *The Principles of Psychology*. Cambridge, MA: Harvard University Press, [1890] 1981.

James, William. "The Sentiment of Rationality." In *The Will to Believe, and Other Essays in Popular Philosophy*, edited by William James, 63–110. New York: Longmans, Green, and Co., 1905.

James, William. "The Thing and Its Relations." In *Essays in Radical Empiricism*, edited by William James, 92–122. New York: Longmans, Green, and Co., 1912.

James, William. "What Is an Emotion." *Mind* 9, no. 34 (1884): 189–190.

James, William. *The Will to Believe: And Other Essays in Popular Philosophy*. New York: Longmans, Green, and Co., 1912.
James, William. "A World of Pure Experience." In *Essays in Radical Empiricism*, edited by William James, 39–91. New York: Longmans, Green, and Co., [1912] 1996.
Jaspers, Karl. "The Axial Period." In *The Origin and Goal of History*, translated by Michael Bullock, 1–21. London: Routledge & Kegan Paul, 1953.
Jones, Janine. "The Impairment of Empathy in Goodwill Whites for African Americans." In *What White Looks Like: African American Philosophers on the Whiteness Question*, edited by George Yancy, 65–86. London: Routledge, 2004.
Kant, Immanuel. *Groundwork of the Metaphysics of Morals*, edited by Mary Gregor. Cambridge: Cambridge University Press, [1784] 1998.
Keen, Suzanne. *Empathy and the Novel*. New York: Oxford University Press, 2007.
Keysers, Christian. *The Empathic Brain: How the Discovery of Mirror Neurons Changes Our Understanding of Human Nature*. Lexington, KY: Social Brain Press, 2011.
Kilteni, Konstantina, Raphaela Groten, and Mel Slater. "The Sense of Embodiment in Virtual Reality." *Presence* 21, no. 4 (2012): 373–387.
Knox, Jean. "'Feeling for' and 'Feeling with': Developmental and Neuroscientific Perspectives on Intersubjectivity and Empathy." *Analytical Psychology* 59, no. 4 (2013): 491–509.
Knox, Robert. *The Races of Men: A Philosophical Enquiry into the Influence of Race over the Destinies of Nations*. Cambridge, MA: Harvard University Press, [1850] 2008.
Kögler, Hans Herbert, and Karsten Stueber. *Empathy & Agency: The Problem of Understanding in the Human Sciences*. New York: Routledge, 1999.
Kohut, Heinz. "On Empathy." *International Journal of Psychoanalytic Self Psychology* 5, no. 2 (1981): 122–131.
Konstan, David. "Epicurean 'Passions' and the Good Life." In *The Virtuous Life in Greek Ethics*, edited by Burkhard Reis, 194–206. New York: Cambridge University Press, 2006.
Korchin, Sheldon J. *Modern Clinical Psychology: Principles of Intervention in the Clinic and Community*. New York: Joanna Cotler Books, International Edition, 1978.
Krznaric, Roman. *Empathy: Why It Matters, and How to Get It*. New York: Random House, 2014.
Lamm, Claus, C. Daniel Batson, and Jean Decety. "The Neural Substrate of Human Empathy: Effects of Perspective-Taking and Cognitive Appraisal." *Journal of Cognitive Neuroscience* 19, no. 1 (2007): 42–58.
Langfeld, Herbert Sidney. *The Aesthetic Attitude*. New York: Harcourt, Brace, 1920.
Lawson, John, Simon Baron-Cohen, and Sally Wheelwright. "Empathizing and Systemizing in Adults with and without Asperger Syndrome." *Journal of Autism and Developmental Disorders* 34, no. 3 (2004): 301–310.
Lee, Thomas. *An Epidemic of Empathy in Healthcare: How to Deliver Compassionate, Connected Patient Care That Creates a Competitive Advantage*. New York: McGraw Hill Education, 2016.

Lemon, Narelle, and Sharon McDonough, eds. *Mindfulness in the Academy: Practices and Perspectives from Scholars*. New York: Springer, 2018.

Levenson, Robert W., and Anna M. Ruef. "Physiological Aspects of Emotional Knowledge and Rapport." In *Empathic Accuracy*, edited by William Ickes, 44–72. New York: Guilford Press, 1997.

Lightbody, Brian. *Philosophical Genealogy: An Epistemological Reconstruction of Nietzsche and Foucault's Genealogical Method*, Vol. 1. New York: Peter Lang, 2010.

Lightbody, Brian. *Philosophical Genealogy: An Epistemological Reconstruction of Nietzsche and Foucault's Genealogical Method*, Vol. 2. New York: Peter Lang, 2010.

Lijphart, Arend. *Democracy in Plural Societies*. New Haven, CT: Yale University Press, 1977.

Lipps, Theodor. *Ästhetik: Psychologie des Schoenen und der Kunst*. Leipzig, Germany: L. Voss, 1914.

Lipps, Theodor. "Das wissen von fremden ichen." *Psychologischen Untersuchungen* 1, no. 4 (1907): 694–722.

Lipps, Theodor. "Einfühlung und Ästhetischer Genuß." *Die Zukunft* 54, no. 16 (1906): 100–114.

Long, Anthony Arthur, and David N. Sedley. *The Hellenistic Philosophers, Volume 1*. Cambridge: Cambridge University Press, 1987.

Lotze, Hermann. *Microcosmus: An Essay Concerning Man and His Relation to the World*, Vol. 1, 4th ed. Edinburgh: T. & T. Clark, 1856.

Luz, Menahem, ed. *Cosmic Sympathy: The Teachings of Posidonius*. Albany, CA: Berkeley Hills Books, 2005.

Maibom, Heidi L. "Introduction: Almost Everything You Ever Wanted to Know about Empathy." In *Empathy and Morality*, edited by Heidi L. Maibom, 1–40. New York: Oxford University Press, 2014.

Malcolm, Norman. *Knowledge and Certainty: Essays and Lectures*. Englewood Cliffs, NJ: Prentice-Hall, 1963.

Mathur, Divya, Alyssa Bost, Ian Driver, and Benjamin Ohlstein. "A Transient Niche Regulates the Specification of Drosophila Intestinal Stem Cells." *Science* 327, no. 5962 (2010): 210–213.

Mathur, Vani A., Tokiko Harada, Trixie Lipke, and Joan Y. Chiao. "Neural Basis of Extraordinary Empathy and Altruistic Motivation." *NeuroImage* 51, no. 4 (2010): 1468–1475.

Matravers, Derek. *Empathy*. Malden, MA: Polity Press, 2017.

McBride III, Lee A. *Ethics and Insurrection: A Pragmatism for the Oppressed*. London: Bloomsbury Press, 2020.

McFee, Graham. "Empathy: Interpersonal vs. Artistic?" In *Empathy: Philosophical and Psychological Perspectives*, edited by Amy Coplan and Peter Goldie, 82–98. Oxford: Oxford University Press, 2011.

Mead, George Herbert. *Mind, Self, and Society: From the Standpoint of a Social Behaviorist*, edited by Charles W. Morris. Chicago: University of Chicago Press, 1934.

Meltzoff, Andrew. "Imitation, Memory, and the Representation of Persons." *Infant Behavior and Development* 17, no. 1 (1994): 83–99.

Meltzoff, Andrew. "Newborn Infants Imitate Adult Facial Gestures." *Child Development* 54, no. 3 (1983): 702–709.

Meltzoff, Andrew, and Keith Moore. "Imitation of Facial and Manual Gestures by Human Neonates." *Science* 198, no. 4312 (1977): 75–78.

Meltzoff, Andrew, and Keith Moore. "Imitation in Newborn Infants: Exploring the Range of Gestures Imitated and the Underlying Mechanisms." *Developmental Psychology* 25, no. 6 (1989): 954–962.

Mercer, Phillip. *Sympathy and Ethics: A Study of the Relationship between Sympathy and Morality with Special Reference to Hume's Treatise*. Oxford: Clarendon Press, 1972.

Montalan, Benoît, Thierry Lelard, Olivier Godefroy, and Harold Mouras. "Behavioural Investigation of the Influence of Social Categorization on Empathy for Pain: A Minimal Group Paradigm Study." *Frontiers in Psychology* 3, no. 389 (2012): 2–5.

Moran, Dermot. "The Problem of Empathy: Lipps, Scheler, Husserl, and Stein." In *Amor Amicitiae: On the Love That Is Friendship; Essays in Medieval Thought and Beyond in Honor of the Rev. Professor James McEvoy*, edited by Thomas A. F. Kelly and Philipp W. Rosemann, 269–312. Leuven, Belgium: Peeters, 2004.

Morrell, Michael E. *Empathy and Democracy: Feeling, Thinking, and Deliberation*. University Park, PA: Penn State University Press, 2010.

Morrell, Michael E. "Empathy and Democratic Education." *Public Affairs Quarterly* 21, no. 4 (2007): 381–403.

Moss, David A. *Democracy: A Case Study*. Cambridge, MA: The Belknap Press of Harvard University, 2017.

Munteanu, Dana LaCourse. *Tragic Pathos: Pity and Fear in Greek Philosophy and Tragedy*. Cambridge: Cambridge University Press. 2012.

Nagel, Thomas. *Mortal Questions*. New York: Cambridge University Press, 1979.

Nash, David. "Ethics, Empathy, and the Education of Dentists." *Journal of Dental Education* 74, no. 6 (2010): 567–578.

Nichols, Shawn. "Mindreading and the Cognitive Architecture Underlying Altruistic Motivation." *Mind & Language* 16, no. 4 (2001): 425–455.

Niezink, Lidewij, and Katherine Train. *The Self in Empathy: Self-Empathy*. South Africa: Lidewij Niezink and Katherine Train, 2021.

Nussbaum, Martha. *The Therapy of Desire*. Princeton, NJ: Princeton University Press, 1994.

Peck, Tabitha C., Sofia Seinfeld, Salvatore M. Aglioti, and Mel Slater. "Putting Yourself in the Skin of a Black Avatar Reduces Implicit Racial Bias." *Consciousness and Cognition* 22, no. 3 (2013): 779–787.

Peirce, Charles Sanders. "How to Make Our Ideas Clear." In *Philosophical Writings of Peirce*, edited by Justus Buchler, 124–141. New York: Dover, [1878] 1992.

Pinker, Steven. *The Better Angels of Our Nature*. New York: Viking, 2011.

Plato. *Complete Works*, translated by John M. Cooper. Indianapolis, IN: Hackett, 1997.

Plato. *Meno*, translated by Georges Maximilien Antoine Grube. Indianapolis, IN: Hackett, 1976.

Plato. *Republic*, translated by Georges Maximilien Antoine Grube. Indianapolis, IN: Hackett, 1992.

Popper, Karl. *The Myth of the Framework: In Defense of Science and Rationality*. London: Routledge, 1994.

Preston, Stephanie D., and Frans de Waal. "Empathy: Its Ultimate and Proximate Bases." *Behavioral and Brain* Sciences 25, no. 1 (2002): 1–20.

Prinz, Jesse. "Against Empathy." *The Southern Journal of Philosophy* 49, supp. 1 (2011): 214–233.

Prinz, Jesse. *Gut Reactions: A Perceptual Theory of Emotion*. Oxford: Oxford University Press, 2004.

Prinz, Jesse. "Is Empathy Necessary for Morality?" In *Empathy: Philosophical and Psychological Perspectives*, edited by Amy Coplan and Peter Goldie, 211–229. New York: Oxford University Press.

Ramachandran, V. S. "Mirror Neurons and Imitation Learning as the Driving Force behind 'the Great Leap Forward' in Human Evolution." *Edge.org*, May 29, 2000.

Rifkin, Jeremy. *The Empathic Civilization: The Race to Global Consciousness in a World in Crisis*. New York: Jeremy P. Tarcher, 2009.

Rizzolatti, Giacomo, Luciano Fadiga, Vittorio Gallese, and Leonardo Fogassi. "Premotor Cortex and the Recognition of Motor Actions." *Cognitive Brain Research* 3, no. 2 (1996): 131–141.

Rogers, Carl. "Empathy: An Unappreciated Way of Being." *The Counseling Psychologist* 5, no. 2 (1975): 2–10.

Rogers, Carl. "The Necessary and Sufficient Conditions of Personality Change." *Journal of Consulting Psychology* 21, no. 2 (1957): 95–103.

Rogers, Carl. "A Theory of Therapy, Personality and Interpersonal Relationships as Developed in the Client-Centered Framework." In *Psychology: A Study of Science: Formulations of the Person and the Social Context*, edited by Sigmund Koch, 210–211. New York: McGraw Hill, 1959.

Rorty, Richard. *Philosophy and Social Hope*. Middlesex: Penguin Books, 1999.

Rorty, Richard. *Philosophy and the Mirror of Nature*. Princeton, NJ: Princeton University Press, 1979.

Rorty, Richard. "Pragmatism, Relativism, and Irrationalism." In *The New Social Theory Reader: Contemporary Debates*, edited by Steven Seidman and Jeffrey C. Alexander, 147–155. New York: Routledge, [1980] 2001.

Rousseau, Jean Jacques. *The Social Contract and Discourses*. London: J. M. Dent and Sons, [1761] 1923.

Sadurski, Wojciech. *Legitimacy: The State and Beyond*. Oxford: Oxford University Press, 2019.

Scheler, Max. *The Nature of Sympathy*. London: Transaction Publishers, [1923] 2009.

Schwaber, Evelyne. "Empathy: A Mode of Analytic Listening." *Psychoanalytic Inquiry* 1, no. 3 (1981): 357–392.

Seneca. *Letters from a Stoic*, translated by Robin Campbell. London: Penguin Classics, 1969.

Sigman, Marian D., Connie Kasari, Jung-Hye Kwon, and Nurit Yirmiya. "Responses to the Negative Emotions of Others by Autistic, Mentally Retarded, and Normal Children." *Child Development* 63, no. 4 (1992): 797–807.

Singer, Tania, and Claus Lamm. "The Social Neuroscience of Empathy." *Annals of the New York Academy of Science* 1156, no. 1 (2009): 81–96.

Slote, Michael. *The Ethics of Care and Empathy*. New York: Routledge, 2007.

Slote, Michael. *Moral Sentimentalism*. New York: Oxford University Press, 2010.

Smith, Adam. *Theory of Moral Sentiments*, edited by David Daiches Raphael and Alec Lawrence Macfie. Indianapolis, IN: Liberty Fund, 1779.

Spinoza, Baruch. *Ethics: Proved in Geometric Order*, translated by Michael Silverthorne and Matthew J. Kisner. Cambridge: Cambridge University Press, 2018.

Staub, Ervin. "Commentary on Part I." In *Empathy and Its Development*, edited by Nancy Eisenberg and Janet Strayer, 103–115. New York: Cambridge University Press, 1990.

Stein, Edith. *On the Problem of Empathy*, translated by Waltraut Stein. The Hague: Martinus Nijhoff, 1917.

Stitcher, Matt. *The Skillfulness of Virtue*. Cambridge: Cambridge University Press, 2018.

Stueber, Karsten. *Rediscovering Empathy: Agency, Folk Psychology, and the Human Sciences*. Cambridge, MA: MIT Press, 2010.

Stuhr, John. "Democracy as a Way of Life." In *Philosophy and the Reconstruction of Culture*, edited by John Stuhr, 37–58. Albany, NY: State University of New York Press, 1993.

Stuhr, John. "Introduction: Classical Philosophy." In *Pragmatism and Classical American Philosophy: Essential Readings & Interpretive Essays*, edited by John Stuhr, 1–9. New York: Oxford University Press, 2000.

Stuhr, John. *Pragmatic Fashions: Pluralism, Democracy, Relativism, and the Absurd*. Bloomington: Indiana University Press, 2016.

Stürmer, Stefan, Mark Snyder, and Allen M. Omoto. "Prosocial Emotions and Helping: The Moderating Role of Group Membership." *Journal of Personality and Social Psychology* 88, no. 3 (2005): 532–546.

Titchener, Edward B. *Lectures on the Experimental Psychology of the Thought-Processes*. New York: MacMillan, 1909.

Turnbull, Colin. *The Forest People*. New York: Simon & Schuster, 1961.

van Baaren, Rick B., Jean Decety, Ap Dijksterhuis, Andries van der Leij, and Matthijs L. van Leeuwen. "Being Imitated: Consequences of Nonconsciously Showing Empathy." In *The Social Neuroscience of Empathy*, edited by Jean Decety and William Ickes, 31–42. Cambridge, MA: MIT Press, 2009.

Vischer, Robert. *Empathy, Form and Space: Problems in German Aesthetics, 1873–1893*, edited by Harry Francis Mallgrave and Eleftherios Ikonomou. Santa Monica, CA: Getty Center for the History of Art and the Humanities, 1994.

Willett, Cynthia. *Interspecies Ethics*. New York: Columbia University Press, 2014.

Willett, Cynthia. *Uproarious: How Feminists and Other Subversive Comics Speak Truth*. Minneapolis: University of Minneapolis Press, 2019.

Williams, Bernard. *Moral Luck*. Cambridge: Cambridge University Press, 1981.

Wispé, Lauren. *The Psychology of Sympathy*. New York: Plenum Press, 1991.

Xu, Xiaojing, Xiangyu Zuo, Xiaoying Wang, and Shihui Han. "Do You Feel My Pain? Racial Group Membership Modulates Empathic Neural Responses." *Journal of Neuroscience* 29, no. 26 (2009): 8525–8529.

Zaki, James. *The War for Kindness*. London: Penguin, 2019.

Zembylas, Michalinos. "The Politics of Trauma: Empathy, Reconciliation, and Education." *Journal of Peace Education* 4, no. 2 (2007): 207–224.

Zinn, John Kabat. *Mindfulness for Beginners: Reclaiming the Present Moment and Your Life*. Boulder, CO: Sounds True, 2016.

Index

abductive reasoning 152, 164
active listening 152–53
aestheticism 56–57, 61, 63
affect attunement 87, 199nn.42-4
affects 27, 29, 32, 34–35
Against Empathy (Bloom) 126
The Age of Empathy (De Waal) 100
Age of Enlightenment 48–53, 62, 69, 71, 194n.25
akrasia 162
altruistic motivation 11, 125
animal sciences 78, 81
Apatheia 29, 117
appreciation 150–51
Aquinas 29–31, 41, 189–90n.37
architecture 55, 83
arete see virtue
Aristotle,
    and the cosmos 117
    description 24–25, 27, 187n.17
    and habits 140–41
    and moral luck 161–62, 210n.5, 211n.8
    and *pathé* 30–32
    and *pathos* 40
Augustine 29–30, 189nn.31, 35
autism 145–46
aversion 30, 33

Baron-Cohen, Simon 98, 121
Batson, C. D.,
    definition 3, 11
    and empathetic care 95–98, 103, 200n.8
    and empathetic concern 18–19, 183n.25
    and empathetic connection 74, 197n.16
    and morality 116, 121, 127, 203–4n.8
The Better Angels of Our Natures (Pinker) 102
biology 54–55, 80, 82, 85, 99, 137
birds 82
Bloom, Paul 126, 205n.37
Blumer, Herbert 79
body language 2, 5, 18, 84, 151

body-mapping 81
Bubandt, Nils 124–25
Buddhism 117, 157

Candice (example) 67
car accident example 1–4
categorical imperative 49, 118, 173
Charmides (Plato) 70
chimps 81
Christianity 29, 31–32, 40–41, 43, 118, 189n.30
Chrysippus 27–28, 70, 187n.20, 188n.23
Cicero 27–29, 70, 115, 187n.17, 196n.8
City of God (Augustine) 29
Cole (example) 21–23
concupiscible passions 30
Confucianism 117
consciousness 7, 53, 59, 73–74, 85, 99, 120, 142, 149–50, 160
Coplan, Amy 8–12, 182n.16
cosmic sympathy 70, 195–96nn.4–5
cosmos (hyle) 26, 70, 195–96n.5
Counter-Enlightenment 47–50
critical thinking 151–52
Curtis, Robin 59

Damasio, Antonio 41
Danziger, Nicolas 82, 101
Darwin, Charles 37–38, 80, 99
'Das wissen vom fremdem ichen' (Lipps) 73
Davidson, Donald 113, 203n.4
Decety, Jean 82, 101
democracy 165–71, 176, 211n.12, 212n.15
Democratic People's Republic of Korea 170
Democritus 25, 186n.10
Descartes, René 31–35, 37–38, 41–42, 118, 190nn.43, 47–8, 193n.64
de Waal, Frans,
    definition 12–13
    and empathetic care 90, 97, 100–101, 199n.4, 200n.18, 201n.21

and empathetic connection 81–83
and morality 122–23, 127
Dewey, John 110, 169–71, 172
Die Lehrlinge zu Sais (Novalis) 53
Dilthey, Wilhelm 50, 76
Diogenes Laertius 27, 187n.15
disease (*nosēma*) 27–28
distress 6, 11, 21, 28, 42, 81, 95–96, 101, 103, 107
Dixon, Thomas 29
Doric columns 57–58
dualisms,
  adequacy/inadequacy 35, 191n.54
  death of 21–24
  exorcizing the ghostly 37–44
  falling into trap of 82
  nature/nurture 137–39
Duhigg, Charles 143

early childhood development 79–80, 198n.31
Einfühlung,
  development of 145–46
  and empathetic connection 69, 72–73, 75–78, 86
  and empathic care 93
  and empathic projection 55–60, 62, 64–65
  meaning 7, 46
Einfühlungsvermögen 46
Eisenberg, Nancy 98
Elements of Law (Hobbes) 33
Eliot, T. S. 111, 203n.1
Elliott, Richard George 59
empatheia 78
empathic accuracy 4, 82, 180n.3
empathic care 6–8
empathic concern 6–7, 11
empathic connection 81–82
empathic inference 4, 6, 81
empathic mimicry 5, 57, 79, 81
empathic perspective-taking 3, 6
empathic projection 49
empaths 131
empathy-altruism hypothesis 11, 96
'Empathy: An Unappreciated Way of Being' (Rogers) 94
Empathy: From Bench to Bedside (Decety) 101

'Empathy: It's Proximate and Ultimate Bases' (Preston/de Waal) 12
Enlightenment *see* Age of Enlightenment
Epicurus 25–26, 40, 117, 185–86nn.8–10
ethics 12, 24, 114–15, 119, 130, 140, 173
ēthikós 140
ēthos 24–25, 27, 140
eudaimonia 25, 161–62
eupathies 28, 32
eupathy 26–29
evolutionary biology 82, 99
evolutionary psychology 99
The Expression of the Emotions in Man and Animals (Darwin) 37–38
extended reality (XR) 155

Fabes, Richard A. 98
Fagiano, Mark 110, 203n.42
fallibility 136, 138, 170, 173, 207n.8
familiarity 49, 107
fate 27, 40, 160, 177
fear 2, 5, 24–25, 28, 30, 34, 74, 101, 186
feeling 57–65, 83–87, 91–94, 97, 102–9, 124–25, 202n.41
fellow-feeling *see* sympathy
Fichte, Johann Gottlieb 51–52
fixists 138–39
Freud, Sigmund 77

Galen 27
Galton, Sir Francis 99
generalized other 79–80
global social meliorism 123
glory 33
God 26, 29–31, 34, 40–41, 118, 188n.29, 189n.30
grammatical interpretation 76
Great Chain of Being 30–31, 33, 41
Greece 70, 133, 150, 171, 212–13n.20
Groos, Karl 56–58, 60, 62–64, 72, 82

habit 141–43
Handbook of Physiological Optics (Helmholtz) 55
Hannah (example) 67
happiness 32
Hardenberg, Georg Friedrich Phillip von *see* Novalis
Hausheer, Roger 48

Hegel, G. W. F. 55
Heinrich von Ofterdingen (Novalis) 53
Helmholtz, Hermann von 55
helping behavior 7–8, 20, 92, 95–96,
  98–103, 107, 122, 153
Herder, Johann Gottlieb,
  and empathetic connection 72–73, 76,
    88
  and empathic care 93
  and empathic projection 8, 49–54, 56,
    59–60, 62–64, 193–94n.12
  and mindfulness 149
  and moral empathy 127
hermeneutics 72, 75–76, 78, 85, 97
hexis 25
Hickok, Gregory 83
Hinduism 157
Hippocrates 26–27, 33, 40
Hitler, Adolf 170
Hobbes, Thomas 32–35, 166, 191nn.51–2
Hoffman, Martin 97–98, 123, 127
Homer 134, 206n.2
Hook, Sidney 110, 170
hope 171, 212–13nn.19-20
horses 82
human happiness 32
human reason 42, 118
Hume, David 10, 36, 38, 71, 121–22,
  140–41
Husserl, Edmund 74–75, 79

Ich 79, 145
Ickes, William 4, 82, 180n.3
imagine-other perspective 3
imagine-self perspective 3–4
impulses 27–28, 41–43
in/out-groups 107
intellectual emotions 32
internal emotions 32
irascible passions 30
irrationalism 129
Ituri Forest 89

Jahoda, Gustav 61
James, William,
  development of empathy 135,
    206–7n.4, 210n.32
  and dualisms 42–43
  and empathetic projection 63–64

and habit formation 141–43
and moral empathy 111–14, 120, 129
and pluralism 14–16
and relations 16, 184n.41
and strenuous mood 172–73
The Jeweled Net of Indra 157–59
joy 28, 188.24
judgment 24, 28, 41–43, 47, 153
jury example 6

Kandinsky, Wassily 45
Kant, Immanuel,
  and empathetic connection 73, 77, 79
  and empathetic projection 49–52, 56, 59
  and morality 162, 210–11n.6,
    212–13n.20
  and principlism 118
kindness 105–6, 121, 125, 153, 208n.26
Knox, Jean 102
Kohut, Heinz 79, 88
Kropotkin, Petr 99
Krznaric, Roman 123

Lamm, Claus 82, 102
Leviathan (Hobbes) 34, 166
liberalism 171
Lipps, Theodor,
  and empathetic care 95, 97
  and empathetic connection 72–77, 85,
    197n.17
  and empathetic projection 56–60,
    62–65
  and mindfulness 149
  and morality 127, 129
logos see reason
Lotze, Hermann 54, 56–57, 59–60, 62–64,
  72, 149
love 7, 29–31, 41, 89, 146, 177
luck 162

Matryoshka dolls 100
matter (*hyle*) 26, 30, 32–33, 40, 55
Maurita (example) 67
Mbuti tribe 89–91
Mead, George Herbert 79–80, 85, 95, 97,
  127
meliorism 123, 136, 164, 171–72
Meno 133–36, 144
metriopatheia 25, 30

mice 81
Middle Ages 117
mindfulness 17, 46–47, 87, 149, 155, 208n.23
mindreading 4, 82
mirror neurons 83, 97, 123
mobilists 138–39
modernism 87
monkeys 83
mood 21, 59, 111, 131, 172, 174
morality,
    of empathy 111, 121–28, 204n.22
    establishing/legitimizing principles 116–18
    portraits of 114–18, 203n.7
    and relational empathy 130–32
    and relativism 128–30, 206n.45
    shortcomings of principlism 118–20
    and William James 111–14
moral luck 161–64, 170, 177, 211nn.9-10
The Moral Philosopher and the Moral Life (James) 120
moral sentiments 36
Moran, Dermot 75
motivation 6, 11–12, 96, 107, 121, 171
Mussolini, Benito 170
Mutual Aid (Kropotkin) 99

narcissism 146
The Nature of Sympathy (Scheler) 74–75
nature vs. nurture 137
net/web example 157–59
neuroscience 78–80, 83, 85, 88, 99, 101, 103, 137, 146
Nia (example) 21–23
Nicomachean Ethics (Aristotle) 24–25, 162
Novalis,
    and empathetic care 93
    and empathetic connection 73, 77, 79
    and empathic projection 51–54, 56, 59–60, 62, 64
    and mindfulness 149
    and morality 127
    and nature 8, 182n.11

ordinary luck 162

'parts-to-whole' approach 136
passio (passion) 29–31, 33–34, 188n.28

passivity 13, 26, 30–31, 41, 58
pathé see pathos
pathéma 26
pathology 26–29
pathos,
    and dualisms 21–24
    and modern philosophy 31–44, 190n.41
    neutral conceptualizations in antiquity 24–26
    pathology and eupathy 26–29, 187nn.20-1, 188n.22
    reason for controlling unruly 118
    and relational empathy 17, 20, 184n.42
    worldly flesh/heavenly love 29–31
Peirce, Charles Sanders 139, 141–43
perturbation (*perturbatio*) 28–29, 31, 41–42
phenomenology 55, 60, 72–75, 78–79, 85, 97, 129, 176
Pinker, Steven 102–3
Plato 70, 117, 140, 166, 194–95nn.1-3
The Play of Man (Groos) 56
pleasure 24–25, 28, 30, 33, 42, 54, 56–57, 117, 140
pluralistic pragmatism 14–16, 183n.30, 184n.40
Popper, Karl 129, 205–6n.44
Posidonius 27
The Power of Habit (Duhigg) 143
pragmatic benevolence 153
Preston, Stephanie 12–13, 100, 200n.18, 201n.21
primatology 79–80
principles of justice 161
principlism 117–20, 130
Prinz, Jesse 10–11, 125
Prkachin, Kenneth M. 82, 101
pseudo-empathy 9
Psychology: Briefer Course (James) 142
psychopaths 26, 146
pure experience 16

Ramachandran, Vilayanur 123
rational compassion 126
rationality/rationalism 42–43, 51, 119
ravens 81
reason 23–27, 32, 40–42, 118, 152, 164, 187nn.19-20
relational empathy 15–16, 17–20, 44, 129

Rhetoric (Aristotle) 24, 185n.2
Rifkin, Jeremy 123
Rogers, Carl 79, 94–95, 103, 127
romanticism 47, 49, 53–54, 61, 64, 88
Rome 70
Rorty, Richard 128, 171, 175
rugged individualism myth 99

Scheler, Max 74–75
Scherner, Albert 55
Schleiermacher, Friedrich 75–76
The Science of Evil (Baron-Cohen) 98, 121
Scottish Enlightenment 36, 47
selectivity bias 107
self-care 105
self-empathy 47, 149–50
selfishness 106
self-knowledge 59
self-reflection/awareness 47
self-regarding 106
self-transformation 52
Seneca 34
sensus 17
sentimentalism 10, 43, 122
sich hineinfühlenn 46, 52
sickness (*arróstmata*) 26–28
Singer, Tania 102
skepticism 10, 72–75, 84–85, 136
Slote, Michael 9–12, 121–22, 125
Smith, Adam 3, 36–38, 47–48, 71, 180n.1, 192n.58, 193n.2, 196n.12
social amnesia 159
social-cognitive anarchy 129
social Darwinism 99, 160, 200n.15
social gathering example 3–4
socialization stages 79
social meliorism 136, 164
social psychology 79, 93, 95
sociopaths 146
Socrates 70, 133–36
sophrosyne 150
soul/psyche 27, 186n.11
Spencer, Herbert 99
Spinoza, Baruch 34–35, 118
squirrel example 112–13
Stalin, Joseph 170
Stein, Edith 74–75, 145, 197n.18

Stoicism 26–28, 31–32, 34–35, 40–43, 70, 117, 186n.11
strenuous mood 172–74
Stuhr, John 110, 172, 175
sunrise 45
symbolic interactionalism 78–79
symhedonia 104
sympathy 36, 70–72, 75, 124–25, 195–96nn.4–5, 9–10

Taoism 117
technology 154–55, 208–10nn.27–31
teleology 117
tenor 27
Titchener, Edward 78
torture 124
traditional relativism 166
tranquility (*ataraxia*) 28
transcendental ego 51, 79
Turnbull, Colin 89

Über das Optische Formegefühl: Ein Beitrag zur Ästhetik (Robert Vischer) 55
United States 159

virtue 25, 133–37, 206–7nn.2–4
Vischer, Friedrich Robert 55–57, 59–60, 64, 149
Vischer, Robert 55–57, 60–61, 64, 149

The War for Kindness (Zaki) 121, 138
whales 82
'What Is an Emotion?' (James) 38
What Pragmatism Means (James) 111–12
Whitman, Walt 60–61, 64
Willer, Jean-Claude 82, 101
Willerslev, Rane 124–25
Willett, Cynthia 176
'Will the Real Empathy Please Stand Up?' (Coplan) 9
Wissenschaftslehre (Fichte) 51

yawn contagion 81

Zaki, Jamil 121, 138
Zeno 27

www.ingramcontent.com/pod-product-compliance
Lightning Source LLC
Chambersburg PA
CBHW062136300426
44115CB00012BA/1945